The Idea of Europe in Literature

Edited by

Susanne Fendler
*Assistant Professor
University of Würzburg
Germany*

and

Ruth Wittlinger
*Lecturer in European Studies
University of Durham
Stockton Campus*

Foreword by Bernard Crick

in association with
University of Durham

First published in Great Britain 1999 by
MACMILLAN PRESS LTD
Houndmills, Basingstoke, Hampshire RG21 6XS and London
Companies and representatives throughout the world

A catalogue record for this book is available from the British Library.

ISBN 0-333-72189-6

First published in the United States of America 1999 by
ST. MARTIN'S PRESS, INC.,
Scholarly and Reference Division,
175 Fifth Avenue, New York, N.Y. 10010

ISBN 0-312-21985-7

Library of Congress Cataloging-in-Publication Data
The idea of Europe in literature / edited by Susanne Fendler and Ruth Wittlinger.
p. cm.
Includes bibliographical references and index.
ISBN 0-312-21985-7 (cloth)
1. European literature—History and criticism. 2. Europe—In literature. 3. Literature and society—Europe. I. Fendler, Susanne, 1966– . II. Wittlinger, Ruth, 1961– .
PN701.I53 1999
809'.93324—dc21   98-54303
                                                  CIP

Selection and editorial matter © Susanne Fendler and Ruth Wittlinger 1999
Foreword © Bernard Crick 1999
Text © the various contributors 1999

All rights reserved. No reproduction, copy or transmission of this publication may be made without written permission.

No paragraph of this publication may be reproduced, copied or transmitted save with written permission or in accordance with the provisions of the Copyright, Designs and Patents Act 1988, or under the terms of any licence permitting limited copying issued by the Copyright Licensing Agency, 90 Tottenham Court Road, London W1P 9HE.

Any person who does any unauthorised act in relation to this publication may be liable to criminal prosecution and civil claims for damages.

The authors have asserted their rights to be identified as the authors of this work in accordance with the Copyright, Designs and Patents Act 1988.

This book is printed on paper suitable for recycling and made from fully managed and sustained forest sources.

10 9 8 7 6 5 4 3 2 1
08 07 06 05 04 03 02 01 00 99

Printed and bound in Great Britain by
Antony Rowe Ltd, Chippenham, Wiltshire

DISCARDED

THE IDEA OF EUROPE IN LITERATURE

Also by Susanne Fendler

ENTSTEHUNG UND DARSTELLUNG VON INDIVIDUALITÄT
IN DER RENAISSANCE IN DER ROMANZEN VON GERVASE
MARKHAM, MARY WROTH, ANNA WEEMYS UND JOHN
REYNOLDS

FEMINIST CONTRIBUTIONS TO THE LITERARY CANON
Setting Standards of Taste

In memoriam
Gertrud Wittlinger
11.3.1920–23.6.1998

Contents

Foreword by Bernard Crick   ix

Notes on the Contributors   xv

Acknowledgements   xviii

Introduction: The Idea of Europe – the Contribution of Literature by Susanne Fendler and Ruth Wittlinger   xix

Part I Portrayal of the Continent

1. Charlotte Brontë's Alternative 'European Community'   3
   Jan B. Gordon

2. 'Nation and Narration': Continental Europe and the English Novel   31
   Silvia Mergenthal

3. *Schlosses* and the Scent of Pine: Images of Austria and Germany in the English Historical Romance and Gothic Romance since 1945   44
   Ulrike Horstmann

4. Discovering 'Europe' in the Process of Repatriation: Primo Levi's *La Tregua*   64
   Angela Flury

Part II Inner/Outer Perspectives in Comparison

5. World Fiction: the Transformation of the English/Western Literature Canon   85
   Marion Frank-Wilson

6. France and its DOM: the Ambivalence of European Identity   101
   Ute Fendler

7. Immigrants in Britain: National Identities and Stereotypes   119
   Susanne Fendler

8 A Never Closer Union? The Idea of the European
   Union in Selected Works of Malcolm Bradbury   138
   Paul G. Nixon

Part III   The Idea of Europe and National Identity

9 A Romanian View of Europe: George Uscatescu   159
   Liliana Mihut

10 Eyvind Johnson and the History of Europe: Many
   Times in One Place   173
   Rolf Hugoson

11 Englishness from the Outside   192
   Ruth Wittlinger

12 Memories of Hell: Kieslowski's Vision of European
   Subjectivity   207
   Roy Boyne

13 Europeans: Foreigners in Their Own Land   225
   Sylvie Gambaudo

Index   240

Foreword

When I was asked to write a foreword to this thoughtful gathering of studies and essays, a tune of Offenbach's forced its way into my head to divert me in the heaviness of the task. In *La Belle Hélène* the knowing offspring of Zeus taunt him with a teasing song to a jolly melody, 'it was a bull that met Europa, as every schoolboy will know'. The mythical, ravished daughter of Agenor, king of Tyre, who gave us her name, was like Dionysus, of course, 'out of Asia'. The erotic myth quickly gained a vague geographical and an equally vague but forever compulsive (among the Greeks, the Romans and all their heirs) cultural connotation. Those like Herodotus and the early Christian theologian, Lactantius, who tried to rationalize or reform the old mythic narrative still kept the Asian origins, or contrast. For the question 'What is Europe?' could be readily answered (as could later be a brief enough summary of Hegel's phenomenology of history): 'Not Asia. We are not like them.' But for Asia, would we think of a Europe at all? We might have been 'The Greater Polis' or 'Megapolis', the continent of the city, the unique civic culture of citizens – however much reality, until the very yesterday of today, conflicted with that eternal and enabling memory.

'Asia', like 'Orientalism' in our times, or 'Islamic extremism' (somewhat untypical of Islam, by the way), had its uses. In the so-called Middle Ages 'Christendom' began to replace Europe as a reasonably clear concept, but it could not survive the break-up of Christian unity in the Reformation, and had already had some conceptual difficulty on the north-eastern and eastern borders; not so much with Slavic paganism, as with the Greek and Russian orthodox churches, let alone substantial Coptic minorities in Muslim North Africa, then plainly part of Asia – were they, or were they not, part of Christendom? Slavophile Europhobes have been most useful to a (too) clear sense of modern European identity – plainly not 'us' in their antagonism to an 'us' seen as embodying secular modernism; but Russian liberals of both the nineteenth century and today have posed greater problems, being seemingly more clear, or eager to be clear, about a European identity than those who can, like myself (and most of the contributors to this book), almost bathe with lazy wisdom in the warm cross-currents of dual or even multiple identities. 'Lazy' is perhaps unfair. Most of the contributors to this volume are admirably energetic in trying to define their, or more often their chosen subject's, identity. But ambiguity can be useful both as a literary and as a political strategy.

Think of the great generation of writers of the Irish literary revival, mainly an Anglo–Irish movement; some torn between Irish and English identities, others consciously using (even affecting) that tension for artistic effect. And politically think of modern Turkey, internally torn by 'Europe–Asia', but externally playing the ambiguity as a strong card in international politics. And would modern Greeks think of themselves so intensely as European were it not for Turkey to their east, enabling them to view the European credentials and pretensions of their northern Albanian and Macedonian neighbours with some irony and even scorn? Jan Gordon nicely contrasts the Europe as 'surfeit of history' of Dorothea Brooke's antiquarian husband in *Middlemarch* with Europe as Shelley and Byron's great escape from the burden of an oppressive national history. But, of course, George Eliot, quintessentially English but English in a radical mode, was jibbing not at 'Europe' but rather at an antiquarian version of Europe, not her own commitment to the modern Europe of German philosophy and the new scientific biblical criticism. Contrasts, as the editors well say, are part of identity. And borders always raise difficulties of definition, as well as unexpected pleasures for the intellectual wayfarer. But the fact that one can only very rarely draw a clear line, and that such lines always change, does not render concepts meaningless. 'Where do you draw the line?' is not to be treated as an objection in principle, but as a request for one's own subjective response to a real question; and the question should be returned to the questioner: 'Where do *you* draw the line?' Think of the theory of language and meaning in late Wittgenstein. We search in vain for the core of meaning around which clusters of differing but related associations revolve. There is no hard, central or essential core of meaning to 'Europe' and 'European', but these ideas define, as it were, a magnetic field around which particles revolve, some moving with time or contingent events into a harder centrifugal mass, others spinning off to the periphery or out of sight and mind entirely. Indeed over-zealous attempts to define terms more clearly than is readily possible on the borderlands of a national or trans-national identity (often literally borderlands) can create purist witch-hunts in the very heartlands of a meaning. Silvia Mergenthal, for instance, traces how the English cultural elite could in the course of the (long) eighteenth century turn from an image of Europe as the enlightenment of universal values to Gothic and romantic particularity – spiritual illuminations and horrors alike. For myself, for instance, I am sceptical (unlike another of the contributors to this volume) that there is something deliberately intended as and sensibly called 'a European novel', even if there are certain novels that cross national and linguistic boundaries more easily than others; and not just 'the greats', such as Tolstoy, Dickens and Thomas Mann, but also, one notes, while suppressing any old-fashioned pre-postmodernist value judgements, westerns, sci-fi, English-American pop-romances and Mills and Boon. When novels were more widely read and serious-enough novels more accessible to the common reader, a writer such as Alexandre Dumas was famous throughout Europe. But Ulrike Horstmann delineates only too well the casual chauvinism and the silly stereotypes of 'abroad' or Europe in the Barbara Cartland genre of English popular novels.

The idea of Europe, however, was older than any clear idea that territories were best composed of nations or that nations *should* constitute states, still less that non-national or multi-national states to survive in the modern world had to construct or fabricate a sense of common nationality and common history among their inhabitants. As a political philosopher by training and now also a historian by vocation, I have been greatly impressed (before I ever thought of writing about George Orwell) with how much more our perceptions of national identity and of political and social justice are shaped by literature than by formal history. I am an Englishman, with half-Welsh children, living in Scotland, who visits Northern Ireland a great deal, and therefore much interested in questions of identity, both academically and personally. The Scottish National Party (SNP) about ten years ago came up with a clever and quite effective slogan: 'Independence in Europe'. The party, by adopting this, sought to get rid of an image that separatism would mean a retreat from the modern world into Celtic mists and myths. Most of their activists now seem to believe that, even though they are true Scots, they are also good Europeans, more so than the English are; and that this duality is enhancing and more authentic than the diminishing belief of most other Scots that they are Scottish *and* British. Books and articles written from a nationalist perspective now stress those elements of Scottish history that linked Scotland to the continent of Europe. This is easy enough to do, of course; not by what you must put into the narrative but by what you leave out. There are some real cultural links, undeniably, but the driving force and greater reality were military and dynastic alliances in the seventeenth century and Jacobite intrigue and tribal rebellions in the seventeenth and eighteenth centuries. While cultural links can be found with France and are vaunted (the 'auld alliance' and all that), the obvious and far greater cultural bondings and *mutual* influences are with England. Just as the Luther Bible began to elevate German from vernaculars into a common language of state and high culture, so the Protestant reformation brought the English of the Cranmer Bible into general use as the printed and written language of Scotland. The spoken vernacular, however (an autonomous development from Middle English, not a corrupt Standard English), has proved strong and hardy, even to this day. Novels and plays, as in Wales and Ireland, can be written either in the vernacular or in standard English – often, of course, in both according to the characters.

SNP orators and even those who have campaigned for a federal-like Scottish parliament within the United Kingdom would often cry 'If we do not have a parliament, we will lose our national identity!' This was a common slogan and favourite figure of political rhetoric, but completely untrue. A strong and distinctive Scottish culture has survived without a political institution since the ending of the Scottish Parliament in 1707, and what is more, has modernized itself – *Trainspotting* is far removed from the Waverley novels. The vernacular language of *Trainspotting* or *Lanark* poses linguistic problems for translators, but the social setting of the text, the sociology that can be inferred, is not unfamiliar to, say, Hamburg, Lille or Turin, just as the Danzig or Gdansk of Günter Grass is both highly peculiar, and peculiar in a way that can only seem European. The old Russian culture of the literary intelligentsia, good and bad, survived 60 to 70 years of political indoctrination by a powerful state. If one actually reads the 'Appendix' to *Nineteen Eighty-Four* and treats it as part of the text, not an incompetent authorial afterthought, one will find that the translation of the classics of English literature into Newspeak has been postponed into a distant future (that is to say, impossible, if we read that as satire on the futility of state control of language).

My personal digression was simply to assert and applaud what seems to me to be the presupposition of this volume of what an older generation would have called 'Studies in the Idea of Europe': that imaginative literature is both the main source of most people's understandings of 'Europe' and a potent factor from way, way back in the construction of the concept. I say 'Studies' deliberately because it is important that the editors have not tried to impose any thematic general answers to the grand question, 'What is Europe?' That is a virtue, not a failing. Many grand questions, such as 'What is life?', are better lived with in a mood of unresolved critical curiosity rather than constantly stirred to a fever-pitch of alleged crisis or crises – what is Europe? will the nation-state survive? is sovereignty meaningful? is hypertext the end of the book? is television the end of the novel? who am I? No, in these essays (I use this uncommon term in the original French sense) there are no general theories, but a rich sense of common context. That is integrative enough. Attempts to use literature as a means of speeding political integration would, I suspect, lead to ludicrous and unwelcome results, both politically and aesthetically. Complex novels that help us to think, help us to empathize with other people, circumstances and ideas (and may, after all, be a source of delight for readers as well as subjects for study in the academy), are products of free minds and are usually found in reasonably free, civic societies. If they are all that, they are integrative enough. The novel, as much a European invention as free politics and natural science, is to modernity and modern science what the cathedral was to Christendom – both meeting-ground and mirror of all the facets of society.

For economic and peace-keeping reasons, Europe needs stronger and more integrative political institutions; but for its respect and understanding in the outside world it needs a literature or literatures that reach out as well as in – that arouse interest in those parts of the world that were once involuntary parts of an imperial context, as well as in those parts that are, while clearly not of Europe, but Canadian, Australian or American (Latin American as well as North American), yet are nonetheless in some undeniable sense European in culture, or clear modulations thereof. Ute Fendler's study of the French Caribbean shows that these ambiguities are not a matter of the English- or the Spanish-speaking worlds alone. And Susanne Fendler sees that the immigrant into the UK can often have a sharper sense of the actual content of 'Englishness' and 'Britishness', as well as of the different connotations between them, than does the 'native Brit'. Elsewhere I have argued that there is still great confusion about 'Englishness' and 'Britishness', especially among the English themselves. The British government signed with the Irish government an 'Anglo-Irish Agreement', to which presumably the Scottish and the Welsh are party; and the 'Deutsche-Englische Gesellschaft' do not intend to limit their interests to England.

'British' does not connote a culture in the full sense. Who talks of a British novel, rather than an English novel – either meaning written in English or, more often, to distinguish it from an Irish (in English) novel, a Scottish, a Welsh or an Indian (English) novel, and so on? 'British', most usefully and clearly, simply denotes a political culture (as social scientists would say): parliament, the crown, the laws and other institutions common to the United Kingdom. So when the Hindu Indian calls himself or herself a British-Indian or British-Asian they are announcing their allegiance, their respect for the laws, or claiming the protection of the laws, but not necessarily claiming or wanting to be English in a full cultural sense, indeed by implication are claiming if not rights, certainly space and tolerance for their own culture.

In thinking of Europe as a whole, as of any multi-cultural or pluralistic state within Europe – say the United Kingdom, Spain, or Belgium, and, taking a deep breath and a long leap, Russia – we must never confuse assimilation with integration. Assimilation is becoming one, integration is two or more entities intermingling or living side by side, reasonably peacefully, hopefully with mutual respect, sometimes with a creative tension – in art as well as life, in so far as art, shaping our perceptions as well as being shaped, is not life. Roy Boyne puts this so well in talking of memory as being the key theme in Kieslowski's films – a voice from a border that illuminates central preoccupations in the heartland of European culture:

> The lesson for philosophies of European integration is both positive and cautionary: positive, since it suggests that new political forms will not erase the formative regional narratives of identity formation, and will therefore not empty out European subjectivities to create the feared spectre of homogeneity *in vacuo* at the heart of European identity; cautionary, because the pursuit of European integration becomes an extraordinarily complex affair requiring a pervasive sensitivity to the defining histories of European subjectivities as they are currently constituted.

The essays in this interesting volume reach no common conclusion, but they revolve with 'a pervasive sensitivity' around an important but always perplexing theme – what is it to be European? Literature throws at least as much light on this as does history, sometimes more.

BERNARD CRICK
Edinburgh

Notes on the Contributors

Roy Boyne is Professor of Sociology at Durham University. He has published extensively on French cultural theory, and works at the interface of aesthetics and the sociology of culture. He is a member of the editorial board of *Theory, Culture and Society*. His next book, *Weak Subjectivity*, is soon to be published.

Susanne Fendler (PhD in 1996) studied English and German literature and history at the universities of Bayreuth and Passau, Germany. From 1992 to 1996 she taught English literature at the University of Passau. Since 1996 she has been Assistant Professor at the University of Würzburg, Germany. Her publications include a book and articles on English romances of the Renaissance, and various articles, mainly on women's literature; she edited *Feminist Contributions and the Literary Canon: Setting Standards of Taste* (1996). She is currently working on the concept of fragmentation in nineteenth-century English poetry.

Ute Fendler graduated from the University of Bayreuth in Germany. Her PhD is in Romance Literatures. In 1991–92 and 1993 she spent some time in Guadeloupe and Martinique for research. From 1992 to 1997 she was Assistant Professor at the University of Ouagadougou (Burkina Faso). She has published a book on interculturality in Francophone Caribbean literature, and various articles on Caribbean and African literature. She is currently working on Spanish travel literature of the eighteenth century and on film aesthetics.

Angela Flury is a PhD candidate in the Comparative Literature Department at the University of California, Davis. She is currently researching her dissertation on fashion, colour and race in the context of contemporary visual culture.

Marion Frank-Wilson is a graduate of Bayreuth University in Germany (PhD 1992). Her extensive field research resulted in the publication of *AIDS Education through Theatre* (Bayreuth African Studies Series, Bayreuth, 1995). She is Librarian for African Studies at Indiana University.

Sylvie Gambaudo is a lecturer in European Studies at the University of Durham, Stockton Campus. Her research interests address issues of psycholinguistics applied to gender, literature, post-subjectivity and cyberspace.

Jan B. Gordon, Professor of Anglo-American Literature at the Tokyo University of Foreign Studies, is the author of *Gossip and Subversion in Nineteenth-Century British Fiction: Echo's Economies* (1997). His work on representations (and misrepresentations) of Europe in British fiction has appeared in a number of international journals. He is currently working on the theme of 'transparency' in the literature and visual arts of the *fin-de-siècle*.

Ulrike Horstmann, University of Würzburg, is writing her doctoral thesis on the names in Spenser's *The Faerie Queene*. Besides literary onomastics, her main fields of interest are fantasy fiction and popular literature.

Rolf Hugoson is currently finishing his PhD thesis at the Department of Political Science, Umeå University. He has been working as a lecturer at the Centre for Research and Debate on Cultural Policy, at the University College of Borås. His research concerns relationships between rhetoric, governance and the arts.

Silvia Mergenthal studied German and English at the universities of Erlangen, Austin/Texas, and St Andrews/Scotland. From 1988 to 1997 she taught English literature at Erlangen. She is now a Professor at the University of Konstanz. Her publications include books on Scottish literature and on the construction of gender roles in eighteenth-century fiction and non-fiction as well as a number of articles on contemporary literature. She is currently engaged in research on constructions of Englishness in contemporary fiction.

Liliana Mihut graduated from the Faculty of History and Philosophy, Babes-Bolyai University, Cluj-Napoca, Romania (PhD in Philosophy in 1982). She was a Visiting Scholar at the Ohio State University, Columbus during 1993–94, thanks to an American Studies Fellowship awarded by the American Council of Learned Societies. She is Associate Professor and Chair of the Department of Political Science, Faculty of Law, Babes-Bolyai University, and author of several books and articles, including *Dilemele stiintei politice* (Dilemmas of Political Science) (1995) and *Despre pluralism in America* (Pluralism in America) (1997).

Paul G. Nixon is Senior Lecturer in Comparative Social Policy and European Projects Co-ordinator in the Community Informatics Research and Applications Unit at the University of Teesside. He is Visiting Professor at the Department of Political Science, Mid-Sweden University – Sundsvall. His research interests include reform of the EU and political parties and new technologies.

Ruth Wittlinger is Lecturer in European Studies at the University of Durham, Stockton Campus. Her main research interest is in the area of politics and literature, particularly in Britain during the 1980s.

Acknowledgements

First of all, we would like to thank T.M. Farmiloe at Macmillan for showing an interest in our project right from the beginning and Professor Michael Prestwich at the University of Durham for readily agreeing to include it in the joint series published by Macmillan and the University of Durham. We would also like to express our gratitude to the contributors for their co-operation and goodwill. Special thanks go to Professor Bernard Crick, a scholar with a longstanding record of using literature as a source for political understanding, for his interest in our collection and for writing the Foreword. Warm thanks also go to the administrative staff at Stockton Campus, who willingly helped in moments of panic. Last but not least we would like to thank Kevin for making up for the editors' deficiency in not being native English-speakers by patiently proofreading the whole volume although it contains nothing on Sunderland AFC.

Introduction: the Idea of Europe – the Contribution of Literature
Susanne Fendler and Ruth Wittlinger

Traces of an interest in Europe, and the idea of Europe as a cultural and/or political entity can be found throughout history. Thus, the idea of Europe comes in various different shapes and forms and in this respect, it might have been more appropriate to entitle this volume *Ideas of Europe in Literature*. Politicians, diplomats and scholars from various, if not all, academic disciplines, have taken part in the discourse on Europe, in an attempt to construct (or, more recently, deconstruct) an entity which allegedly can be defined by its political, geographical and/or cultural characteristics.

The actual practice in the form of what is now known as the European Union might not be too closely related to previous ideas of Europe and excludes large parts mainly on economic grounds, but it nevertheless constitutes the most serious attempt so far to overcome the borders of nation-states and work together on more and more issues in an increasingly interdependent world. Having said that, it should be pointed out that more than 40 years after the signing of the Treaties of Rome, which prescribed an 'ever closer union among the peoples of Europe', the nation-state is still the most important political (f)actor in the context of European integration. Accordingly, the nation-state has also dominated theories which have been put forward in order to explain and analyse the integration process so far, as well as those prescriptive theories which attempt to suggest the way ahead. Both for optimistic supranationalists whose aim is to transcend the nation-state in a federal framework and for intergovernmentalists who favour the idea of co-operation between individual sovereign national governments, the nation-state remains the basic entity around which events as well as theories revolve in the context of European integration. However, nations – although on a political level in the form of nation-states very real – are to some extent only 'fictitious entities'.

Their definitions are flexible and adapt to changing political realities. In spite of, or perhaps because of, this fluidity, politicians among many others continue to discuss the role of individual nations, claiming legitimation for their actions by reminding us of the 'national interest' they are allegedly pursuing and by evoking the spectre that is haunting Europe in the context of further integration, the 'loss of national sovereignty'. Nations and other political and cultural units which have been created for identificatory purposes, such as the United States, are always to some extent 'fictitious', meaning that they are based on contracts and concepts that have been constructed and either agreed upon or imposed (as in Africa) from the outside. Accordingly, they can be deconstructed and redefined as recent history shows in the case of the former Yugoslavia or the former USSR, where former sub-nationalisms were turned into nationalisms. Leaving economic factors aside, what makes a nation a stable construct for some time at least is the consent of the majority constituting this nation. Regarding this element of consent to nationhood, Ernest Renan remarked in a lecture delivered at the Sorbonne in 1882: 'A nation's existence is, if you will pardon the metaphor, a daily plebiscite, just as an individual's existence is a perpetual affirmation of life.'[1]

Usually, part of the process of becoming a nation is to define oneself by identifying the 'otherness' of one's neighbours. National stereotypes and prejudices are employed towards this end. Other means are national myths and history. A nation – or the European Union – can only continue to exist when people identify with it on a rational *and* an emotional level, employing mechanisms of exclusion and inclusion. The rational level is to some extent handled by politicians and journalists, whereas literature is an ideal vehicle to transmit and possibly even expose the emotional level. In Naipaul's *Enigma of Arrival*, the author-narrator points to the core concern of imaginative writing and the different priority it has compared with other narratives produced by, for example, academic disciplines: 'The historian seeks to abstract principles from human events. My approach was the other; for the two years that I lived among the documents I sought to reconstruct the human story as best I could.' (*EA*, p. 94)

In the context of European integration, the British Prime Minister Tony Blair recently pointed out that the people have to catch up with the institutionalization of Europe. In other words, if Europe is to become a unified 'country' then the union has to take roots on the micro-level and cannot get stuck in administrative structures. Towards the end of his life, Jean Monnet suggested that he would start the European project with culture were he given another chance. We obviously cannot start again, but what we can do is give literature, as an important constituent part of a culture, a more prominent place in the discussion on European integration. Thus, this volume brings together essays which look at representations of Europe and its nation-states in literature. As indicated above, literary sources have the distinct advantage that they do not have to pretend to be rational but, because of their literary nature, are allowed to be subjective and emotive, describing feelings and prejudices, which provides an additional dimension to the discussion on the idea of Europe. Using literature also makes it possible to look at existing prejudices and stereotypes which make a union and an understanding between the different nations so difficult.

This volume consists of three parts which deal respectively with different perspectives on Europe. Part 1 discusses the 'Portrayal of the Continent' and draws on literary sources produced by Europeans about Europeans. The second part, 'Inner/Outer Perspectives in Comparison', deals with views of Europe 'from within' compared with those 'from the outside'. The final part, 'The Idea of Europe and National Identity', consists of contributions that discuss questions of identity in the European context.

There is one last point that requires a brief clarification regarding the contributors' 'ideas' of Europe and literature as separate concepts. Our 'idea' of Europe is not restricted to the European Union member states; hence one contribution focuses on Romania, and others include Eastern Europe in their analyses, and our 'idea' of literature also allows for a discussion of cinematic and televized material.

NOTE

1. Ernest Renan, 'What is a Nation?' *Nation and Narration*, ed. Homi Bhabha (London: Routledge, 1990), pp. 8–22, 19.

Part I
Portrayal of the Continent

1 Charlotte Brontë's Alternative 'European Community'
Jan B. Gordon

Thanks to the morbid estrangement which the lunacy of nationality has produced and continues to produce between the people of Europe, thanks likewise to the short-sighted and hasty-handed politicians who are with its aid on top today and have not the slightest notion to what extent the politics of disintegration they pursue must necessarily be only an interlude – thanks to all this, and to much else that is unmentionable today, the most unambiguous signs are now being overlooked [...] which declare that *Europe wants to become one*.[1]

In past days there had been, said history, an awful crisis in the fate of Labbassecour, involving I know not what peril to the rights and liberties of her gallant citizens [...]. Tradition held that patriots had fallen: in the old Basse-Ville was shown an enclosure, solemnly built in and set apart, holding, it was said, the sacred bones of martyrs. Be this as it may, a certain day in the year was still kept as a festival in honour of the said patriots and martyrs of somewhat apocryphal memory – the morning being given to a solemn Te Deum in St Jean Baptiste, the evening devoted to spectacles, decorations, and illuminations, such as these I now saw [...].
  That festal night would have been safe for a very child. Half the peasantry had come in from the outlying environs of Villette, and the decent burghers were all abroad and around, dressed in their best. My straw-hat passed amidst cap and jacket, short petticoat, and long calico mantle, without perhaps attracting a glance; I only took the precaution to bind down the broad leaf gipsy-wise, with a supplementary ribbon; and then I felt safe as if masked.[2]

Lucy Snowe's dream of a provisional, unitary European community in which all classes might celebrate a shared historical past occurs in *Villette* only after she has been drugged by her mentor/tormentor and rival for Monsieur Paul's attentions, Madame Beck. In Charlotte Brontë's account, the midnight visitation to the *Place of the Martyrs*, that symbolic Hôtel de Ville of European consciousness, and its celebratory fete – as it turns out, a kind of nocturnal *Déjeuner sur l'herbe* – is narratively and syntactically indistinguishable from the contents of the drug-induced dream whose recursivity it shares. Even the attentive reader of *Villette*[3] is uncertain whether Lucy Snowe's passive participation really occurred, or is merely one more part of the repressed nightmare of European history as imagined by isolated British expatriates on the continent. Like Nietzsche's equally induced pan-European utopia, this alternative community could be either the product of a repressing 'individual interest' or its cause. What is being celebrated may (doubly) never have occurred: the consequence of a 'somewhat apocryphal' personal and political record, which is nonetheless accepted as true and held in the collective memory of the nation, Lucy Snowe, and the reader. If this annual celebration of European revolutionary unity is in fact a collective fantasy, then echoing Lewis Carroll, we might justifiably ask, of both Nietzsche and Lucy Snowe, who, precisely, is the subject of these repressed dreams?

The overly 'sincere' Lucy Snowe does not quite fit in with the festivities. Though ostensibly 'safe for a very child', she feels insufficiently secure so as to necessitate a disguise. And that disguise is remarkable, for amidst what is a very cosmopolitan group representing all classes and vocations, she marginalizes herself with the mask of the darkened gypsy, the original borderless: people of the European imagination – transnational, but persecuted. Having dedicated herself to assimilation in the life of Labbassecour and its Franco-Flemish culture and having mastered to some degree the French language (in whose fluency Lucy Snowe shows such sustained improvement in the course of Charlotte Brontë's novel that it begins to subvert English), in its penultimate pages, the heroine reverts to the posture of the Euro-sceptic on the periphery, the spy who must have a 'cover' if she is to attend the ritual of European unity or its dreams.

To be sure, hers is not the only nineteenth-century British fantasy in which any participation in European life is conditional upon some act of false consciousness. For Wordsworth in *The Prelude*, the French Revolution, like the imaginary long poem for which his own twelve-book epic was to be but the prelude, was the betrayal of a hoped-for apocalyptic order. With Napoleon's advent, Europe became the place where dreams became nightmares on a truly grand scale. In the by now infamous passage in Book V, the so-called 'Simplon Pass' episode, Wordsworth was to link the ideology of revolutionary betrayal to the failures of the poetic imagination: transcendence, politically or imaginatively, can be experienced only after the fact, as an inability to dwell in the immediacy of the moment, save as the imagination has (always-already) transformed it into the secondary – one of those recoverable, but for that very reason inauthentic, 'spots of time'. Devoting all his hopes and energies to the ascent of whatever geographic, political or imaginative heights, the speaker/traveller has access to it only derivatively, in the conversations of those who have already descended the slippery slopes of romantic self-consciousness. Experientially apparently, as well as politically, the majesty of Europe and the brotherhood of man have become, in the first quarter of the nineteenth century, a kind of sublime 'syncope', to borrow from Catherine Clément, that inexpressible interruption or interlude in the putative syntagmatic order of the British literary imagination.[4]

Although Europe continues to have a place in the canonical works of British Romanticism, it is often part and parcel of the geography of this interruption. The abrupt heights and dizzying abysses of late eighteenth- and early nineteenth-century gothic fiction found a congenial topography on the continent where distinctions of gender and genre, and those enforced by political boundaries, were less fixed and, consequently, disguise and substitutions created an economy of potentially perpetual dissimulation, so evident in the works of Mrs Radcliffe. The displaced heir, the purloined (but possibly counterfeit) or lost manuscript, the Catholic penchant for illusion, demons, and imaginative transubstantiations found a more receptive home on the continent, rather than in a Britain which privileged philosophical empiricism and a pragmatic religion coterminal with the state and its interests. Gothic novels with their 'framed' narratives, conditional status as 'found' texts, and infinitely regressive corridors and plots, were a perfect medium for the discontinuous, sublime *frisson*.[5] Emotional and topographical amplitude were shared by the map of Europe and that of the tormented, gothic soul in the early-nineteenth-century British literary imagination. If the Byronic Grand Tour with its implicit association of sexual licence and political freedom, the prerogative of a British patriarchy with enough wealth or time on its hands, is one representation of the nineteenth-century European 'visitation' in the popular consciousness, surely George Eliot's Dorothea Brooke on her ill-fated Roman honeymoon with an academic pedant more than twice her age, on the eve of the First Reform Bill, is another. For it is in that city of presumptive transcendental illuminations that, in contradistinction to Lord Byron's experience, the potential revolutionary perceived her future life as a closed 'basin', her meliorative projects confined by a suffocating marriage. Europe, for George Eliot, is the surfeit of history rather than, as for Shelley or Byron, the prospect of flight from its burdens. If Europe is the site of limitless metaphysical and ideological vistas on the one hand, it can easily become a prison house of the imagination on the other – or even both simultaneously, as in Mary Shelley's *Frankenstein*, with its highly internationalized protagonists.

As a figuratively (and often commercially) underground literary form, the gothic novel often alternates between the two extremes. Perhaps Fairfax Rochester of *Jane Eyre* is a case in point. Although part of the British landed aristocracy, his estate, Thornfield, even etymologically, belongs to the post-lapsarian world, the edenic gone to seed as a consequence of its master's sexual secret in the attic. Yet, his attraction for Jane Eyre, so often clad in her drab Quaker-grey cloak, lies in his skill at disguise and dissimulation. Early on in her stay as a governess at Thornfield, during an evening's dramatic performances and charades, Rochester cloaks himself in the garb of the gypsy fortune-teller in order that he might surreptitiously fathom the secrets of Jane Eyre's heart. As in *Villette*, a European education, no matter what its culturally cosmopolitan attraction, is experienced by the devoutly Protestant British governess or schoolmistress as latently deceptive, willing to disguise itself (as ventriloquy or an equivalent sartorial dissimulation, the harlequinage of the gypsy) in order to lure the insular and inexperienced to its doom. This danger is, paradoxically, part of Rochester's sensual appeal; his marriage proposal mixes new prospects with the promise of shedding sunlight on his Byronic past.

> 'I shall bear my treasure to regions nearer the sun: to French vineyards and Italian plains; and she shall see whatever is famous in old story and in modern record [...].'
> 'Shall I travel? – and with you, sir?'
> 'You shall sojourn at Paris, Rome, and Naples; at Florence, Venice, and Vienna: all the ground I have wandered over shall be re-

trodden by you [...]. Ten years since, I fled through Europe half mad; with disgust, hate, and rage, as my companions: now I shall revisit it healed and cleansed, with a very angel as my comforter.' (*Jane Eyre* II, ix, p. 272)

In a remarkable metaphoric transposition, however, his heliotropic marriage proposal becomes in her own mind an occluding darkness, which threatens the stern faith in which she has been raised: 'he stood between me and every thought of religion, as an eclipse intervenes between man and the broad sun' (*Jane Eyre* II, ix, p. 272). Despite the passionate pull of a Mediterranean warmth, Europe's darkness is the threat to her salvational faith. In order for such passion and violent history to be made open to full British participation, several conditions must be met, all of which are fulfilled in the highly symmetrical plot of *Jane Eyre*.

The deceptive libertine must seek atonement for past sexual, political, or economic profligacy. This is accomplished by a symbolically reflationary economic manoeuvre: Jane Eyre must be shown to be born to wealth, self-sufficient enough to challenge Rochester's own independence. Jane Eyre is revealed to be neither the discontinuous orphan nor some destitute appendage, but someone defrauded of expectations and hence potentially Rochester's social equal. This can be accomplished only by forcing a European sensibility to become dependent upon Britain's rather specialized skills, by impoverishing those very cultural values which had previously appeared as indomitable as the Mediterranean sun. When Thornfield burns, becoming the gothic ruin *par excellence*, impairing Rochester's sight and mobility in a conflagration initiated by his unacknowledged past, he beckons Jane Eyre to symbolically redeem a pernicious influence of European history.

If not the absolute saviour of that which torments her dreams, Jane Eyre must become the Florence Nightingale who sets the diseased and handicapped upon the road to social assimilation. As his economic and physical status is demeaned, hers is raised, making a marriage of 'interests' possible, within the confines of some symbolic equivalent of an emotional exchange rate mechanism. Additionally, however, she must turn her back on an alternative, historically antecedent interest, an equally alien but more familiar Empire which makes similar, threatening demands. This is achieved in the plot of Charlotte Brontë's novel by Jane's denial of St John River's request that she retain her quasi-ecclesiastical habit (in some double sense) by accompanying him in the hybrid role of unacknowledged wife (disguised as a 'sister') in a missionary enterprise to India, an alternative region where the sun seldom sets for long! There, she would combine a sexless 'marriage', social service to the socially handicapped, and an unacknowledged colonial impulse in a *mélange* of false consciousness.

Read admittedly as a rigid political allegory, Britain (Jane Eyre) has a permanent (marital) interest in Europe only when it serves as a restraining counterweight to the dominant power which threatens civilized, moral values: an entirely acceptable description of British foreign policy *vis-à-vis* Europe during most of the nineteenth century. Simultaneously, in the British literary (and perhaps political) imagination, Europe appears as a potential rival to that Empire whose similarly needy heathen made similar (imaginary?) demands upon British civilization and its moral values. The burgeoning British Empire, however, was at least metaphorically – and perhaps more than metaphorically, given the proliferating designations, like OBE and CBE, used to define the precise nature of the subject's relationship to a continuous political 'family' – not part merely of the country's interests, but 'of us', in a quasi-biological sense. Given the impossibility of extending the Empire to the continent (and perhaps owing something to Britain's penchant for colonizing mythically 'empty' countries on other continents), Europe historically continued to be portrayed in her literatures as a temptation of history, to be avoided as a potentially harmful entanglement or, given the dominance of Roman Catholicism in the Mediterranean rim, a subversive threat. Very late in the nineteenth century and even until his so-called 'major phase', Henry James was still portraying Europe as a deceptive antique shop where the likes of Gilbert Osmond or Madame de Cintre lure the innocent and unwary puritan imagination into morally compromising positions and collusive social gestures even as they pay homage to the 'honour' of another, antecedent 'family' of sexual or economic interests. Rather special 'ambassadorial' missions and interventions are often necessary to extricate the 'innocent abroad' – be he British or American – from European entanglements.

If Europe was to be seen not as a temptation to solid British isolation or the museum of history turned into a gothic ruin it must be made to appear as an internal British political 'interest', like that of the Empire, in which the Crown had a proprietary share. That early letter of Charlotte Brontë wherein she announces a desire to reside in Belgium rather than the continental *bête noir*, France, suggests a new country which gave indications of qualifying: 'I would not go to France or to Paris. I would go to Brussels, in Belgium [...]. I could improve greatly in Italian and even get a dash of German, i.e. providing my health continued as good as it is now'.[6] In contradistinction to the illusory and self-deluding Mediterranean vistas of *Jane Eyre* (1847) that temporarily extinguished the heroine's religious faith, Belgium apparently offered an alternative foreign community, more easily assimilable to Britain's self-image. In the later *Shirley* (1849), *Villette* (1853) and *The Professor* (published posthumously in 1857), Belgium is represented as the one continental country whose social, political and economic interests were imagined to be so coincidental with Britain's that a more or less emotional free trade, without the tariffs that imposed physical or emotional handicaps, was possible. Charlotte Brontë, in these less familiar late novels, came to terms of course with her early experiences as both student and docent in Monsieur Heger's Brussels *pensionnat* where, apart from a nursery maid, she was the sole Protestant. But these late novels, if read politically rather than as the revelation of a secret romantic attachment to Monsieur Heger, as is often the case in critical commentary, might suggest an opening for an altogether different British 'involvement'.[7] Rather than the fear of threats to sovereignty, mutual distrust, and persistent advancement of claims of exceptionalism, which collectively continued to define British attitudes toward Europe during the nineteenth century, and may well characterize its posture toward the European Union at the end of the twentieth century, Belgium, at least in Charlotte Brontë's imagination, is the one continental country in which Britain might find a kind of soul-mate. Many of her heroes and heroines do precisely that.

To be sure, Belgium was a new and, in its ideological associations, an 'empty' European country when Emily and Charlotte Brontë took up residence there in 1842. Occupied by the French during the Revolutionary Wars, the country was transferred from Austria to France by the Treaty of Campo Formio. After the defeat of Napoleon at Waterloo (south of Brussels) in 1815, the territory now denominated as Belgium was granted to the newly formed Kingdom of the Netherlands under the provisions of the Congress of Vienna. Under the reign of King William I of the Netherlands, the Belgians came to resent measures that discriminated against them, primarily in the areas of language and religion, in favour of the Dutch. Belgian independence was established after a rebellion in Brussels in 1830. The attempt of William I to suppress the uprising failed when France and England intervened in 1832. In a sense, then, Belgium's foundational 'revolution', like Great Britain's 'near miss' at approximately the same time (when the 'Catholic Question' in Ireland and the agitation for extended suffrage which led to the passage of the First Reform Bill coalesced) was more 'virtual' than real, brokered by a last-minute consensus among unlikely allies. At the London Conference of 1831–2, an Anglophile, Prince Leopold of Saxe-Coburg-Gotha, became King of the Belgians as Leopold I. In 1838–9, at a second London Conference, a final Dutch-Belgian peace treaty was signed, and the perpetual neutrality of Belgium was guaranteed by the major European powers, including Prussia. With its security guaranteed, Belgium dedicated itself to rapid industrialization and investment in infrastructure. Even in Africa, Belgium's colonies were a useful buffer between French West Africa and British interests in South Africa and Rhodesia: the 'protected' neutral necessary to a balance of power and any economic prosperity which ensued.

If Belgium was indeed a new kind of nation, relatively immune to the arbitrary political winds which threatened the economic viability and even the national security of the nations of Europe during the wave of abortive liberalizations which briefly brought 'citizen-kings' to power in the 1830s, we might logically expect to encounter this uniqueness in British literature of the period.[8] And, sure enough, when William Crimsworth of *The Professor*, in flight from familial servitude, initially responds to Belgium as an impecunious refugee looking for employment, it is the landscape of the tiny country which strikes him as, well, 'buffered'. He takes great pains to assure the reader of Charlotte Brontë's novel that the route by stagecoach from Ostend to Brussels is neither 'flat' nor 'dull', the two common British extremes which have shaped his sensibility, but nonetheless aesthetically pleasing, as a 'plotted' middle distance susceptible to imaginative improvements by those willing to accept a reduced visual scale:

> Well! and what did I see? I will tell you faithfully. Green, reedy swamps; fields fertile but flat, cultivated in patches that made them look like magnified kitchen-gardens; belts of cut trees, formal as pollard willows, skirting the horizon; narrow canals, gliding slow by the roadside; painted Flemish farm-houses; some dirty

hovels; a grey, dead sky; wet road, wet fields, wet housetops: not a beautiful; scarcely a picturesque object met my eye along the whole route; yet to me all was beautiful, all was more than picturesque. It continued fair as long as daylight lasted [. . .]. (*The Professor* VII, p. 87)

Although lacking his customary attributes of natural beauty, the Flemish landscape is nevertheless beautiful in Crimsworth's reflections. Miraculously, a leaden grey sky becomes fair in a revisionary gesture within the same paragraph. Similarly, during his first night at a foreign hotel, a slatternly Flemish housemaid 'with an air the reverse of civil' is transformed into something 'charming', whom the speaker conceives of, again, as 'very picturesque' (*The Professor*, VII, p. 89), as he attempts to make her conform to increasingly restrictive categories of aesthetic comprehension.[9] The Belgian landscape, standards of physical charm and beauty, and apparently even appellations have a squishy variability, like that of the mysteriously named Zoraïde Reuter, at least in Crimsworth's narrow imagination:

[. . .] the Continental nations do allow themselves vagaries in the choice of names, such as we sober English never run into. I think, indeed, we have too limited a list to choose from. (*The Professor* VII, p. 97)

Those limits are surely apparent to any reader attempting to keep the generational lines clearly demarcated in *Wuthering Heights*!

Thus, ever so subtly, the Professor's native England becomes home to a civilization whose arbitrary limits extend from fixed definitions of the picturesque, through a host of other aesthetic responses and social practices. And yet, the insufficiency of binary distinctions in easing the Briton's exposure to Belgium remains a feature of his professional life. Confronted by what he believes to be a combination of low intelligence and student insubordination in Monsieur Pelet's classrooms where he has taken up employment as an English master, Crimsworth's strategy reflects his own radical protestant upbringing: 'I offered them but one alternative – submission and acknowledgment of error, or ignominious expulsion' (*The Professor* VII, p. 98). Prey to pedagogical predestination, his students can retain only the illusion of free choice; to borrow from the categories of the heterodox Joseph of *Wuthering Heights*, the 'fallen' must submit to judgment as (only) potentially 'chozzen' – and then, only after an exhaustive catechism – or are banished as so much 'rubbidge'.

Puritan antinomies are part of Crimsworth's personal effects which accompany him to Brussels and must ultimately be discarded.

Although partially explicable given the religious convictions of the Reverend Patrick Brontë, the arbitrary, unpredictable nature of God's Creation – and derivatively of Great Britain itself – is truly remarkable. In all of Charlotte Brontë's novels, as the so-called Tawney-Weber thesis might suggest, the indeterminacy and instability of man's future heavenly prospects are reflected in the precarious state of his financial position; the 'wager' of faith and the vagaries of capitalist risk create a life of spiritual and economic doubt.[10] Albeit the descendant of a landed family, Crimsworth's refusal to marry a first cousin (and hence to maintain familial wealth within the parameters of a biological model of 'succession') places him at the mercy of his abusive brother, Edward, a mill-owner who demands increasing expressions of loyalty with no economic reciprocity. In other words, William Crimsworth's emigration to the Belgian classroom is an attempt to replace now empty marital and economic prospects, similar to the impulses which shaped the British Empire in the early years of the nineteenth century. This 'turn to Europe' is narrated as a loosening of hitherto fixed categories of aesthetic, theological and social habits of response.

We almost forget how fiscally insecure and unstable Britain appears in the Brontë novels. Jane Eyre, albeit in reality the unacknowledged dependant of a secure, propertied uncle, is orphaned to extraordinary poverty and physical deprivation at Gateshead and, after a marital injunction which renders Fairfax Rochester (temporarily as it turns out) ineligible, is banished, guilty, to a literal wilderness in which she wanders without sustenance until found and partially redeemed by St John Rivers's family and faith. The acknowledgment of kinship by the unknown uncle alone restores her to the traditional prospects of the landed, part of the proceeds of which she shares with St John Rivers – to whom she incidentally discovers a shared genealogical relationship. Jane Eyre undergoes two cycles of 'riches to rags' and back, before she settles in to something resembling upper middle-class comfort in a burned-out Thornfield which must be 'improved' along with its handicapped master. Reduced to its economic dimension, *Jane Eyre* intimates that personal 'worth' and financial wealth continue to have their joint origin in the *family*: wealth can be shared only by the recuperation of a foundational family 'name' from which one has been estranged, but is not otherwise 'made' or redistributed by virtue of some implicit social contract.

Shirley commences with a similar portrayal of widespread economic inequality *across* social classes and a commensurate volatility within those classes accustomed to stability, from which only a very secure clergy remains exempt. Although the 'abundant shower of curates' (*Shirley* I, p. 39) which characterized the bloated bureaucracy of the Church of England in the 1840s had not yet flooded the landscape, already in the first decade of the nineteenth century (in the chronologically displaced setting of Charlotte Brontë's novel), the clergy alone among the so-called Establishment exhibit an extraordinary sense of social and economic security and the leisure time that accompanies it. They lavish their energies on an 'unfailing supply of enjoyment' (*Shirley* I, p. 40) not entirely approved of by those in other communities:

> a rushing backwards and forwards, among themselves, to and from their respective lodgings: not a round – but a triangle of visits, which they keep up all the year through, in winter, spring, summer, and autumn. Season and weather make no difference; with unintelligible zeal they dare snow and hail, wind and rain, mire and dust, to go and dine, or drink tea, or sup with each other. (*Shirley* I, p. 40)

If the vaunted English weather is symbolic of the heights of environmental unpredictability, the lives of minor curates are peculiarly resistant.

The insecurity of Robert Gérard Moore, the Anglo-Belgian immigrant in Yorkshire, is in marked contrast to those of the natives. Although he will ultimately be assimilated into a more Europeanized Britain, at the outset of Charlotte Brontë's novel he shares in a mutually felt hostility to the presence of a visitor with two social strikes against him: foreign birth and no land holdings. Born and partially reared in Antwerp, Moore had been heir to a two-hundred-year-old merchant trading company which had fallen upon bad times and ultimate ruin during the period of speculation which accompanied the French Revolution. That collapse had necessarily had an impact on the English and Yorkshire subsidiary of the Anglo-Dutch parent company, so that the 'hybrid' (*Shirley* II, p. 60) is forced to rent a derelict cloth mill in a remote district at high rent in order to repay the family debts and restore the trading house to its former glory.

With his accented English and single-minded, somewhat parsimonious (Flemish?) ambition, Moore has some success, even with limited capital, in replacing obsolete and inefficient machinery and 'rationalizing' productive and distributional practices. Yet, as an immigrant from Europe, he remains aloof from participation in the community life of Fieldhead and its environs, which in some sense defines British provincial life. This isolation from the normal rounds (or triangles) of social life, traced by the British clergy and those they call upon, is attributed to the divided political allegiances of someone who is, after all, only half-British, and therefore neither entirely acceptable nor accepting:

> [...] it is probable he had a hybrid's feeling on many points – patriotism for one; it is likely that he was unapt to attach himself to parties, to sects, even to climes and customs; it is not impossible that he had a tendency to isolate his individual person from any community amidst which his lot might temporarily happen to be thrown [...]. (*Shirley* II, p. 60)

Any isolation from the 'lived life' of Fieldhead, no matter how boring and tedious, is translated in the community's speculations about the *arriviste* speculator into a manifestation of a new kind of homelessness. Not the parasitical vagrancy of the growing hordes of unemployed and underemployed, to be sure, but nonetheless potentially destabilizing of 'inherent' cultural values. For the 'hybrid' mill-owner is imagined to be interested only in 'push[ing] the interests of Robert Gérard Moore, to the exclusion of philanthropic consideration for general interest' (*Shirley* II, p. 60). Having no landed stake in his fledgling enterprise, Moore compounds the accusation of nomadism by a consistent hesitancy to identify any recognizable political or linguistic loyalty, as is evident in a conversation with the minimally articulate Joe Scott, employed in the mill's counting room:

> 'Is there mony o"your mak' i" your country?' inquired Joe, as he folded up his temporary bed, and put it away.
> 'In my country! Which is my country?'
> 'Why, France – isn't it?'
> 'Not it indeed! The circumstances of the French having seized Antwerp, where I was born, does not make me a Frenchman.'
> 'Holland, then?'
> 'I am not a Dutchman: now you are confounding Antwerp with Amsterdam.'
> 'Flanders?'
> 'I scorn the insinuation, Joe! I, a Flamand! Have I a Flemish face? – .... Joe, I'm an Anversois.' (*Shirley* V, p. 87)

A native of a state only *in situ*, as it were, in the period between 1807 and 1820, the chronological setting of Charlotte Brontë's narrative, Moore is a forerunner of the late twentieth century's international businessmen, at home everywhere ... and nowhere. His theological next-of-kin is to be found in Lucy Snowe of *Villette* who, fleeing her narrow Protestantism with its dependence upon empirical verification of the signs of election, but resistant to the Jesuitical Monsieur Paul's attempts to convert her to the magical transubstantiations of Roman Catholicism, becomes almost impossibly ecumenical in the same Belgium with which Robert Gérard Moore will come to (minimally) identify:

> Père Silas, it seems, had closely watched me, and ascertained that I went my turns, and indiscriminately, to the three Protestant Chapels of Villette – the French, German, and English – *id est*, the Presbyterian, Lutheran, Episcopalian. Such liberality argued in the Father's eyes profound indifference – who tolerates all, he reasoned, can be attached to none. (*Villette* XXXVI, p. 513)

This reluctance to embrace steadfastly any single faith ultimately extends to a remarkable degree of tolerance, given Lucy Snowe's (and the Brontë) religious education. Presented with a gift-volume that 'preach[es] Romanism', by her imaginary lover, Miss Snowe recognizes the familiar even in what she originally (and prejudicially) believed to be anathema:

> [...] portions of it reminded me of certain Wesleyan Methodist tracts I had read when a child; they were flavoured by about the same seasoning of excitation to fanaticism. (*Villette* XXXVI, p. 508)

As the differences between the main European faiths begin to narrow in her mind, Lucy Snowe's rich fantasy life, subsidized by the secret passages of Madame Beck's behaviour and institution, comes to be amplified: the heroine begins to recognize that her condemnation of the unverifiable nature of the visionary in Roman Catholicism is unwarranted. Once one begins to have dreams which mix real experiences, local history, and oppression, such as the one prefixed to this essay as an epigraph, Monsieur Paul's generalization, 'Protestants are rarely superstitious' (*Villette* XXXV, p. 502), becomes an ironic commentary upon Lucy Snowe's slow departure from some of her faith's more rigorous tenets. Her increasing affection for him involves, if not the wholesale acceptance of his faith, at least the realization that she must find common ground, exempt from the prejudices attendant upon what was, after all, an historical schism.

This progressive modification or flattening of a faith which depends upon a belief in *extremity* – the separation of those elected for salvation from the permanently lost – has its parallel in a similar political ecumenicism which comes to affect everyday life in *Shirley*. The search for a common 'interest' between an isolated Great Britain and the rest of Europe was originally prompted, one suspects, by a nightmare – as was the case with Lucy Snowe's search for a unified faith in *Villette*. In the period between 1807 and 1810, Napoleon waged economic war against Britain through the so-called Continental System which closed, in progressively more repressive measures, all north German ports to British trade. The British reciprocated with 24 Orders in Council which imposed stringent control and excessive customs duties on all neutral trade with Europe. In concert, the two measures caused acute economic distress, exaggerating an already serious monetary crisis in Britain; had it continued beyond 1811, it may well have resulted in the total defeat of Britain, for whom a favourable balance of trade was crucial in financing the European opposition to Napoleon. With markets for his finished cloth all but closed off, Moore, the entrepreneurial mill-owner in *Shirley*, has begun to cut costs, first through redundancies, but later by installing new, more efficient mechanized looms and frames.

As the novel opens, his impoverished former employees have begun to organize themselves into increasingly militant associations, one of which conspires to attack the mill and destroy the new machinery. The collapse in the British standard of living wrought by the Continental System – rather than military warfare – 'trickles down' as an armed domestic insurrection which erupts in *Shirley* as a midnight raid on the Fieldhead mill. This threat demands that the community, and especially the Establishment, take sides with either the disenchanted workers or the landlords and mill-owners who, in this case, happen to be of European, francophone descent. As the ironies of history would have it, security guarantees for nations (based upon treaty and/or traditional alliances) and employment guarantees for workers (based upon an unwritten feudal obligation between landlords and dependants) – each of which were believed to be crucial to the maintenance of international and domestic peace, respectively – were revealed by the Continental System to be simultaneously worthless without economic prosperity.

As *Shirley* commences, political battle lines are sharply drawn. The High Tory Rector of Briarfield, Helstone, laments the depredations of private property and the widespread disaffection with constituted authority, his prescribed cures being 'vigorous government interference, strict magisterial vigilance; [and] when necessary, prompt military coercion' (*Shirley* IV, p. 83). Believing in a foundational Establishment which presumably united church and state in such a way as to make them organically inseparable from the individual will, the cleric cannot understand the interests of the people detaching themselves from the institutions in which and by which they are formed. But Hiram Yorke, that 'gentleman of the old school' (*Shirley* IV, p. 79), whose family was the first and oldest in the district, sees the same widespread disaffection with constituted authorities as politically promising. Although he concedes the genuine grievances of the masters and mill-owners, Yorke realizes that government interference cannot ever feed the hungry. His complaints centre upon the weaknesses of a governing order, 'king-ridden, priest-ridden, peer-ridden [...] where [...] a pampered, persecuting established Church was endured and venerated' (*Shirley* IV, p. 83). The international entrepreneur and investor, however, refuses to take sides. This is the first step in shaping a new *via media* which will put a premium neither on law and order nor upon radical changes in the political system which has historically defined British life and its governance:

> 'I dare not stay all night with a rebel and blasphemer, like you, Yorke; and I hardly dare ride home with a cruel and tyrannical ecclesiastic, like Mr Helstone.' (*Shirley* IV, p. 85)

At first glance, Anglo-Belgian ideological neutrality seems of a piece with community expectations of the British mercantile and merchant classes who come in for their share of rebuke at the hands of Charlotte Brontë's omniscient narrator who, as would the Brontë version of the Divine, stand in judgement:

> Many of them are extremely narrow and cold-hearted, have no good feeling for any class but their own, are distant – even hostile to all others; call them useless; seem to question their right to exist [...]. They do not know what others do in the way of helping, pleasing, or teaching their race; they will not trouble themselves to inquire: whoever is not in trade is accused of eating the bread of idleness, of passing a useless existence. Long may it be ere England really becomes a nation of shopkeepers. (*Shirley* X, p. 184)

In this patriotic rebuke of Napoleon's judgement of British mercantile interests, Charlotte Brontë's narrator, like Robert Gérard Moore, will occupy a position advocating compromise: patriotically opposed to the 'nation of shopkeepers' but also critical of the positions of Britain's two political parties. Like the narrator, Moore early on sets himself apart from those who think 'too exclusively of making money' (*Shirley* X, p. 183), with an extraordinary act of self-criticism.

For, though he initially insists that his only interest is self-interest – the protection of his mill and its future unrealized assets against the vandalism of disenchanted operatives – he nonetheless asks to be remembered in his cousin (and *fiancée manquée*), Caroline Helstone's, prayers. Brought up 'only to make money [...] and scarcely breath[ing] any other air than that of mills and markets' (*Shirley* VII, p. 144), Moore fears perpetual exclusion from the nest of any 'benignant heart' that might hopefully 'harbour him'. As a refugee, struggling to 'wipe clean from [his] bourgeois scutcheon the foul stain of bankruptcy' (ibid.), the defensive and solitary Moore fears that his heart has become similarly exiled among the ledgers of his mill's counting-house. That delicate equipoise which Matthew Arnold was later to find only in the perfect balance of Hebraic strictness of conscience with the Hellenic love of beauty and spiritual expansiveness, Moore would hope to find in combining the motives instilled by Christ with those dictated by Mammon.

Ever so gradually, Robert Gérard Moore will embrace, if not economic union with Europe, at least the free-trade doctrines which were a nineteenth-century antecedent in so far as they recognized the possibility of shared economic interests. We almost forget, given the emotional baggage which has historically attached itself to 'free trade' and open markets in the post-capitalist era, that in the so-called 'hungry 1840s' the notion of free trade offered a political 'seam' between the Tory defence of the Establishment and Whig criticism of its monopoly upon British political, economic and religious life, and the increasingly desperate plight of labourers, mill hands, and renters.[11] The change in Moore's bourgeois self-interest and contempt for the lower social orders which threaten it and the ultimate assimilation of the international businessman into British life, effected through a marriage to the comfortable Caroline Helstone, similarly 'smudged' by a genealogical blot on the scutcheon, is surely a precursor of later attempts to privilege a certain kind of mutually beneficial, *complementary* international relationship like that privileged in E.M. Forster's novel, *Howard's End* (with its elliptical epigraph, 'only connect').[12]

Those who supported the doctrine of free trade, as opposed to its mere practice, tended to be radicals in the context of the 1840s, a radicalism which Charlotte Brontë projects backward in time to the first decade of the nineteenth century. They were generally advocates of a *laissez-faire* policy which included individualism; a resistance to empire; non-intervention in foreign affairs; minimal state interference in commerce and industry (hence Moore's reliance upon a civilian co-operative in defence of his mill); and finally, the replacement of the old paternal relationship between owner and dependant by a contractual relationship between employer and employed. The so-called Free Traders were initially organized by the radical Richard Cobden, cotton printer and pacifist, and John Bright, a Quaker, as merely an Anti-Corn Law League, campaigning for the abolition of protective tariffs which had raised prices of staples for the poor.[13] But, gradually, as extended through the 'Manchester School', free trade came to encompass an assortment of anti-monopoly attitudes: the abolition of the means whereby landlords had maintained the great estates in the hands of a few people or the abolition of the monopoly held by the Church of England on the country's behalf. Because these real or imagined monopolies were associated with sovereignty and hence, by implication, national security, free trade came to be seen in some quarters as a potentially dangerous internationalism with a concomitant threat to the 'local'.

Having once escaped his brother Edward's malignity and the servitude of the counting-house (where one of his duties was the translation of European business correspondence), William Crimsworth is befriended by another mill-owner, the mysterious Mr Hunsden, whose varied international 'contacts' result in William's appointment as a professor in Belgium. To the astonishment of his British guest, the international 'mover and shaker', Hunsden, imbibes Rhine wines and coffee (as opposed to tea) while enjoying an equally cosmopolitan intellectual diet, as revealed by his library shelves:

> French and German works predominated, the old French dramatists, sundry modern authors, Thiers, Villemain, Paul de Kock, George Sand; in German – Goethe, Schiller, Zschokke, Jean Paul Richter; in English there were works on Political Economy. (*The Professor* IV, p. 65)

Later in the novel, Hunsden's international tastes are seen to be matched by an equally eclectic circle of social acquaintances, one of whom appears, at least to Crimsworth's wife, the former Frances Henri, to have 'tout l'air d'un conspirateur' (*The Professor* XXV, p. 282).

This suspicion of a nefarious political or amatory space beneath social existence and conventions is a recurrent experience among those Britons exposed to continental life and its ideologies in Charlotte Brontë's fiction. Abetted, at least initially, by limitations in the linguistic comprehension of the British expatriates, these pockets of secrecy, subterfuge, and incompletely overheard conversations come to impact on the proxemics governing the ways in which people, institutions, and social conventions are related. Typically, the 'shadow-world' (*Villette* XIII, p. 185) surrounding the assorted international schools in which her British teachers find refuge (or employment, depending upon the reader's perspective) comprehends a covert *allée* whose access initially, but only initially, appears as restricted or otherwise enjoined to the non-initiated:

> The windowless backs of houses built in this garden, and in particular the whole of one side was skirted by the rear of a long line of premises – being the boarding-houses of the neighbouring college. This rear, however, was all black stone, with the exception of certain attic loop-holes high up, *opening* from the sleeping rooms of the women-servants, and also one casement in a lower story said to mark the chamber or study of a master. But, *though thus secure, an alley, which ran parallel with the very high wall on that side of the garden*, was forbidden to be entered by the pupils. It was called indeed 'l'allée défendue', and any girl setting foot there would have rendered herself liable to as severe a penalty as the mild rules of Madame Beck's establishment permitted. (*Villette* XI, p. 174, italics added)

This sacred lane, park, fountain, or plaza – not unlike the one which the drugged and disguised Lucy Snowe visits in the lengthy epigraph to this chapter – is more often than not the site of some historically local legend, now supplemented by rumours and celebration, the two most common forms of social reproduction in Charlotte Brontë. The point of course is that these spaces of real or apocryphal conspiracy in Charlotte Brontë – the dwelling of literal or figurative historical ghosts – are in reality never private, but *always-already* under surveillance by a subaltern or his informers. This creeping de-privatization of what had been a locally sacred discursive monopoly so that its narratives are no longer confined, but equally distributed among (suitably cosmopolitan or those disguised as cosmopolitan) foreigners and natives alike, is in effect an 'opening' to public speculation, not unlike that provided by the 'attic loop-holes' overlooking the lovers' *allée* in *The Professor*.[14] Structurally and economically, this might represent some challenge to, if not an actual penetration of, the local, so feared by 'Eurosceptics' then and now.[15]

If gossip signals a divestment from the discursive *self*-possession known, with perhaps some etymological resonance, as *prop*riety, then those previously stable values which it puts into 'play' resemble the more material speculations favoured by the new breed of international businessmen, less attached to landed, that is imaginary, permanent values. Both economic and discursive forms of 'speculation' add value (as exchange-value) in social reproduction and, for that very reason, represent a departure from the British/Protestant privileging of fixed or 'stored' value, often comprehended in that marvellous description of character, 'British reserve'. As the remarkably precocious young Rose Yorke (who, appropriate to her ideology, fancies the highly speculative novels of Mrs Radcliffe with their continental settings) corrects Caroline Helstone, parson's niece, and, along with her knitting basket, a perfect representative of British diffidence, at least early in the novel:

> '[. . .] if my Master has given me ten talents, my duty is to trade with them, and make them ten talents more. Not in the dust of household drawers shall the coin be interred. I will *not* deposit it in a broken-spouted tea-pot, and shut it up in a china-closet among tea things. I will *not* commit it to your work-table to be smothered in piles of woollen hose.' (*Shirley* XXIII, p. 385)

This emotional economy based upon 'multiplying talents' is in sharp contradistinction to the patient storing of some originary, inherited share, the puritan philosophy which maintains a waiting Caroline Helstone in her provincial prison. Typically in Charlotte Brontë's fiction, the limits of self-sufficiency are only recognized after some acute physical indisposition that incapacitates a previously self-reliant individual, much as Napoleon did the British economy with the Continental System.

As this de-localizing speculation with value added at each stage of a (re)productive process begins to displace more historically (or biologically) privileged determinations, it would *appear* – as in fact does so much of the international capital flow at the end of the twentieth century – to be ideologically a-political. The borderless investor and William Crimsworth's symbolic benefactor in *The Professor*, Hunsden, may appear to Frances Crimsworth (*née* Henri) to be hosting anarchists and conspirators among his international friends devoted to free trade, but Charlotte Brontë emphasizes the pragmatic nature of a nomadic politics free of articulated belief:

> What English guests Hunsden invites, are all either men of Birmingham or Manchester – hard men, seemingly knit up in one thought, whose talk is of free trade. The foreign visitors, too, are politicians; they take a wider theme – European progress – the spread of liberal sentiments over the Continent; on their mental tablets, the names of Russia, Austria, and the Pope are inscribed in red ink. I have heard some of them talk vigorous sense [...]; also, I have heard much twaddle, enounced chiefly in French and Deutsch, but let that pass. Hunsden himself tolerated the drivelling theorists; with the practical men he seemed leagued head and heart. (*The Professor* XXV, p. 282)

Even the most radical of the foreign visitors to the salon at Hunsden Wood would reduce instances of European tyranny to an impact upon trade: red ink. Moreover, the financially astute Hunsden advises the relatively impecunious Crimsworth and his wife how to invest their meagre savings from teaching school so as to secure a comfortable future in the country of their choice:

> [...] as soon as we had capital to invest, two well-skilled counsellors, one in Belgium, one in England, viz. Vandenhuten and Hunsden, gave us each a word of advice on the sort of investment to be chosen. The suggestion made was judicious; and, being promptly acted on, the result proved gainful – I need not say how gainful. (*The Professor* XXV, p. 280)

Apparently, however, gainful enough to finance a return to England, a genuinely 'picturesque dwelling' (by English standards) and an Eton education for their son – not bad at all for the Crimsworth who had declined the security of a clerical vocation and rich wife chosen by his family and avoided the boom-and-bust cycle which afflicted his brother Edward's provincial mill.

Obviously, Charlotte Brontë is depicting not merely an alternative European community within her novels, but an a-filiative body furnishing (competing) (information) that enables the familial or financial exile to be repatriated along with his foreign-sourced wife and money into a 'realized [...] independency' (*The Professor* XXV, p. 280). The number of poor men truly 'self-made' from international investments (even with a little help from their friends!) in British fiction of the 1840s is infinitesimal.[16] By the conclusion of *Shirley*, with the end of both the Continental System and the countervailing Orders in Council, a remarkably anglicized Robert Gérard Moore, who had even entertained the thought of emigration to America at the height of his mill's difficulties, finds, like William Crimsworth of *The Professor*, that peace on the continent has brought dividends:

> 'The repeal of the Orders in Council saves me. Now I shall not turn bankrupt; now I shall not give up business; now I shall not leave England; now I shall be no longer poor; now I can pay my debts; now all the cloth I have in my warehouses will be taken off my hands [...] this day lays for my fortunes *abroad* [...].'
> (*Shirley* XXXVII, p. 594, italics added)

The problem is precisely how this individual financial 'salvation' can become part of a more general liberal impulse, thereby separating itself from the radical individualism characteristic of Protestant notions of salvation. Given the abortive citizens' revolutions of the 1830s which betrayed so many bourgeois hopes across Europe, governments are apparently limited in their ability to improve the common weal on a permanent basis. To be sure, there is, with peace, free trade, and unhindered capital flow and personal exposure, some 'trickle down' effect upon the working classes:

> 'Now, I can take more workmen; give better wages; lay wiser and more liberal plans; do some good; be less selfish: *now*, Caroline, I can have a house – a home which I can truly call mine [...].'
> (*Shirley* XXXVII, p. 594)

And, presumably, with his marriage to Caroline Helstone, share in the consumer society which his beliefs and energies have helped to bring about. But, in the context of *Shirley*, the rise in general commercial fortunes does not lift all displaced refugees equally. And the newly financially emancipated Moore realizes that he must work to create a primitive social safety net for those workers unable to reap the benefits of increased trade, exchange of information, or the bachelor's luxury of emigration to America. In Charlotte Brontë's novel, Moore's emergent social consciousness is recognized in his successful attempt to 'outplace' the destitute William Farren, made redundant by automated looms, as a gardener for the elder Yorke's orchards.

Retrospectively, this 'world' of Charlotte Brontë's less familiar achievement resembles the so-called New World Order which has attracted the allegiance of politicians and economists in the waning years of the twentieth century. The weaker, merely secular infiltration of ideas and goods resulting from daily encounters and trade – as well as the international and (near) interdenominational marriages of her late novels – may have an effect in reshaping traditional identity politics and allegiances in separate political regimes. Free, rational choices aimed at achieving a better life (defined in rather crudely material terms of rising income and economic growth) are presumed to impel both private and public behaviour toward peace, compromise, the rule of law, and mutual accommodation. Because violence or war represent disruptions to or departures from social and national order, those responsible for it (like the antinomian Michael Hartley in *Shirley*) must be punished, albeit not so harshly as to be altogether banished from the social order. The multiplication of peaceable contacts and the slow amelioration of the economic conditions of life become more or less universal social policy. Implicitly, rationalism is yoked with a universalism, much as it was during the eighteenth-century Enlightenment.[17]

Yet it is precisely this rational universalism (or pan-European order) which demands the more challenging sacrifice of individual autonomy or institutional sovereignty and monopoly, a sacrifice achieved only with great effort and patchy success in nineteenth-century European politics. Although the question of whether more economically open societies *necessarily* lead to heightened individual freedom remains unanswered in the context of Charlotte Brontë's novels, there would appear to be some redistribution of wealth and ideas *away* from what had been represented as monopolies. By the end of *Shirley*, in a chapter ironically titled 'The Winding Up' (as if commercial and narrative debts could be jointly 'settled' by such shared interests), Mr Donne, the clergyman whose life was so committed to idleness and high levels of conspicuous consumption in the novel's opening chapter, has taken to 'beg[ging] for all his erections' (*Shirley* XXXVII, p. 588) in order to support an Establishment which shares in neither the new commercial 'opening' to the continent, nor in socially ameliorative projects. When not defending itself from gossip and scandals, the Church's energies are entirely dedicated to bureaucratic self-maintenance.

Shirley Keeldar, previously an independent feminist who had constructed an elaborate myth by which originary Amazons usurped the role of classical Titans, must perforce learn how to share power with the mild, even effeminate French tutor, Louis Gérard Moore, in a domestic equivalent of a divided government, like that which will later come to dominate European politics:

'Louis,' she said, 'would have never learned to rule if she had not ceased to govern: the incapacity of the sovereign had developed the power of the premier.' (*Shirley*, XXXVII, p. 592)

Once having been reunited with her previously unacknowledged biological mother, Caroline Helstone requests of her new husband that the woman, whom she alleges to be 'the personification of *reserve* and discretion' (*Shirley* XXXVII, p. 595, italics added), be admitted as a resident mother-in-law in their new home.[18] So unthreatened is Moore now by financial and discursive speculation that he informs his wife of his lack of concern, even should she prove herself a gossip, that potentially intrusive, a-filiative threat to their marital 'internal affairs'. For those like the irreligious Anglo-Belgian, accustomed to 'homelessness' in an environment where religious or political radicals 'speak in tongues', there is precious little discursive or ideological sovereignty to surrender. His *via media* would de-construct rigid cartographies of nationality, faith, or family as surely as the most extreme forms of nomadism – or William Crimsworth's pseudo-picturesque Belgium.

If Charlotte Brontë's late novels in fact recognize an alternative European community within a new political regime, it is (already) present as a repressed latency in her most popular novel. In the infamous scene wherein a cruelly deceptive Fairfax Rochester, disguised as a female gypsy fortune-teller, entertains himself by pretending to foretell the future of an impoverished governess without one, Jane Eyre is startled by his prognosis. This is the same Jane Eyre who frequently harbours her soul's integrity by self-isolation from visual reciprocity and social communities, even as she tacitly admits enjoying the 'confusion of many voices [giving me] a welcome sense of liberty' (*Jane Eyre* I, vi, p. 57) or translating languages with which she lacks familiarity. Rochester's combination of palm-reading and phrenology 'sees' what she eventually comes to abandon – to him:

'I see no enemy to fortunate issue, but in the brow; and that brow professes to say, – "I can live alone, if self-respect and circumstances require me to do so. I need not sell my soul to buy bliss. I have an inward treasure, born with me, which can keep me alive if all extraneous delights should be withheld; or offered only at a price I cannot afford to give [. . .].'" (*Jane Eyre* II, iv, p. 211)

Were he describing not Jane Eyre's clearly contradictory character – her waning (religious as well as economic) conviction in some Protestant 'inward treasure born with me' – but Britain's increasingly accommodative, less self-reliant image in some imaginary Allegory of an Alternative Community, he would be no less accurate. A predestined, Protestant self-sufficiency, based upon an inherited, hence metaphorically 'landed share', is being subtly subjected to a *political* critique.

Maybe, such an allegory in fact exists, albeit in another medium. In the Tate Gallery in London, in a room otherwise devoted to Turner's grand scenes from famous encounters in Greek and Roman antiquity, stands *Heidelberg* (*circa* 1845), contemporaneous with Charlotte Brontë's later novels. In the background is the hillside castle of the Electors Palatine, on whose balcony is seated Elector Friedrich V and his young wife, Elizabeth, daughter of James I, whom he married in 1613. Clearly it is a festive occasion; the newlyweds look down the Neckar Valley to a gathering throng of burghers, peasants, and visiting nobility among whom are British guests, conspicuous by their oddly colourless dress and heavy shoes. Turner clearly celebrates, along with the guests, a Golden Age of Britain's 'constructive engagement' with continental life, before competing power rivalries in the New World, the French Revolution, and the defensive posture which accompanied the rise of Napoleon put an end to political ecumenicism. But just perhaps also in anticipation of that Pax Brittanica ensuing upon the marriage of a nineteenth-century monarch to a continental with limited skills in her language that produced a 'family' of interrelated European royalty. In the foreground of Turner's hillside *fête*, lower left, is a band of approaching gypsies.

NOTES

1. Friedrich Nietzsche, *Beyond Good and Evil*, #256.
2. *Villette*, XXXVIII, pp. 550–1. All citations from the work of Charlotte Brontë are taken from the following editions, with the relevant volume (where applicable), chapter, and page number: *Jane Eyre*, edited and with an introduction by Margaret Smith (Oxford and New York: Oxford University Press, 1993); *Shirley*, edited by Andrew and Judith Hook (Harmondsworth: Penguin, 1985); *Villette*, edited by Mark Lilly with an introduction by Tony Tanner (Harmondsworth: Penguin, 1985); *The Professor*, edited by Heather Glen (Harmondsworth: Penguin, 1989).
3. Lucy Snowe's dream vision has an uncanny afterlife in the new 55-hectare amusement park named 'Villette', which opened in 1993 northeast of Paris. It is the only public park in France which remains open throughout the night, and one of the experiences to which visitors can gain admission – along with acrobats, circus performances, 'alternative' concerts, etc. – is the incredible *Jardin des effrayantes enfants* in which loudspeakers amplify the screams and cries of children in distress. This mixture of entertainment, punishment, the return of the repressed and therapy is remarkably like the experience of Lucy Snowe in her midnight stroll in Charlotte Brontë's novel.
4. See Catherine Clément, *Syncope: the Philosophy of Rapture*, translated by Sally O'Driscoll and Deidre Mahoney (Minneapolis and London: University of Minnesota Press, 1994).
5. Some reasons for the widespread use of European settings in gothic fiction (1770–1820) is suggested, using the logic of post-structuralism, in my 'Narrative Enclosure as Textual Ruin: the Archaeology of Gothic Consciousness', *Dickens Studies Annual* XI (1983): pp. 209–38 and also in Eve K. Sedgwick, *The Coherence of Gothic Conventions* (New York and London: Methuen, 1986).
6. Reprinted in Juliet Barker, *The Brontës* (New York: St. Martin's Press, 1996) p. 362.
7. Ever since Mrs Gaskell's *Life* of Charlotte Brontë (1857), many of her critics and biographers have speculated on the nature of her attachment to Monsieur Heger while in Belgium. Her most recent biographer, Juliet Barker, though superb in assessing Heger's influence upon Charlotte Brontë's apprenticeship as a writer, finds no evidence of any other emotional relationship.
8. For an excellent survey of the role of Belgium (and its guarantors) in the democratization of western Europe in the nineteenth century, see Henri Pirenne, *Belgian Democracy: Its Early History* (New York: AMS Press, rpt. edition, 1996). For some evidence of the more rapid evolution of women's role in educational institutions in Belgium (compared with the UK), see Patricia M. Hilden, *Women, Work, and Politics: Belgium 1830–1914* (Oxford: Oxford University Press, 1994).
9. See Christine Alexander and Jane Sellars, *The Art of the Brontës* (Cambridge: Cambridge University Press, 1995) for an account of the stylistic evolution of the 'picturesque' in Charlotte Brontë's drawings, commencing with her interest in Bewick's work. In *Jane Eyre* (I, xiii,

pp. 131–2) Fairfax Rochester subjects three of the watercolours in the heroine's portfolio to a rigorous critique. The third of these landscapes depicts the pinnacle of an iceberg piercing a polar winter sky in whose foreground lies a 'colossal head, inclined toward the iceberg, and resting against it'. A ring of white flame overlooks the iceberg and head. Pictorially insufficiently realized, the entire scene lies athwart a 'solemn depth', not unlike Coleridge's infamous 'romantic chasm'. The blurring of traditional aesthetic categories (human/transcendent; landscape/skyscape; realism/symbolism; body/empty space) causes Rochester to characterize the work as 'elfish', and the reader to see the sketches as some stage in the elaboration of perhaps some religion of the imagination, as an alternative to Jane's narrowly Protestant faith. This de-compartmentalization of pictorial or imaginative 'planes' is precisely what confronts Crimsworth in Belgium's 'patchwork' countryside.

10. Although the so-called Tawney–Weber thesis encompasses many sets of relationships between capitalist behaviour and religious practice, the relationship of economic 'saving' to salvation is perhaps most applicable here. Postponed gratification enabled the individual to 'store' assets which would be held accountable on Judgement Day, creating a transcendental subsidy for personal parsimony – and derivatively, the advent of banking and credit. So many of Charlotte Brontë's heroines combine feelings of inwardness – the 'soul's cell' of Jane Eyre (*Jane Eyre* I, ii, p. 36) – with a deep longing for the loosened bonds of one who 'values visions' (*Villette* XXXVII, p. 520). A free-flowing imaginative or material economy is often elided with spatial liberation (traffic as opposed to 'local' accumulation).

11. By chronologically displacing the debate over free trade from the late 1830s and 1840s back to the period 1807–15, Charlotte Brontë is hypostasizing its origins not in the domestic poverty which accompanied protective tariffs or the Irish famine (as argued by Terry Eagleton), but as historically continuous with Britain's resistance to political or economic involvement with continental affairs. Everyone in *Shirley* is affected in one way or another, even those whom we might expect to be exempt – not merely or only the lower classes.

12. Limitations of space do not allow an exploration of the political implications of 'international marriages' in British fiction. But it is worth recalling that many trading companies and government ministries frowned upon marriages of their representatives with the 'natives' of Empire. One way of overcoming these stated or unstated injunctions was to make of either the foreigner or the expatriate Briton (or both) an individual of 'mixed' blood of which only half was identifiably non-English, as is the case with Carolyn Helstone and Robert Gérard Moore in *Shirley*. Cloudy or unknown origins allows internationalism to disguise itself as recuperation, thereby in terms of the plot making such a rebellious act more tolerable.

13. Because Bright and Cobden were pacifists either by religion or ideology, the Anti-Corn Law League was suspect to those who, albeit in sympathy with its economics, questioned the patriotism of its members.

Similarly, Robert Gérard Moore's pacifism at the outset of *Shirley* seems a product, at least initially, of self-interest and survival rather than belief. Because he is not entirely British, any suspicions of his patriotism are more understandable to his few friends.
14. For a more elaborate discussion of the threat which gossip (as speculation) posed to religious or amatory monopolies in Emily Brontë, see my 'Parlour's *Parler*: The 'Chattering of Tongues Within...' *Wuthering Heights,' Gossip and Subversion in Nineteenth-Century British Fiction: Echo's Economies* (London and Basingstoke: Macmillan, 1996) 97–154.
15. This fear of the demise of the local is perhaps best articulated by a well-known cosmopolitan European in search of belonging, the late Sir James Goldsmith, leader of the British Referendum Party which would force the Conservatives to hold a referendum on Britain's future in Europe. In his best-selling *The Trap* (Fr. *Le Piège*) the Anglo-French, Catholic-Jewish hybrid international businessman urges support for 'primal societies' where man's relationship with nature is 'not one of exploitation', but of harmony. A recurrent romantic streak among Eurosceptics in Britain is shared by Sir James's defence of 'authentic communities' against a presumably artificial world of multi-national businessmen. His ideological flip-flops are no less interesting than those of Moore in *Shirley*, or for that matter, the Peel who ultimately voted to repeal the Corn Laws. See Ian Buruma, 'Fear and Tembling in Europe', *The New York Review of Books* 43.16 (17 October 1996): pp. 55–60.
16. In many ways Dickens's Pip of *Great Expectations*, who self-deceptively assumes that he has 'named himself' in the graveyard of Chapter I, represents some urge to become economically 'self-made', rather than assuming the *nomination* of class or broken family to which he is born. The fantasy of economic self-nomination (since one can lose money as well as make it) heightens the nomadism to which Pip is prey.
17. Recently, in a number of his public statements, former US Secretary of State, Henry Kissinger has argued that ideology should take a back seat to the attempt to establish a wide range of shared mutual interests among countries whose political systems differ. Although specifically addressing the US–China relationship and its disagreements over human rights initiatives, Kissinger's attempt to equate rationalism with internationalism (and an enlargement of the range of discursive interests) seems of a piece with eighteenth-century mercantilism. See J.G.A. Pocock, 'The Political Economy of Burke's Analysis of the French Revolution', *Virtue, Commerce, and History* (Cambridge: Cambridge University Press, 1985) pp. 193–212.
18. The loosening of a hitherto privileged British 'reserve' may have an additional significance as an economic metaphor, given the early nineteenth-century setting of *Shirley*. To the permanent chagrin of romantics like Cobbett, first America, then France (in the form of *assignats*) had adopted paper money as almost an emblem of their respective revolutions. Earlier, Adam Smith had argued that paper money was 'a sort of waggonway through the air' and that no state should be dependent upon 'pools' brought by such 'Daedalian wings'. But between

February 1797 (when cash payments were suspended in Britain) and the recommendations of the Bullion Committee in 1811, after considerable debate, paper in England was made convertible with metal. Virtue thereby came to be gradually defined not as dependence upon property and/or independence from the power of the State, but as (initially) an interdependence among all a nation's 'estates' and later, an interdependence among nations who accepted each other's 'representations' of value on 'credit', a truly universal belief system. Neither words nor money had an intrinsic value, but only a value-in-exchange. See Marc Shell, *Money, Language and Thought* (Berkeley: University of California Press, 1982).

2 'Nation and Narration': Continental Europe and the English Novel
Silvia Mergenthal

> Dear Miss Morland, consider the dreadful nature of the suspicions you have entertained. What have you been judging from? Remember the country and the age in which we live. Remember that we are English, that we are Christians. Consult your understanding, your own sense of the probable, your own observation of what is passing around you – Does our education prepare us for atrocities? Do our laws connive at them? Could they be perpetuated without being known, in a country like this, where social and literary intercourse is on such a footing; where every man is surrounded by a neighbourhood of voluntary spies, and where roads and newspapers lay everything open?[1]

Catherine Morland, in Jane Austen's *Northanger Abbey*, is an avid reader of horror stories. According to her lover Henry Tilney, like herself English and a Christian, Catherine's fault is that she mistakes fiction for fact, or rather, that she, the protagonist of a novel of manners, insists on casting herself as the persecuted maiden of the eighteenth-century Gothic novel. Catherine, in other words, is in the wrong book – and in the wrong country. The books she would have preferred to have been in generally choose continental Europe for their setting: for example, France and Italy in Ann Radcliffe's *The Romance of the Forest* (1791), and Spain and Germany in Matthew Lewis's *The Monk* (1796). These authors cater to their readers' fascination with foreign countries, a fascination which also caused unprecedented numbers of upper-class and educated eighteenth-century British travellers to embark on the so-called 'Grand Tour', with its rigid code of places to be visited, sights to be seen, and goals to be achieved.[2]

Outside the Gothic novel, it is primarily the travelogue which appeals to this taste for the geographically remote. However, as the case of Laurence Sterne's *A Sentimental Journey through France and Italy* amply illustrates, the boundary lines between these two literary modes are often blurred. Hence, historians of the novel, for example Percy Adams in his *Travel Literature and the Evolution of the Novel*[3] have frequently drawn attention to the importance of travel writing for fiction although they do emphasize that 'abroad' may well serve different narrative purposes in each mode – or, for that matter, in each given text. In both modes, and here we return to Henry Tilney, the geographically remote is also frequently perceived to be historically backwards – a preoccupation with history being, of course, another dominant feature of eighteenth-century intellectual life. Phenomena which can still be observed by eighteenth-century tourists abroad – or by their armchair traveller counterparts – are assumed to have become obsolete at home, in eighteenth-century England: quaint customs and civil unrest, superstitions and tyrannical governments, or, in terms of *Northanger Abbey*, husbands who murder their wives and fathers who force their children into loveless marriages. Whether *Northanger Abbey* as a whole supports this self-congratulatory point of view – the point of view expressed by Henry Tilney – or whether it uses foreign countries and remote periods as screens onto which a dissatisfaction with contemporary England can be projected, has been a matter of some critical discussion. What does emerge from the text, though, is a dialectic of national auto-stereotypes and hetero-stereotypes which, like the fascination with foreign countries and with history, has been recognized as yet another prominent feature of eighteenth-century England. It is no coincidence that the century of the 'Grand Tour' can also be designated the century of the 'Home Tour', and that travel writing on the British Isles proliferates alongside travelogues describing trips abroad.[4] As Stephen Haseler demonstrates, it is in the course of the eighteenth century that the English cultural elite, unlike progressive forces in France and in America, turns its back on Enlightenment concepts of 'universal man', of universal human rights, and of social and political reforms on the basis of rational and abstract principles. Instead, it embraces what Haseler calls the '"non-ideological" ideology of Englishness', an ideology based on a conjunction of 'land, class, and race'.[5]

Key texts in this process are David Hume's 'Of National Characters' (1749), and Edmund Burke's *Reflections on the Revolution in France* (1790). While Hume, in *Philosophical Essays Concerning Human Understanding*[6] (1748), had stated that 'mankind are so much the same, in all times and places', he adopts a much more particularist view in 'Of National Characters'.[7] He employs numerous strategies for constructing cultural otherness which he borrows from the historians, ethnologists, and travel-writers of his time. Like them, he tries to find a pithy epithet to describe the dominant feature of a given nation, pits two nations against one another, and finds physical causes for their differences. The most striking feature, however, is his ethnocentrism: Hume argues that what distinguishes the English from all other peoples is their individuality, that is, the way in which they, unlike the Italians, the Spaniards or the French, resist facile categorization. And while Hume, who, after all, sets out to refute Montesquieu's adaptation of Jean Bodin's climatologist view of historical development, succumbs to it himself when he discusses other peoples, the reasons he – like his worthy disciple Henry Tilney – adduces for the English 'national character' are strictly non-physical and 'moral': a mixed constitution, a liberal government, and the resulting 'sympathy and contagion of manners'.

A similar movement from the universal to the particularist and national can be traced in Burke's *Reflections on the Revolution in France*. At the same time, Burke, like Hume, defines national identity largely through negation, that is, by establishing a counter-identity and constructing a 'we–they' dichotomy. While Burke had drawn on Enlightenment positions in his 1770s defence of the American Revolution, he now associates these very positions with the deplorable events in France, and contrasts them with what he perceives to be the characteristics of the English political system, a system not so much founded on reason as on emotion; specifically, on the chivalrous sentiment evinced by the strong towards the weak. What emerges from *Reflections* is the economic and political model of a society developing organically and continuously over time and space, and by its very continuity superior to all other social systems:

> I wish my countrymen rather to recommend to our neighbours the example of the British constitution, than to take models from them for the improvement of our own. In the former they have got an invaluable treasure. They are not, I think, without some causes of apprehension and complaint; but these they do not owe to their constitution, but to their own conduct. I think our happy situation owing to our constitution; but owing to the whole of it, and not to any part singly; owing in a great measure to what we have left standing in our several reviews and reformations, as well as to what we have altered or superadded. Our

people will find employment enough for a truly patriotic, free, and independent spirit, in guarding what they possess from violation.[8]

Thus, at the end of the eighteenth century, instead of universal ideas of individual freedom, it is the collective identity of 'Englishness', that is, of nationalism and national subjecthood, which becomes the staple of political propaganda and which is to be defended in the wars against revolutionary France – wars, incidentally, against the background of which *Northanger Abbey* must be read. The ultimate irony is, of course, that two of the most influential proponents of this collective identity should be a Scot, Hume, and an Irishman, Burke, respectively.

In a recent volume of articles entitled *Nation and Narration*,[9] Homi K. Bhabha and others, notably Timothy Brennan, argue that nation is closely linked to narration in general – to its search for origins, to its building of continuity through time, and to its inclusiveness – and to the novel in particular. Conversely, the novel can be said to both reflect and contribute to the way in which a nation conceives of itself. In this context, our passage from *Northanger Abbey* opens up a complex field of questions. Specifically, it shows how literary representations of 'we–they' dichotomies both call for more narrowly textual considerations – what do these representations actually *do*, in a given literary genre, and in a given literary text – and for more broadly contextual considerations – how do these literary representations respond to as well as contribute to constructions of otherness, as a means of defining the (national) self, in a given society? In a further step, one can then trace the development of these dichotomies over a longer historical period, paying particular attention to those moments in history in which notions of nationhood may be assumed to have required readjustment. In the case of 'Englishness', those moments are Britain's imperial expansion in the nineteenth century, the two world wars in this century, and, following the loss of worldpower status after 1945, the triple pressures of cultural Americanization, of economic globalization, and of economic and political integration into the European Community.

As a result of these pressures, Stephen Haseler predicts that 'Englishness', while not disappearing altogether, 'will lose what was its uniquely powerful hold on the psychic identity of the people of England'.[10]

David Lodge's novel *Out of the Shelter* and Ian McEwan's novel *The Innocent or The Special Relationship*[11] are both set in 1950s Germany, in Heidelberg and Berlin respectively, and show symptoms of that unease over Britain's postwar role to which I have just alluded. As the protagonist of *The Innocent* reflects: 'His Englishness was not quite the comfort it had been to a preceding generation. It made him feel vulnerable.' (*Innocent*, p. 8)

David Lodge, in the afterword to the 1985 revised edition of *Out of the Shelter*, describes his novel as 'a combination of the *Bildungsroman* [...] and the Jamesian "international" novel of conflicting ethical and cultural codes' (*Shelter*, p. 275). The protagonist in *Out of the Shelter* is the aptly named adolescent Timothy Young, whose views of Germany are conditioned by childhood memories of the London Blitz, by bedtime stories in which the Nazis, or Nasties, figure as bogeymen, and by comics and films. A Ministry of Information documentary newsletter on the importance of films as a medium of propaganda from 1940 gives an impression of the type of film Timothy would have seen:

> *German ideals and institutions in recent history.* This might include an historical film on the growth of Pan-German ideas from Bismarck onwards. There should be a number of themes for films in the activities of the Gestapo stressing, as more easily credible, the sinister rather than the sadistic aspect, but the Germans should also be shown as making absurd errors of judgment.
> *Animated cartoons*: These are a very flexible medium of propaganda and have the advantage that ideas can be inserted under cover of absurdity. They can present (as in Mickey Mouse) a system of ethics in which independence and individuality are always successful, bullies are made fools of, the weak can cheek the strong with impunity, etc.[12]

Thus, when Timothy goes to Heidelberg to spend his summer holidays with his older sister, who works for the American army, his baggage contains a number of childish preconceptions – prejudices, quite literally – about the Germans. In the course of the novel, through personal encounters with Germans and helped by various mentor figures, he learns to recognize these prejudices for what they are, and to share his sister's view that Germans, after all, 'seem just like other people'. But which other people *are* they like, the English or the Americans? Throughout the novel, the narrator makes it clear that, to return to Lodge's definition of the international novel, the English and the Americans hold conflicting 'ethical and cultural codes'. In other words, it is the Americans who activate the 'we–they' mechanism and function as counter-identity to the English characters: Timothy is given a foretaste of American consumerism as well as of a distinct American youth culture. As Lodge explains in the afterword, these features of American expatriate life in Heidelberg would soon be aspired to, and to an extent enjoyed, by the English: 'a life of possessions, machines and diversions, of personal transportation, labour-saving devices, smart cheap clothing, mass tourism, technologically-based leisure and entertainment' (*Shelter*, p. 276). The epilogue of the novel shows that Timothy, now in his late twenties, has been granted a share of 'the good life'. Whether this presents a new freedom for him, or a new enslavement, Timothy's author is not prepared to say. Lodge does, however, alert us to the fact that *Out of the Shelter* is not only a *Bildungsroman* and an international novel, but also a historical novel which recognizes, with the benefit of hindsight, the year of Timothy's journey to Heidelberg, 1951, as a year of 'crucial transition, the hinge on which our society swung from "austerity" to "affluence"' (*Shelter*, p. 276). In the novel, 'austerity' is associated with England, 'affluence' with America; one of the most important concerns of the novel is, surely, the Americanization of English material culture.

Out of the Shelter is mainly narrated from Timothy's point of view, that is, from the point of view of a naive central consciousness. In a 1984 interview,[13] Lodge admits that this narrative method is somewhat restrictive, and the numerous stylistic alterations he introduces into the 1985 revised edition of the novel can be seen as strengthening what Lodge calls a 'covert' authorial voice; in other words, they are distancing devices articulating Timothy's 'adolescent sensibility with a slightly more eloquent and mature style than Timothy himself would have commanded' (*Shelter*, p. 282). It is the task of this covert authorial voice to alert the reader to Timothy's initial errors of judgement, and to reward him for having learnt his lessons. However, while Timothy is a diligent student, his narrator (or his author?) is rather more remiss. We have already seen that he endows the English and the Americans with conflicting value systems. In addition, although he tries hard to explode the myth of the Nazi bogeyman, he (or Lodge himself?) succumbs to the influence of other – older – stereotypes of 'the German', namely, that of the musical German and that of the German student as immortalized in the film *The Student Prince*:[14]

The bar comprised two rooms, one at a lower level than the other, both furnished with long bare wooden tables deeply scarred with initials and mottoes. The ceiling was dark with smoke and heavily beamed: the grimy walls were almost covered with posters, banners, and old-fashioned photographs of young men in strange clothes and funny hats. The drinkers sat on benches with thick mugs of beer before them. Most wore open-necked shirts with rolled-up sleeves, and some wore grey leather shorts. [...]

After a while, the singing started. A man sitting at the head of one of the long tables rapped on it with his beer mug and intoned a phrase. The rest of the men at the table took up the song in resounding chorus, sitting up very straight and staring before them with stern concentration. (*Shelter*, p. 171)

Like *Out of the Shelter*, *The Innocent* charts what might be called its protagonist's progress from innocence to experience, and describes the rites of passage which this protagonist has to undergo, *vis-à-vis* Germany and the Germans, and also *vis-à-vis* the Americans with whom he comes into contact. Leonard Marnham, the protagonist of *The Innocent*, is several years older than Timothy, but for Leonard, as for Timothy – and as, indeed, for any other young Englishman – it is 'impossible [...] to be in Germany for the first time and not think of it above all as a defeated nation, or feel pride in the victory'. (*Innocent*, p. 5) Leonard is an employee of the Post Office and is sent to Berlin to assist in a tunnel project, 'Operation Gold', which aims at tapping communication lines between the Soviet forces in Eastern Europe and their high command in Moscow. This part of the novel is, incidentally, based on real events, though Leonard himself is a fictitious character: 'Operation Gold' was a joint CIA–MI6 venture operating for just under a year until April 1956. In a second plot-line, Leonard falls in love with a German woman, Maria, and helps her kill her estranged husband, Otto. The two plot-lines, previously linked through Leonard and, on a metaphorical level, through the imagery of burrowing and excavation, finally converge when Leonard is driven to hiding Otto's mutilated body in the tunnel, and to betraying the tunnel to the Russians – a futile gesture, this, as the Russians, thanks to a double agent, have known about 'Operation Gold' all along.

This brief summary of the plot indicates that McEwan's novel can also be discussed fruitfully in the context of two other fictional conventions: namely, the tradition of the spy novel and the tradition of the historical novel. As Bernd Lenz has shown,[15] the spy novel, like the international novel, is by definition dichotomous, leaving its practitioners with the option of either rigorously observing, and indeed reinforcing, the boundary lines between two opposing political camps, or of trying to blur these lines. While Ian Fleming, for instance, opts for the first type in his James Bond novels, Graham Greene, John Le Carré, or Len Deighton paint portraits of secret agents who find it increasingly difficult to cling to ideological certainties in a world of moral ambiguities; *The Innocent* clearly belongs to the second of these two types. Consequently, the political world of *The Innocent* is one of shifting allegiances, from the anti-German war alliance between Britain, the United States and the Soviet Union, to post-war confrontation between East and West, and from a 'special relationship' between Britain and America to closer links between America and Germany. 'The Special Relationship' is, of course, the subtitle of the novel.

McEwan's use of the historical novel reinforces this blurring of boundaries: the postscript of *The Innocent* describes Leonard's return to Berlin in 1987, a Berlin which, with its architecture, its shops, and its tourist crowds, has become 'a European city like any other a businessman might visit' (*Innocent*, p. 231). In addition, there are portents of imminent political change: the last sentence of the novel implies that the Berlin Wall is about to come down – an event which had already occurred when the novel was published in 1990, and which figures prominently in the 1993 film based on *The Innocent* and scripted by McEwan himself. It is this event, followed by the emergence of democracy in Eastern Europe and ultimately by the collapse of the Soviet Union, which puts an end to 'the special relationship'. As Haseler explains in *The English Tribe*:

> During the cold war Britain had something of a role. Whether it was the Americans' 'unsinkable aircraft carrier' or the intelligence partner of Washington or the cultural bridge between America and Europe in NATO and the Atlantic Community, Britain at least possessed a niche, and, moreover, one which allowed its political class to retain a certain detachment from continental Europe. Now, though, the end of the cold war would mean serious American retrenchment, and, as a consequence, the loss of postwar Britain's geopolitical *raison d'être*.[16]

From the point of view of 1990, the self-important cloak-and-dagger, or rather telephones-and-tunnels, world of 1950s Berlin seems strangely anachronistic, not to say supremely ridiculous.

As we have seen, David Lodge, in *Out of the Shelter*, strives towards a similar blurring of boundaries, but his efforts or, perhaps more accurately, those of his protagonist, are, to an extent, sabotaged by the covert authorial voice. Therefore, it seems requisite to take a brief look at McEwan's handling of narrative perspective. Paradoxically, narrative perspective in *The Innocent* is both close to and detached from the protagonist. To start with the second of these two possibilities: on several occasions throughout McEwan's novel, we share Maria's perception of her relationship with Leonard. This, of course, seems likely to trigger what I have called the 'we–they' mechanism, and at first glance this is exactly what happens. At one point, Leonard apologizes to Maria, who reflects: 'It was almost unbearable to watch this clumsy, reticent Englishman who knew so little about his feelings lay himself open. He was like a prisoner at a Russian show trial.' (*Innocent*, p. 113) While the first of these two sentences appears to conform to a widespread stereotype of the Englishman, the second immediately relocates this behaviour pattern in a completely different context – and changes its nationality in the process. For another example of this kind of strategy, we can look at a letter Maria writes to Leonard: 'It was wrong of you to retreat with your anger and your silence. So English! So male.' (*Innocent*, p. 242) Again, Maria initially constructs a 'national' dichotomy, only to deconstruct it again by redefining its terms on the grounds of gender rather than nationality.

What about Leonard, then? Unlike Lodge's covert authorial voice, McEwan's resists the temptation of establishing a reality of 'Germanness' beyond what Leonard perceives as such. Hence, the most important pub scene in *The Innocent* – a scene in which the natives neither wear leather trousers nor engage in singing competitions – reads as follows: Leonard has already had several pints, and in the course of the fifth his comprehension of German begins to improve miraculously:

> There was no doubt about the word Tod, death, and a little later, Zug, train, and the verb bringen. He heard spoken wearily into a lull, manchmal, sometimes. *Sometimes these things were necessary.* The conversation gathered pace again. It was clear that it was driven by competitive boasting. To falter was to be swept aside. Interruptions were brutal, each voice was more violently insistent, swaggering with finer instances than its predecessor. Their

consciences set free by a beer twice as strong as English ale and served in something not much smaller than pint pots, these men were revealing when they should have been cringing in horror. They were shouting their bloody deeds all over the bar. (*Innocent*, p. 7)

It is only much later, when his German has improved even while not under the influence, that Leonard finds out what these Germans had, in fact, been discussing: not genocide, but the weather, the food, the government. 'The usual pub grumble', in other words – with the word 'pub' deliberately chosen to stress links to practices at home, as Leonard usually thinks of the German equivalent as 'Kneipe'.

By way of conclusion, I shall now return to the set of questions raised by the passage from *Northanger Abbey*. First of all, we have seen that literary representations of 'we–they' dichotomies are governed by the conventions of their respective genres or subgenres, in the case of *Out of the Shelter* and *The Innocent* by the conventions of the *Bildungsroman*, the international novel, the spy novel, and the historical novel. In the *Bildungsroman* context, Germany is the testing-ground where Timothy and Leonard must show their mettle before they can return to their own societies; while Timothy is, literally as well as metaphorically, brought out of his shelter, Leonard fails his test because he refuses to assume responsibility for Otto's death. As international novel and spy novel, respectively, *Out of the Shelter* and *The Innocent* presuppose the existence of a non-English other or, more precisely, of non-English others; in both novels, these others are the Germans and the Americans. As historical novels, both *Out of the Shelter* and *The Innocent* examine 'we–they' dichotomies in a specific historical situation, the early 1950s, and re-evaluate them from a later perspective, that of the early 1970s (*Out of the Shelter*) and that of the late 1980s (*The Innocent*).

The second question is whether *Out of the Shelter* and *The Innocent* can be said to respond to constructions of otherness in postwar English society. Both Lodge and McEwan show that their protagonists' attitudes towards Germans and Americans are rooted in their wartime childhood or adolescence and derived from wartime propaganda. Corresponding auto-stereotypes can be traced back to the same sources. Thus, Timothy reflects on his way to Germany:

> He might have been a French boy, or a German... What would *that* have been like? To grow up in that benighted country, knowing

that everybody in other countries hated and despised you, because of Hitler, because of the concentration camps, because of the war which your country had started and lost. Actually, when he thought of the Germans, the ones living in Germany now, he felt no hatred, only a kind of embarrassment. It was far more likely that they hated *you*. And that was what made him, at the deepest level, apprehensive about the weeks to come. A solitary English boy, he thought, would not be particularly welcome in occupied Germany. They would think he had come to gloat. (*Shelter*, p. 70)

And here is Leonard, on his first walk through Berlin:

He had spent the war with his granny in a Welsh village over which no enemy aircraft had ever flown. He had never touched a gun, or heard one go off outside a rifle range; despite this, and the fact that it had been the Russians who had liberated the city, he made his way through this pleasant residential district of Berlin that evening – the wind had dropped and it was warmer – with a certain proprietorial swagger, as though his feet beat out the rhythm of a speech by Mr Churchill. (*Innocent*, p. 5)

However, there are two major differences between the two novels: while Lodge, as we have seen, deconstructs some hetero-stereotypes – and thus, given the dialectic of auto-stereotype and hetero-stereotype, some auto-stereotypes as well – he perpetuates others. The more prominent among the latter are not necessarily the ones relating to Germany and the Germans; in fact, although the American characters in *Out of the Shelter* are comparatively more diversified than the German characters, and although Timothy's mentor Don is cast as an 'un-American' American, the prevailing image of 'the American' is one of immaturity, shallowness, and conspicuous consumption. This image is sanctioned by the narrator, and presumably by the author. One should perhaps add, by way of parenthesis, that Lodge's later international novels, notably *Changing Places* and *Small World*, heavily draw on these stereotypes of 'the American' as well. McEwan, on the other hand, carefully avoids giving the stamp of authorial approval to any of the hetero- or auto-stereotypes with which *The Innocent* abounds. All of them are consistently marked as social constructions filling individual as well as collective psychological needs.

The second difference between the two novels can be described as follows: although 'The Special Relationship' is the subtitle of McEwan's novel, it is *Out of the Shelter* which brings into the foreground the relationship between the English and the Americans, a relationship to which Heidelberg merely provides a picturesque background. Hence, after a few days in Heidelberg, Timothy 'had already acquired a sense of two communities [. . .]: underneath, the Germans, and on top of them, floating, or skimming over them with minimal contact, like dragonflies or waterboatmen, the Americans.' (*Shelter*, p. 98) Not surprisingly, Timothy's first sexual encounter is with an American girl, and the epilogue of the novel is set in America. *The Innocent*, on the other hand, focuses on what can legitimately be called a love triangle. We have already seen how, in political terms, America moves from 'the special relationship' with Britain to closer relations with the former enemy, Germany; on the personal level, this is reflected in the marriage between Maria, Leonard's German lover, and the American Glass. And, in a move which suggests that McEwan 'writes back' to Lodge, the epilogue of *The Innocent* is set in Berlin: after all, by 1990, Britain had become what Stephen Haseler calls 'Uncle Sam's deserted child',[17] face to face with, to quote Haseler once again, 'a federal destiny'[18] – within Europe.

NOTES

1. Jane Austen, *Northanger Abbey* (1818), Vol. II, Ch. IX.
2. For the most recent account of the 'Grand Tour' see Andrew Wilton and Ilaria Bignamini, eds, *Grand Tour: The Lure of Italy in the Eighteenth Century* (London, 1996).
3. Percy Adams, *Travel Literature and the Evolution of the Novel* (Lexington: Kentucky University Press, 1983).
4. S. Korte, Barbara, *Der englische Reisebericht: Von der Pilgerfahrt bis zur Postmoderne* (Darmstadt: Wissenschaftliche Buchgesellschaft, 1996).
5. Haseler, Stephen, *The English Tribe: Identity, Nation and Europe* (London: Macmillan, 1996), p. 22.
6. Commonly known under the title of the 1758 edition, *An Enquiry Concerning Human Understanding*.
7. For an analysis of 'Of National Characters' see Franz K. Stanzel, 'Schemata und Klischees der Völkerbeschreibung in David Hume's Essay "Of National Characters"', *Studien zur englischen und amerikanischen Sprache und Literatur. Festschrift für Helmut Papajewski*, eds Paul G.

Buchloh, Inge Leimberg, and Herbert Rauter (Neumünster: Wacholtz, 1974), pp. 363–83.
8. Edmund Burke, 'Reflections on the Revolution in France, and on the Proceedings of Certain Societies in London Relative to that Event', *Works*, Vol. II (London: Bohn, 1855), p. 516.
9. Homi K. Bhabha, ed., *Nation and Narration* (London and New York: Routledge, 1990).
10. Haseler, p. 124.
11. *Out of the Shelter* was first published in 1970, and reissued, in a considerably revised version, in 1985. Quotes will be from the 1986 Penguin edition. McEwan's *The Innocent or The Special Relationship* was first published in 1990. Quotes will be from the 1990 Picador edition.
12. Ministry of Information, Programme for Film Propaganda; from *Documentary Newsletter* (1940); repr. in: Judy Giles, and Tim Middleton, eds., *Writing Englishness 1900-1950: an Introductory Sourcebook on National Identity* (London and New York, 1995), pp. 142–3.
13. John Haffenden, *Novelists in Interview* (London: Methuen, 1985), pp. 145–65.
14. For a survey of stereotypes of the German in English literature see Günther Blaicher, *Das Deutschlandbild in der englischen Literatur* (Darmstadt: Wissenschaftliche Buchgesellschaft, 1992). Ironically, one of the characters in the novel refers to *The Student Prince* as 'real schmaltz' (*Shelter*, p. 87).
15. For example in his article '*Game, Set & Match*: Konstanten und Varianten in Len Deighton's geheimer Welt', *Anglistik und Englischunterricht* 37 (1989): pp. 65–97.
16. Haseler, p. 131.
17. Haseler, p. 131.
18. Haseler, p. 137.

3 *Schlosses* and the Scent of Pine: Images of Austria and Germany in the English Historical Romance and Gothic Romance since 1945
Ulrike Horstmann

Images of Europe and Europeans in popular literature are dominated by stereotypes. Russians are passionate but unpredictable, and so, by implication, is Russia itself. Italians are open and voluble but unreliable. The French are charming but deceitful. Germans are diligent but narrow-minded. The British are honourable but stiff. And how could it be different? Popular literature depends on images that can easily be comprehended by the reader, that do not demand any strenuous thinking and differentiating. As a result, such novels offer interesting material for the study of attitudes between neighbours within Europe and ultimately towards the idea of a united Europe. Popular novels are often set abroad, because the foreign setting lends an exotic and exciting touch. In historical romances, this exoticness is further raised by the difference between the reader's present and the period depicted. This double distancing effect – in time and in space – further encourages the use of stereotypes, because no reader of this kind of fiction is really interested in the accuracy of the descriptions; most are happy to encounter easily recognizable images that fit with their expectations. Indeed, historical romances thrive on a blend of 'realism' and fantasy. Helen Hughes speaks of 'the combination of verisimilitude and fantasy which gives such texts their "realism"'.[1] The fantasy element of the historical romance lies in the plots, which have myth and fairy-tale qualities. The 'realism' is conveyed by the settings:

[...] an impression of an accurate representation of a past reality [...] is given by the use of period detail and reference to familiar historical issues. Such representation is both convincing and estranging. The artificially constructed 'past' is presented as 'what really happened', but it is also a suitably exotic context for the romantic motifs which reflect – sometimes by contraries – the concerns of the readers. Historical romance thus provides a useful subject for the study of the ways in which an artificial 'past' can gain 'mythical' significance, confirming attitudes or highlighting fears and hopes which arise from the nature of contemporary society.[2]

Foreign romance settings can be read in the same way as the 'past' Hughes is primarily concerned with. The descriptions are seldom accurate, but filled with sufficient detail to be convincing to the reader. Because a flavour of the place will do, the descriptions rarely exceed stereotypes and superficial details that do not amount to any more than set-pieces. If, as Hughes claims, 'the picture of the past is attractive because of attitudes in the reader which derive from experience in the present, and which are confirmed by reading the text',[3] then the same must be true of the picture of the foreign country. Many of the details that are used for the construction of that picture are influenced by present-day British attitudes and confirm them in turn for the readers.

For this essay I have chosen British historical romances and gothic romances[4] with a German or Austrian setting, although a study of any other combination would have yielded equally interesting results. The relationship between Britain and the German-speaking countries is of special interest, though, because of the ambivalence of British–German relations throughout this century. The British have fought the Germans in two world wars, each time victoriously. From 1945 to 1990, the British army occupied large parts of Northern Germany. At the same time the two countries have dealt as equals in NATO and the EEC. In analysing historical romances and gothics set (or partly set) in Germany and Austria, I want to explore the kinds of stereotypes and popular myths of the German-speaking countries that find expression in the romances and the manner in which real-world relations between Britain and Germany are reflected in the texts. First, I should like to discuss some of the more common stereotypes that are obviously felt to convey a sense of 'Germanness'.[5] In a more detailed study of three novels, I then want to analyse the strategies employed to convey feelings of ambivalence towards Germany and to establish a sense of British national superiority.

For the greatest part, the foreign atmosphere in the romances is created through little details that are felt to be 'German'. Names and food are the ones most easily available.[6] Some authors insert snatches of basic German, mostly spoken by servants and limited to the likes of 'You rang, *gnädige Fraulein*? [*sic*!]' (Cartland, *Angel*, p. 49). Very few of the historical romances set in German-speaking countries depend on specific historical events or periods;[7] mostly, the authors are not interested in giving more than an impression of what is supposed to be the 'mood' of the place. For example, Rosemary Guiley sums up the ingredients that are supposed to create a romance image of Vienna:

> In nineteenth century Europe, Vienna was the center of education, medicine and high society. It was the home of Sigmund Freud, Johann Strauss and others who've left their mark on the world. In its golden era, there were many elegant balls, where dashing Austrian soldiers and their ladies, princes and princesses and dukes and duchesses waltzed 'til dawn. Like the Italians, the Viennese take time every day to enjoy each other's company and watch the world go by while savoring a cup of strong coffee and a sweet, rich pastry.[8]

Add the Prater, the Spanish Riding School, *Heuriger* in Grinzing and 'that warm, easy Viennese charm, which (as Vienna's friends and enemies both agree), "sings the song you want to hear"',[9] and you've got the whole picture.[10] The mood of other places is created with similar set-pieces. Cologne means the cathedral and a walk along the banks of the Rhine;[11] Munich consists of 'Beer-halls' (Cartland, *Angel*, p. 43), cafés and 'the Pinakothek with its wonderful pictures, and the Marienplatz [with] the Glockenspiel' (p. 148).

Beside the guide-book descriptions, there are certain stereotypes that turn up regularly in the romances. One of them is Germany and especially Austria as the land of music. In Heaven's *Castle of Eagles*, the heroine comes to Vienna to study the piano; in each of Hodge's novels set in the imaginary principality of Lissenberg,[12] one of the heroines is employed at the Lissenberg opera as a singer, and a large part of the action centres on the opera. Protagonists of other novels discuss Wagner (Cartland, *Angel*, pp. 23, 110) or go to the opera to watch *Die Fledermaus* (Hylton, *Falcon*, p. 52).

Germany as the source of scientific knowledge does not play a large role – not surprisingly in a genre that focuses on the female protagonists, who have no access to the sciences in the nineteenth century, the period in which most of the novels are set. In Holt's *On the Night of the Seventh Moon*, a sinister doctor claims to have given the heroine a drug after she was supposedly raped, so that her memories of a hurried wedding are no more than delusions. In the course of the novel, however, it appears that everything is part of a plot and he never gave her any medicine at all. Still, the stereotype of the scientist who tests new medicines and treatments, using humans as guinea-pigs, belongs to a literary tradition that goes from Frankenstein to mad Nazi doctors in popular films. In contrast, the heroine of *Secret for a Nightingale*,[13] also by Holt, goes to Germany to be trained as a nurse in a convent. The episode is based on Florence Nightingale's training in Kaiserswerth, which is alluded to in the novel. Here, Germany is shown to be advanced in that women are granted the opportunity to acquire medical training, be it only as a nurse. In Ibbotson's *The Morning Gift*, set in the 1930s, the hero, the heroine and her father are all biologists.

Efficiency and thoroughness seem to be part of the German national character. This can be observed in doctors –

> 'Well, Kratz and Bruckner are very efficient ... very methodical, very conscientious.'
> 'Very German,' added Henrietta.
> 'You could say that. They have made this into an excellent establishment.' (Holt, *Secret*, p. 235)

– as well as housewives –

> 'The bedrooms are ready. All they need is the application of the warming pans.'
> 'Is that what you call German efficiency?'
> 'It is certainly efficiency, and as we are now in Germany you may be right.' (ibid. p. 386)

Unfortunately, this efficiency can lead to what Cartland calls 'a Germanic desire for dominance over those who surrounded [them]' (*Bride*, p. 205). Salisbury's *The Shadowed Spring* features Major von Berg, a Berlin police inspector, who is tall, blond, handsome with pale blue eyes and extremely clever and powerful. When he interrogates the heroine about a murder case, he is completely in control of the situation, and she finds herself unable to hold anything back. The major and the hero (an English colonel) meet in a clash of wills, which is only decided by an order from Bismarck to the major to drop the case.[14] Most interestingly, the scenes with the major are fraught with sexual tension. The heroine is aware of him looking down at her; she finds him confusingly masculine and incredibly masterful.[15] Describing the confrontation with the hero, the narrator uses terms of the battlefield, and the two men are characterized by their iron willpower.[16] It is in this situation of male competition that the heroine becomes aware she has fallen in love with the hero. The powerful personality of the Prussian officer is not conceived of as evil, but as dangerously attractive by Salisbury.

What about the romantic Germany of the Rhine and the Black Forest? The eighteenth-century gothic novelists used to think it a very attractive choice of setting, as can be deduced from the titles quoted in Jane Austen's *Northanger Abbey*, which include *Castle of Wolfenbach*, *Necromancer of the Black Forest* and *Orphan of the Rhine*.[17] Since 1960, only Victoria Holt has made use of this particular stereotype, but she has done so with great thoroughness. All three of her Germany novels[18] abound in similar descriptions:

> When I saw Kaiserwald, I felt as though I had stepped into an enchanted land which belonged in a fairy tale. The house had been a small schloss, with towers and turrets, which had belonged to a nobleman who had given it to the Deaconesses to be used as a hospital. It was situated among mountains – wooded hills and forest. [...]
>
> I could smell the redolent odour of pine; I could hear the water of the falls which tumbled down the mountains. Now and then we heard the tinkle of a bell which, our driver told us, meant that cows were nearby. There was a faint haziness in the air which touched everything with a misty blue. Even before I saw Kaiserwald I was entranced. [...]
>
> Now we were at the schloss. In front of it was a small lake – little more than a pond. Willows trailed in the water and with the mountains in the background it was a sight of breathtaking beauty. (*Secret*, pp. 202–3)

Take the stock motifs: the mountains, the forest with its pine trees, the castles and the cow bells. Add to this 'Gerda the Goosegirl' (p. 202) and 'Old Wilhelm, the woodcutter' (p. 212), fake marriages (*Moon*), local festivals dating back to heathen times (*Moon*), would-be usurpers of the ducal throne (*Moon*), and highborn ladies, half-mad with jealousy, trying to murder their rivals (*Moon* and *Kiss*). Holt creates her Germany like a fairy tale, and the narrator alludes to Grimms' Tales directly:

> In such a setting Hansel and Gretel were lost and came upon their gingerbread house; in such a wood the lost babes had wandered to lie down and sleep and be covered by the leaves. Along the river, although we could not see them, castles would appear to hang on the edge of the hillside – castles such as the one in which the Beauty slept for one hundred years before she was awakened by the kiss of a Prince. This was the forest of enchantment, of woodcutters, trolls, princes in disguise and princesses who must be rescued, of giants and dwarfs; it was the fairy-tale land. (*Moon*, pp. 13–14)

A second strand of mythical images is derived from the Nordic sagas. A young man encountered in the forest is instantly equated with Siegfried (*Moon*, p. 17), and the local festival can be traced back to an old cult of Loke [sic!], god of mischief (*Moon*, pp. 23, 197). The driving force behind some of the unravelling of the plot in *On the Night of the Seventh Moon* is an old woman-servant, who, in her delight in manipulating everybody, gains almost witch-like qualities (pp. 160, 208). The forest itself is a place of seduction, in which the rules of society do not apply. 'And tonight, because I am with you here, because we are in the heart of the forest, because there is magic in the air, you will forget the barriers which you set up for yourself', one hero argues (*Secret*, p. 393).

Holt's romantic Germany is not stable, though, and the nineteenth century intrudes by the end of each novel. The goose-girl has not been seduced by the devil, but by an ordinary pedlar (p. 407). The supposed mock marriage is a prosaic real one (*Moon*, p. 202). The English girl gets to marry the heir to the throne, but he is either supplanted by the baby son of his dead cousin (*Kiss*, p. 373) or dethroned by the new German empire in 1871 (*Moon*, p. 282). The celebration of Loke's festival is abandoned, and the rightful heir to the dukedom, whose life has been at stake for the greatest part of the book, becomes a professor at Bonn university (*Moon*, p. 282). In Holt's novels, Germany serves as a symbolic place where the darker, more primitive desires of the soul can be acted out, a place where the archetypes of the fairy-tale are still true. However, it is tamed by the end of each novel when the bourgeois world claims the protagonists.

The stereotypes of Germany used in the historical romance focus on very few aspects of what is supposed to be the German national character: names, food, the tourist attractions of a few well-known towns, the music, the medical sciences, thoroughness and cleanliness, the forests and mountains of South Germany and Austria, Grimms' fairy tales and Nordic myths. The resulting picture is vague, romantic, and hardly ever explored in any more depth. At first sight, it mostly seems pleasant, the British attitude towards Germany as expressed in the romances a positive one. In order to understand how anti-German and anti-European feelings permeate some of the texts, it is necessary to take a closer look at the way that British protagonists in the novels react to the country they are travelling through. It is interesting to see what strategies are employed by some of the authors to look down on the foreign country and celebrate England and Englishness at the same time.

Of all the novels set in Germany, Cartland's are the ones most obviously written with a copy of *Baedecker's* by the writer's elbow. In particular *A Very Naughty Angel*, which is set in Munich and its surroundings, is filled with short, stereotyped descriptions.

> [...] high above stretching up towards the deep blue sky were the snow-capped peaks of the Bavarian mountains. (p. 37)

> The road wound [...] through a valley with hills rising on either side and silhouetted against the starlit sky were the snowclad peaks of the mountains. (p. 69)

> He was wearing the Peasant costume which looked strange to her eyes but at the same time she thought it extremely attractive. The leather shorts, the green jacket with bone buttons, and on his head a jaunty little green felt hat with a brush at the back of it, all made up a most becoming outfit. (pp. 38–9)

> 'There are Munich specialities. There are white sausages known as Weisswurst, knuckle of pork called Schweinshaxen, and Steckerlfisch, fish on small spits roasted in the oven, which I find particularly delicious.' (p. 56)

> As was to be expected in Bavaria, there were no blankets, but there was a feather eiderdown, a *düchent* [*sic*!], as it was called in German, which was both warm and light. (p. 80)

> 'I will take you to the Picture Gallery at the Alta [*sic*!] Pinakothek. It is built in the Venetian style of the Renaissance and houses

the paintings collected by the Wittelbachs since the 16th Century.' (p. 42)

Many more of these little set descriptions could be added. Cartland's use of them is two-fold: on the one hand, by choosing these very obvious images she makes sure readers will meet their own expectations, thereby creating the 'realism' the romantic novel strives for. On the other hand, the guidebook-like quality of the images makes them a source of information for the reader at the same time. After having read the novel, the reader may feel that she has learnt something about nineteenth-century Bavaria. In one instance, when hero and heroine are discussing the rioting Munich students, the history lesson is made explicit:

> 'They have always been very powerful,' Tilda said. 'After all it was due to them that Ludwig II [*sic*!] was forced to abdicate.'
> 'The trouble in that instance was a lady called Lola Montez,' Rudolph replied, 'but I see that you have not neglected your history lessons.'
> 'It is a mistake to visit a country and know nothing about it,' Tilda replied demurely. (p. 70)

Even though the picture of Bavaria created in the novel is mostly a positive one – after all, the heroine marries the prince of Obernia, a small country next to and rather similar to Bavaria – this is not extended to the rest of Germany. Tilda is sent to Obernia by Queen Victoria for sound political reasons.

> Obernia occupies a very important place in our political strategy concerning Europe. [...] Obernia, as it borders on Bavaria, Austria and Wurthemberg, is a very important factor in the balance of power in that it remains independent. [...] You will, in an indirect capacity, be an Ambassador for England. You must influence your husband to realize that co-operation with us rather than with Germany will be always to his advantage. (pp. 15–16)

The idea of the balance of power in Europe, which is to be controlled by Britain, is expressed openly here. By alluding to a political concern that is as important to British national feelings today as it was in the nineteenth century, Cartland re-establishes the British claim of dominance in Europe in the eye of the reader, happily ignoring the change in political circumstances between 1879, the date of the novel's setting, and 1975, the date of its publication.

A number of worried allusions are made to the behaviour of the Queen's grandson Willy, later Wilhelm II, and to Bismark [*sic!*] (pp. 15–16, 21). At one point, Tilda has a kind of premonition when she considers the recent political changes in Germany.

> Now there were maps of Europe after 1871 when the German Federation had been formed.
> Now the brown of Germany sprawled everywhere from Russia to France with the acquisitions from the Treaty of Prague in a slightly lighter shade.
> 'Brown is the right colour for Germany,' Tilda thought. 'It is a dull, heavy country. At the same time rather sinister!'
> There was something hard and autocratic about the Prussians but, although she had not seen a lot of the Bavarians she found them different in every way.
> They were a smiling people [. . .]. (p. 32)

This passage points clearly forward to the Third Reich and links the heroine's reading of the map with the historical events of the twentieth century, thus giving her attitude validity, although it is originally based on emotion. In this romance, Cartland neatly divides Germany into two parts: 'good' Bavaria and 'evil' Prussia. Positive and negative stereotypes are attached to each one of these countries. As a result, the reader can feel safe; any ambivalent feelings about Germany she may harbour can be dropped in favour of a simple binary construction. This can be extended to modern Germany: the positive Germany, the land of art, music and *Gemütlichkeit*, can be perceived as descended from the 'Bavarian' half of the German soul, whereas the political Germany, derived from the German Empire created by Prussia, can be seen as heir to all the negative characteristics: the desire for dominance, the lack of humour, the know-it-all attitude. Any kind of unprejudiced examination of the other country's character is made unnecessary.

There is hardly any ambivalence in *The Reluctant Bride*. The heroine, Camilla, comes to Germany in 1816 to marry the Prince of Meldenstein. Unfortunately, he turns out to be a drug-addicted, degenerate madman (corrupted by a long stay in China), so she flees with her handsome English escort and marries him instead. Because Germany is not, as for Tilda, a place of romantic fulfilment for Camilla, but only a place of threat, the setting gains a different function and is treated in a different manner.

The picture-book descriptions still occur, but they are reduced to an image of women in national costume here, a fairy-tale palace there. These set-pieces are so vague, in fact, that they could be applied to a romanticized stereotype of any mid-European country, and do not mean anything except 'abroad' and 'before the twentieth century'.

The heroine is the beautiful daughter of an impoverished English baronet who used to be in the diplomatic service. Her suitor is 'His Serene Highness, Prince Hedwig of Meldenstein.' (p. 18) Although Camilla asks herself why she has been chosen (he has never seen her), nobody else wonders for a minute at the disparity of the union in rank and wealth. On the contrary, it is felt that it is Camilla who is honouring the prince by accepting him. As the hero puts it: 'As I have already told you, you are the perfect choice, a girl with both beauty and brains. What Prince could ask for more? These small European Royalty do not usually pull off such an advantageous deal, I can assure you.' (p. 68) As she approaches Meldenstein and adopts the role of a princess on the way, Camilla becomes more and more aware of her national identity. Meeting a reception committee on landing in Antwerp, she is 'proud that being English she was creating a favourable impression as soon as she stepped on foreign soil' (p. 88). When her lady-in-waiting chides her for receiving a young man on her own, Camilla replies haughtily: 'I am English, [...] and I am not yet concerned with the conventions of Meldenstein, or indeed, of Westerbalden.' (p. 160) Faced with the Meldenstein courtiers, again it is awareness of her nationality that gives her strength. '"What right have they," she asked herself, "to criticize or condemn an Englishwoman?"' (p. 168) Camilla, as a proper Cartland heroine, is a timid girl at the beginning of the book. On the continent, though, she acquires the air and the command of the princess she is about to become. Her self-confidence is acceptable, however, because it is grounded on nationality. Like Tilda in *A Very Naughty Angel*, Camilla becomes an 'ambassador' for England, and, representing her country, must behave accordingly.

'Englishness' is raised to an almost mythical quality where the male figures are concerned. When Camilla first meets the courtiers and statesmen of Meldenstein, she is disappointed. '"They seem rather ordinary," she thought, "just like the politicians of any country." And she felt, perhaps unjustly, that they were shorter of stature than they would have been had they been of British blood.' (p. 171) In contrast to all the Meldenstein men, the English hero has this quality: 'she thought how handsome and distinguished he looked. He would have been outstanding, she knew, in any company. Here he seemed like a being from another world, and she knew that world was England.' (p. 172) In this scene, the attributes of the hero are merged with and become a result of his national identity. The hero's Englishness is so obvious that it becomes a threat to the escape of hero and heroine. Camilla 'wondered how, in his superfine grey whipcord coat and polished boots, anyone could mistake him for anything but an English gentleman. But she guessed that the stable-hands were not too bright' (p. 199). Nationality in *The Reluctant Bride* becomes a mythical quality that distinguishes its bearers *per se* and is an important source of their actions.

Besides this indirect establishment of English superiority there is also a direct one in the form of 'the voice of the people'. Camilla's maid, a naive country girl, quotes to her mistress the remarks of the hero's valet on the country they are travelling through.

'Oh, to hear [Fräulein Johann] talk, you would think Meldenstein was more important than England [...] But the Captain's valet, Mister Harpen, is English and says it is only a small country and of little consequence. [Camilla laughs at this.] Personally I would rather believe Mister Harpen [...]. He's a real nice man, miss, and says he's too old to be taken in by them foreigners. He never did approve of an Englishwoman marrying one of them.' (p. 92)

'Mister Harpen gets everything he wants,' Rose said with satisfaction, 'but he does not care much for foreigners – frogs and bullfrogs he calls them – the bullfrogs being the people in this country.'
'Oh hush, Rose,' Camilla said hastily, 'someone might be listening to you. You must not say anything which might offend those who are offering us hospitality.'
'Well, we beat them all, didn't we, Miss?' Rose asked. 'Mister Harpen says the people here hadn't the guts to square up to Boney, however bad he treated them. But we beat him and all those ahanging on to his coat-tails single-handed.'
'Yes indeed we beat Napoleon,' Camilla said, 'and now that we are victorious we must be magnanimous. We must not remind Europe that we are their conquerors, that would be sadly impolite.' (pp. 121–2)

Cartland employs a two-fold strategy to define the relationship between Britain and the continent. The obviously prejudiced opinions of the simple, but patriotic Englishman are quoted at some length. The heroine at first disassociates herself from them by laughter and admonition for the sake of good manners. Still, in spite of that denial, they are printed in the text and thereby given room. Furthermore, when provoked by her mistress's tactfulness, Rose gives an explanation for the English superiority that convinces even Camilla. Mister Harpen's opinions, based on that 'truth', are therefore, in spite of Camilla's earlier protest, justified in retrospect. The simple Englishman, unhampered by the politeness of the upper classes, speaks the obvious truth. Historically, however, he does not. Napoleon was not beaten by the British single-handedly, but by an alliance that included Russia, Sweden, Prussia and a number of smaller German states. At no time during that war did the British 'conquer' Europe. It is questionable, though, whether many English readers of the late twentieth century would know enough about that period to realize this. On the other hand, the valet's remarks accurately describe the opinion some British hold about their country's role in World War II. The condescension shown by Camilla – 'now that we are victorious we must be magnanimous. We must not remind Europe that we are their conquerors, that would be sadly impolite' – reflects an attitude held in twentieth-century Britain, and justifies and strengthens this attitude for the readers of the novel.

Cartland's treatment of the European theme in this novel is not restricted to Germany. England and its people are superior to *all* of Europe. Specific German characteristics (besides the flowerpots and white aprons) are only presented twice, each time in connection with the evil prince.

> He must once have been extremely good-looking in the Germanic way that she could see repeated in the portraits of what were obviously his ancestors round the wall. They all had square heads, fair hair, which in Prince Hedwig's case was now turning grey at the temples, and pale, somewhat cold blue eyes. (p. 180)

The prince's degradation was possible, the hero explains, because his seducers 'pandered to the worst instincts within him – a Germanic desire for dominance over those who surrounded him' (p. 205). Two negative stereotypes of the Germans are evoked here, and interestingly, each time they are connected with the adjective *Germanic*. The term seems to envelop everything bad about the German national character.

Hodge's novel *The Adventurers*[19] is the only English historical romance I have ever come across that is set in Germany during the time of Napoleon's retreat after the battle of Leipzig. England and a number of German states, among them Prussia and Bavaria, are allied against Napoleon. The heroine Sonia, as daughter of a German nobleman and an Englishwoman, has spent all her life in Germany. Both the setting and the personal situation of the heroine would suggest a sympathetic treatment of the German background.

As far as historicity is concerned, the novel is vague and accurate at the same time. As the protagonists follow the Allied Headquarters across Germany, Switzerland and France, the route is the historical one, and the few names dropped, like Schwartzenberg [*sic*!] and Blücher, are those of historical persons who actually were present. At the same time, the author only gives the most superficial details on anything that has not directly to do with the military movements. We are told, for instance, that the castle belonging to the heroine's family, though 'beyond the mountains' (p. 7), is close enough to Leipzig to hear the guns, but we are never informed to which state it belongs. The English governess Miss Barrymore is teased for her love for 'that Goethe' (p. 45) by her half-German pupil, but this remark remains the only token reference to German culture. No Cartland-like recitations of Baedecker knowledge here: Not a single architectural feature – with the possible exception of a 'high gabled window' (p. 69) in Frankfurt – is mentioned.

Although Sonia's father is German and she has never been to England, she emphasizes repeatedly: 'I am English' (pp. 15–16, 108). This attitude is supposed to be based on her family situation, about which contradictory facts emerge. First of all, the late baroness has married against the wishes of her family and has consequently been cut off by her father. These facts would certainly suggest a love match. Nevertheless, the baroness is very unhappy in her married life, suffering under the baron's harsh temper. The reader is told that she used to play cards with her husband, although she is bad at it, as the only device to keep him from drinking. She is so unhappy, in fact, that rumours seep back to England (p. 105) and an Englishwoman comes to keep her company and help her to educate her little daughter. When the hero compliments Sonia on her good English: 'But you – you speak like a native', she explains: 'My mother spoke nothing else.' (p. 21) Now the reader might consider that if the baroness, cut off from her English family and living in Germany, was not prepared to learn the native language of her husband, perhaps it was not exclusively his fault that the marriage turned out unhappily. But such thoughts are not encouraged at all by the text. By inserting these facts so sparingly, the author wants to avoid the construction of a coherent story on behalf of the reader. Every piece of information accounts for one aspect of the background: the baroness must have been unhappy and her husband a brute so that her daughter can reject her German ancestry and be determined to get to England. At the same time, she must have been cut off by her family so that Sonia cannot go to her loving grandparents directly after her father's death. The baroness cannot have spoken any German so that her daughter's command of the English language can be faultless. In all these instances, the foreign country and culture are not taken seriously or given any coherent place in the story, but they are employed according to present needs, using stereotypes and, by using them in such a unreflected manner, actually enforcing them.

In the whole book, not a single likeable figure appears who is German or Austrian. The baron (his attributes are 'broad, leather-clad shoulders' (p. 8) and 'shabby boots' (p. 9)) is so bad-tempered and stubborn that he causes the looting of his own castle and the death of all inhabitants, including himself (pp. 9–11). His late son, Sonia's brother, 'had been just like him, a sportsman, unromantic, short-tempered, and often impatient with what he called her crotchets. Only he called them *launen* [sic!] since, like his father, he thought English a ridiculous language.' (p. 8) Miss Barrymore sums up Sonia's relationship with father and brother: 'Poor child, she's starved for compliments. Her father and brother never did more than admire her sauerkraut or her soup.' (p. 73) The father's sister, with whom Sonia at first plans to take refuge, is equally unappealing: 'A harsh, black widow, she lived a life of near-Trappist solitude, her Calvinism so fierce that anything she found herself enjoying was, automatically, bad. [...] Sonia did her the justice of thinking her stringent life the result of a charity as genuine as it was unlovely.' (p. 17) Cousin Franz, heir to the estate, is a self-righteous lecher with a nasty mind, but the hero deals with him easily: 'On the face of it, they were unequally matched enough, for Von Hugel loomed nearly a head taller than Vincent and broad to match. But his eyes fell first and there was more bluster than confidence in his voice when he spoke.' (p. 54) So much for the heroine's family.

The images presented of other Germans are hardly more attractive. The soldiers are either rude and aggressive, like the Austrian officers

Sonia encounters (pp. 21–2), or '[f]at old men, stinking of schnapps and garlic' (p. 74), who visit the gambling house in Frankfurt. Their main function in the narrative is that of a source of income to the hero, who provides for himself, Sonia and Miss Barrymore as a professional gamester. As a result, they can be spoken of in terms of contempt: 'Haverton and I took on a couple of fat Prussians whose brains, I think, must have been in their stomachs.' (p. 83)

The attitude towards the populace is at least ambivalent. Some mention is made of the villagers' sufferings after the battle of Leipzig (pp. 47–8). The townspeople of Frankfurt are seen in a different light, though. Sonia remarks:

> 'Look at them! Grumble, grumble, grumble all the time about their sufferings under Napoleon – iniquitous taxes, forced levies . . . and all of them as fat as butter, looking as if they'd never suffered in their lives.'
> 'And making a pretty penny out of the Allies too, by all reports.' (p. 70)

This attitude is reinforced by the description of an assembly the protagonists are attending.

> [. . .] the Assembly Rooms were full of plump merchants' daughters, so bejeweled and beribboned that Vincent whispered to Elizabeth it was hard to believe the tales they had heard about Germany's impoverishment at Napoleon's hand. Some of these girls were handsome enough, in a bold and buxom way, but there was none, as Haverton lost no time in telling her, to hold a candle to Sonia. 'Or to Mrs. Barrymore, if it comes to that. How glad I am that I took the precaution of securing dances with both of you in advance: you are going to find yourselves the belles of the ball.'
> It was true, and inevitable. The two Grand Duchesses, though both charming girls, were beings set apart; Lady Burgersh had eyes only for her husband; Sonia and Elizabeth found themselves the most eligible unmarried ladies in the room. (p. 84)

Two sets of stereotypes are employed here, which must be discussed separately. The women at the assembly are disparaged out of hand. They are overdressed, showing off their wealth (presumably acquired by trade). Every one of them corresponds to the national stereotype of the rather large Germanic woman. The condemnation of the 'the fat Frankfurt fräuleins' (p. 78), as another

Englishman puts it, might be based on two grounds. One of them is class. Concerning the historical romance in general, Hughes points out: 'For the most part the notion that lower and upper classes are members of different species [...] is so much taken for granted that the texts never present it for examination.'[20] Descent from the aristocracy, which the Grand Duchesses (sisters to the Czar of Russia) and Sonia can claim, automatically grants them beauty and grace superior to that of mere burghers' daughters. Even the governess, daughter of a clergyman, can claim superiority of class. The other, more subtle reason for the categorization of the women might be nationality and, ultimately, race. Sonia and Miss Barrymore are English, the Grand Duchesses Russian. Their beauty is automatically superior to that of the German women. The passage clearly shows how such stereotypes are enforced: first, when Haverton pays his compliments, the reader might still think that, trying to flatter Sonia, he was exaggerating. But the contrary is the case: the narrative immediately proves Haverton's assessment of the situation to have been entirely and *inevitably* accurate.

The other stereotype that appears in the passage quoted above is a more political one. The Frankfurt citizens are shown to be complaining about their liberators, and they are shown as having gained in the war, although they claim the contrary. Considering this, the date of publication of *The Adventurers* should be taken into account: by 1965, the *Wirtschaftswunder* had brought an undreamt-of economic upturn to the German population, and comparative wealth to most citizens. In Britain, on the other hand, the loss of the colonies was felt quite strongly. The attitude towards the Germans in the novel reflects the attitude of many British at that time towards Germany and the Germans. It was felt that, as they had lost World War II, it was unfair they were better off now than the British – their liberators – were. Even though the novel depicts a historical period, grievances of the present are included in the book.

German history of the twentieth century is prefigured once more in the novel. Officers from a number of countries are squabbling about the political future of France. The discussion culminates in 'a lone Prussian maintaining, *sotto voce*, that only the destruction of Paris could make amends for what had happened at Berlin.' (p. 117) The vindictiveness of this remark clearly points forward to the Prussian–French relations during the next 150 years, culminating in Hitler's attack on France, and it settles who's to blame.

The anti-German attitude of *The Adventurers* is even more apparent when the treatment of the Germans is compared with that of the French. The hero, whose mother was French, claims: 'I see nothing to be ashamed of in being French. We've held the world at bay for twenty years, which is more than you Germans can boast of.' (p. 108) The heroine has witnessed French marauders looting her family's castle, raping a maid and killing all the inhabitants, and accordingly detests the French. Once she arrives in France, though, she has to change her mind: 'They seem so friendly. You can't think of Marthe as an enemy, somehow.' (p. 113). The French are grateful to their liberators (p. 112). When the protagonists are threatened by a French mob later, the landlady runs to the garrison for help, and individual people among the populace speak out for the protagonists and manage to hold back the mob at least for a time. There are good Frenchmen and bad Frenchmen, Sonia (and with her the reader) comes to understand. Any differentiation of this kind is denied as far as the Germans are concerned.

In a novel like *The Adventurers*, the German setting is hardly used for the sake of its exoticism – which would have warranted greater interest in country and customs themselves – but only for the value of the bare historical facts, which serve as a background. On the whole, it is used to reinforce the superiority of Britishness and as a means of cementing the prejudices against the other country.

The treatment of the German setting in Hodge's three Lissenberg novels is quite different. Lissenberg, an imaginary Alpine principality wedged in between Austria, Switzerland and Württemberg in the approximate location of Liechtenstein, permits the 'what if' situation of fantasy. Hodge explores the utopia of a society where men and women are equal – more so than in the real background period, at least. In *First Night* and *Leading Lady*, set in the Napoleonic age, she further uses the country to explore the struggle between revolution and political pragmatism that most European countries had to face in that period. The treatment of Lissenberg is very sympathetic, but Lissenberg is not really a part of Germany. The natives do not speak German as their first language: 'That was Liss, the local language. German with a dash of French and just a touch of Italian. The result of those long winters when no one could get in or out.' (Hodge, *Act*, p. 41) By giving it a separate language, the author has neatly disassociated Lissenberg from Germany and its catastrophic history.

The historical romances' attitude towards the German-speaking countries, when analysed in detail, is, on the whole, a bit disquieting. Considering that general opinions are expressed more freely in popular literature than in more 'educated' texts, the stereotypes and prejudices discussed above will, to some degree, be those held by the British. Some of them are positive, but a greater number negative, and the shadow of the Third Reich looms over many of the texts. Even more interesting is the observation that the texts set in foreign places are less concerned with a depiction of those places than a confirmation of British superiority. This might be a sign of British chauvinism, but it might also be caused by a desire to make sure of one's own national identity in an era when political frontiers as well as cultural differences are slowly dissolving. This, however, need not be a national characteristic of the British. One can assume that German popular literature will, in all likelihood, in a similar manner confirm German superiority and French literature French superiority. It is obvious that the images of one another as presented in the romances are more concerned with creating a distance than creating a community, more interested in differences than in similarities. The concern with one's superiority over other nations points to a degree of national chauvinism that is worrying, though, and that will have to be dealt with to some extent in the near future if the European Union is supposed to go beyond being a mere political tool.

NOTES

1. Helen Hughes, *The Historical Romance* (London & New York: Routledge, 1993), p. 1.
2. Hughes, p. 1.
3. Hughes, p. 5.
4. The terms are used following Kay Mussell, 'Preface', *Twentieth-Century Romance and Gothic Writers*, ed. James Vinson (Detroit: Gale Research Company, 1982), pp. v–vii.
5. Günter Blaicher names a number of typical stereotypes, among them the 'hun', the absent-minded professor, the hard-drinking, duelling student, the stiff Prussian officer, and the exemplary if rather dull housewife in *Das Deutschlandbild in der englischen Literatur* (Darmstadt: Wissenschaftliche Buchgesellschaft, 1992), pp. 13–43. Blaicher describes other stereotypes of the Germans, but they are less relevant to the romance.

6. Almost every novel has a minor character called *Liesel*, *Fritz* or *Wagner*. For some reason, *Rudolph* and *Maximilian* are felt to be fitting names for romantic leads: *Rudolph* is the name the princely hero of Barbara Cartland's *A Very Naughty Angel* (London: Pan, 1975) uses for private occasions; it is the name of the murdered heir to the throne in Victoria Holt's *The Judas Kiss* (London: Collins, 1981); it is further used for the hero's pompous father (a prince nevertheless) in Jane Aiken Hodge's *Last Act* (1979; London: Coronet, 1981). *Maximilian* is the name of the hero both in Holt's *On the Night of the Seventh Moon* (1973; London: Fontana, 1988) and in Sara Hylton's *The Crimson Falcon* (1983; London: Sheridan, 1994) and another young prince in Hodge's *First Night* (1989; London: Coronet, 1990) and *Leading Lady* (1990; London: Coronet, 1991), and it is the official name of Rudolph of *A Very Naughty Angel*. Authors tend to stick to the more typical names partly to avoid mistakes, partly to profit from the names' full power of evocation. Some slips occur, however: Cartland gives the female name of *Hedwig* to an evil prince, and calls one of the courtiers *Frau von Kotze* in *The Reluctant Bride* (1970; London: Arrow, 1972). The hero of Constance Heaven's *Castle of Eagles* (1974; London: Pan, 1977), a nineteenth-century Austrian aristocrat, is called *Julian*. The name is so obviously inappropiate that it was changed to *Alexander* in the German translation. As far as food is concerned, sauerkraut is the all-time favourite, but beer, sausage, dark bread, pastries and, in Austria, Guglhupf fulfil the same function.
7. There are exceptions: Heaven sets *Castle of Eagles* during the 1848 revolution in Vienna, and Eva Ibbotson's *The Morning Gift* (1993; London: Arrow, 1994) depicts the *Anschluss* in 1938, for example. These novels put greater emphasis on the historical background than the others and describe it in more accurate detail.
8. Rosemary Guiley, *Love Lines: a Romance Reader's Guide to Printed Pleasures* (New York: Facts On File, 1983) 123. The description occurs in a list of 'the world's most romantic cities'; Vienna ranks as the ninth.
9. Mary Stewart, *Airs Above the Ground* (1965; London: Hodder, 1967), p. 46.
10. The 'Vienna novels' from which these set pieces were extracted are Heaven, *Castle of Eagles*; Hylton, *The Crimson Falcon*; Stewart, *Airs Above the Ground*; Ibbotson, *Magic Flutes* (1982; London: Arrow, 1993) and *The Morning Gift*; Cartland, *The Enchanted Waltz* (London: Hutchinson, 1955); Clare Darcy, *Letty* (London: Futura, 1980); and Caroline Courtney, *A Lover's Victory* (London: Arlington, 1981).
11. Carola Salisbury, *The Shadowed Spring* (New York: Doubleday, 1980).
12. *Last Act*, *First Night* and *Leading Lady*.
13. (1986; London: Fontana, 1988).
14. Unfortunately, the novel has not been available in English, so the page references apply to the German translation: *Endstation Liebe*, transl. Eva Malsch (Rastatt: Moewig, 1982), pp. 128–38 *passim*.
15. '[Er] blickte auf mich herab, verwirrend maskulin, unglaublich herrisch' (p. 134).

16. 'Das Schlachtfeld war nun klar umrissen, und der Kampf fand nur noch zwischen den beiden Männern statt, der eine blond, der andere schwarzhaarig, beide von eiserner Willenskraft erfüllt, beide von stählerner Härte' (p. 139).
17. Jane Austen, *Northanger Abbey, Lady Susan, The Watsons*, and *Sanditon*, ed. John Davie (Oxford: Oxford University Press, 1980) p. 24.
18. *On the Night of the Seventh Moon*, *The Judas Kiss*, and *Secret of a Nightingale*.
19. (1965; London: Coronet, 1969).
20. Hughes, p. 95.

4 Discovering 'Europe' in the Process of Repatriation: Primo Levi's *La Tregua*
Angela Flury

In the main street, fixed on two stakes driven into the muddy soil, stood a wooden plaque with a map of Europe painted on it, now fading from the sun and rains of many a summer. It must have been used to follow the war bulletins, but it had been painted from memory, as if seen from a great distance; France was decidedly a coffee pot, the Iberian Peninsula a head in profile, with the nose sticking out from Portugal, and Italy a genuine boot, just a trifle oblique, with the sole and heel smooth and straightlined. Only four cities were shown in Italy: Rome, Venice, Naples and Dronero.[1]

Nella via principale, inchiodata su due paletti infissi nel suolo fangoso, era una tavola di legno su cui era dipinta l'Europa, ormai sbiadita per i soli e le pioge di molte estati. Doveva aver servito per seguirvi i bollettini di guerra, ma era stata dipinta a memoria, come vista da una lontananza estrema: la Francia era decisamente una caffettiera, la penisola iberica una testa di profilo, col naso che sporgeva dal Portogallo, e l'Italia un autentico stivale, appena un po'obliquo, con la suola e il tacco ben lisci e allineati. Nell'Italia erano indicate solo quattro città: Roma, Venezia, Napoli e Dronero.[2]

In der Hauptstraße war auf zwei in den schlammigen Boden gerammte Pfähle eine Holztafel genagelt; sie zeigte eine durch Sonne und Regen vieler Sommer verblaßte Landkarte Europas, die dazu gedient haben mußte, Kriegsnachrichten anschaulich zu machen; offenbar war sie frei nach dem Gedächtnis und wie aus großer Entfernung gezeichnet worden: Frankreich glich ausgesprochen einer Kaffeekanne, die Iberische Halbinsel einem

Kopf im Profil, dessen Nase in Portugal hervorsprang, und Italien war ein wirklicher, fast senkrecht verlaufender Stiefel mit schön geradliniger Sohle und eckigem Absatz. Nur vier Städte waren eingezeichnet: Rom, Venedig, Neapel und Dronero, ein winziges Dorf in Piedmont.[3]

Why did the German translators above situate Dronero as a tiny village in Piedmont when neither the Italian author nor the English translator thought it necessary to do so? This question is, for the moment, merely a preface for my essay that takes as its subject the concept of Europe as it emerges in Primo Levi's second book *La tregua*, written after the belated, successful 1958 reception of *Se questo e un uomo*, and published in 1963.[4] Levi remembers and records in the early 1960s traversing a long distance in nine months between January and October 1945 from Auschwitz to Turin, Italy. *La tregua* begins with the German evacuation of the Silesian region, followed by the arrival of the Red Army in Auschwitz. My point of departure for this essay follows closely Levi's own as he leaves Auschwitz and begins the survivor's journey home, for to talk about someone's journey 'is inevitably to engage in it',[5] to go along not so much as distanced observer, merely for the ride, but 'to mime through the movement of one's words that which one is trying to designate with those words'.[6] I accompany Levi in order to show how the body of people(s) whom he links by accounting their particular histories within a metahistorical framework, in numerous camps, and on a post-war continent of soup kitchens, makes up 'Europe'. A long-standing concept, Europe, enters the author-narrator's awareness at a time of political, economic and national crises. Whatever Europe may have been at any time before the events of *La tregua*, and whatever exclusive and inclusive boundaries contained it, are revitalized and revisioned in the immediate aftermath of the war in the process of repatriation. Between war and peace, in the moments of 'the great truce' (*RA*, pp. 59–60) ('la grande tregua', *T*, p. 66; 'die große Atempause', *A*, p. 63), an entangled body of people struggle and strive to situate themselves, like Levi, in accordance with a sense of their national belonging. Many of the characters stand out as individuals, that is to say, as markedly complex, particular subjectivities. Against the metaproject of repatriating nations, a European identity based on the need and desire to make oneself be understood appears, and provides people with unexpected opportunities to forge a community on the move. Among people who do not speak each other's language, interaction can only happen in the act of translation that is a performance. By this I mean quite simply that one's own words in one's own language very often cannot be matched by the other's words in the other's language, and so the process of translation must activate bodies, emotions, gestures, and mimicry in order to convey intended meanings. In *La tregua*, the displacements of people and nations spill over to construct a European landscape framed by Levi's movements towards the East, where this act of translation becomes increasingly a performative *event*. I work most closely with the English translation, because it is the primary language of my understanding, but I read the German translation and the Italian original, as well, to elaborate a major theme of *La tregua*, that is, the way in which questions of translation register differences that can, however, be accommodated and improvised by an emerging, transient European identity.

The first part of the essay looks at Levi's involuntary journey to the European East, that is prompted by a range of circumstances: destroyed train tracks, political chaos, illness, to name a few. The Lager has been left behind, but as Levi passes through a series of camps before he reaches Turin, Lager and camps merge in unsettling and thought provoking ways. Levi's perception of the hierarchies in the Lager anticipates his own struggle in the East versus West, post-war order, when he insists on the validity of this Lager hierarchy. This theme is taken up in part II. *La tregua* revels in the delight in language and representation as its narrator recovers the diversity of European idioms outside of the Lager. Part III explicates the pleasures of acting out meaning among this diversity. The final part shows how representations in the theatrical spaces of Levi's experiences in Belorussia frustrate and entertain the narrator. The conclusion takes up the question of Russia's membership of the European Community.

I. LINGUISTIC LANDSCAPES

How does one orient oneself in places not visited before, amid the anarchy of a post-war landscape in which borders between national territories are unclear even as their proper, absent guardians are substituted by allied forces, while massive movements of people(s) are crossing, trying to get home? And how does one orient oneself and the reader in a narrative whose point of departure is Auschwitz?

La tregua is a book fraught with post-war tensions between an excess of contemplative nation-being and an observant sensibility affected by, and taking into account, complex subjectivities who are divided people. Simply put, people are divided from the *patria* and distinguished by inhabiting multiple cultural, linguistic, ethnic, and racial identities. In contemplating the obligatory bath-ritual to which the formerly incarcerated are subjected by the Soviet Army, the Italian-Jewish narrator-author posits a triangulated largesse of German, American and Russian organizational strategies. These are in keeping with a national character that is, in turn, in keeping with the three nations' political roles and responsibilities. In *La tregua*, however, these characteristically national strategies go hand in hand with the profiles of people like the Greek or Dr Gottlieb, polyglots, whose mysteriousness is founded on their ability to assume more than one nationality in terms of language. Although designated 'the Greek', Mordo Nahum is more than a metonymic embodiment dominated by a general national character. In fact, it is he who provides Levi with the opportunity to observe how one might perform and project a nationality not one's own. In the Italian military camp that, at first reluctantly, admits Levi and the Greek, Mordo Nahum woos his hosts by assuming Italian-ness. Levi observes:

> He possessed the right equipment; he could speak Italian, and (what matters more, and what is missing in many Italians themselves) he knew of what to speak in Italian. He amazed me; he showed himself an expert about girls and spaghetti, Juventus[7] and lyrical music, the war and blennorrhoea, wine and the black market, motor-bikes and spivs [...]. (*RA*, p. 45)

Levi's parenthetical emphasis that many Italians themselves are lacking in the proper thematics needed to perform their national identity suggests that Italian-ness, and by extension national identity in general, can best be fathomed from a distance, from a position outside, among others. Moreover, the cultural thematics of a national identity are better grasped once they are perceived as a performance. Simply put, cultural thematics constitute a reservoir of cultural stereotypes that can be appropriated in the process of including oneself in a nationally based community. In Levi's case as the observer of the Greek's successful attempt to be included (and thus accommodated) in the Italian camp, two kinds of distances, one geographical, the other spectatorial, serve the same purpose: to acquire a sense of Italian national identity. Yet, to be outside of one's national boundaries among others is, in fact, to become European, as I hope to show in the course of this essay.

In addition to national characters utilized by governments and performed by individuals, there is the following observation: 'Only when April came, when the last snows had melted and the mild sun had dried *the Polish mud* [my emphasis], did we begin to feel ourselves truly free.' (*RA*, p. 77) Here the narration relies on the national adjective to situate the consciousness of a freedom in accordance with its surroundings. In this instance, it naturalizes nationality, putting it in the soil, in order to locate that recognition, that is also a remembrance, specifically in time and place. The author-narrator's frequent national attributions to government, subjectivities, and land provoke an uncertain response to the momentum attached to the end of war, on the one hand (a war that must itself be perceived as the battlefield of national(istic) interests and forces), and on the other, cultural differences and particularities at once within and without nationality. The latter warrant Levi's infrequent employment of quotation marks, hyphens, and compounds to clarify the complexity of identities, be they singular or collective. A good example here is a group of Italians, 'civilian and military officials from the Italian Legation at Bucharest' (*RA*, p. 117), who had stayed in Rumania and intermarried, but eventually join the trek home; they are consequently referred to and quoted as 'the Rumanians' (*RA*, p. 178) in a humorous attempt to distinguish between 'Italian-Rumanians and Italian-Italians' (*RA*, p. 117) ('Italiani-rumeni e italiani-italiani'; *T*, p. 139; 'Rumänische Italiener und italienische Italiener', *A*, p. 134). Twentieth-century critics from Hannah Arendt to Tom Nairn have analysed the experience of being caught in between the big picture and its constitutive distinctions. They have discerned the structural ambivalences that mark the nation as a modern construct.[8] The nation is modern and new, a visionary, rational political model *par excellence*, but which wants to be old. This model bases its history on *a* people that are turned into *the* people in an authoritative process that separates representatives from unrepresentables. It claims for itself a stable genesis that does not sufficiently consider the transient nature of the cultural systems and formations that preceded and comprise it. There is in *La tregua* a relationship between the larger, political (dis)order and the individual, that creates at that particular moment in history – in the aftermath of war – an identity surplus classifiable as 'European': a spill-over that is flooding, as it were, deserted streets and the vast emptiness of stretches and plains before Levi in a never-seen-before, unfamiliar landscape. By engaging in Levi's movements towards the East, from an already formerly German-occupied Poland to the former Soviet Union in what is now Belorussia to Northern Italy, I attempt to keep track of the ways in which he designates, describes, analyses and identifies people, strategies, and tactics in terms of national affiliations that comprise a fluid Europe.

As Levi's is the autobiographical account of a man returning home, the all-encompassing *topos* connects itself often through the author-narrator's own citations[9] to a common and popular narrative structure: the journey in European literature. In it, the home is the basis that must be recovered.[10] And yet, in *La tregua* the home has itself been usurped by another point of departure, namely Auschwitz. Levi's stakes are high in that not only must he set an end to the infinite chain of displacements that keeps him moving from one camp to another, but he must regain home as the originary locus at the beginning of his deportation that precedes the beginning of *La tregua* and which is told in *Se questo e un uomo*. He must, in other words, restore a severed beginning, obliterated by the experience in the Lager, and he is thus in a sense caught in an endless chain of narration. The Lager has become the dominant point of departure – in a narrative sense, home – and Levi's comparing every camp thereafter with Auschwitz underlines his conceptual understanding that comes from his experience. He perceives, for example, a Red Cross field kitchen as 'in a certain sense, the Lager upside down' (*RA*, p. 41) ('il Lager a rovescio', *T*, p. 44; 'das genaue Gegenteil des Lagers', *A*, p. 40), and he initially rejoices at finding an Italian army camp: 'I had found a home' (*RA*, p. 44) ('avevo trovato una casa', *T*, p. 47; 'ich hatte ein Zuhause gefunden', *A*, p. 43). At one point, he even discovers that a Lager has been transferred into a transit camp; moreover, all camps are hoped to be 'acceptable substitute[s] for [the repatriates'] homes' (*RA*, p. 39). The disconcerting convergence of Lagers, camps, and homes has an uncanny effect, because it conflates the sought-after familiarity of the origin with its usurpation by German *Konzentrationslager*, leaving the camps meant to bridge the journey home in a precarious place. In the tradition of Western literary discourse, the home is the economic basis, the *oikos*, against which the losses and gains of a journey can be measured.[11] Levi's narrative, that is, his remembrances, are the only gain that can effectively transmit the particularities of his and others' stories (that comprise a figurative survival) against the commonplace of the economic model contained in the traditional travelogue. Thus, Levi is writing against the commonplace even as he writes from within it.

La tregua begins with 'The Thaw' ('Il disgelo'; 'Tauwetter'), the seasonal transition that registers the ending of Levi's incarceration in the concentration camp, the Lager. In the Italian original and in the English translation, the (un)translatability of the foreign term is largely retained throughout the book. By enclosing the prefix 'un' parenthetically, I take a shortcut to circumscribing that the two, translatability and untranslatability, constitute a dialectical relationship that is not easily separated, for while the wish to make evident the singularity of a signifier would seem to suggest that it cannot be translated, its incorporation into a foreign text is an appropriative restatement that, moreover, has to justify the usage, but at any rate, clarify the term.

In the English translation, the Lager remains uncustomarily unitalicized. In this way, it stands to an English reader as familiar in its infamous meaning not to render it formally foreign, that is, italicized, and particular in its meaning as the camp which must be signified as historically determined and thus different from all other camps to follow. A camp is, most generally speaking, a provisional site that enables survival: food and makeshift shelter. The German word for camp, 'Lager', is also commonly used to designate a store room or a warehouse. The economic implications of 'Lager', in view of its common application, are a chilling point of departure for a Holocaust survivor who leaves behind the anatomical remains of a fascist economy based on, and generated by, human beings as expendable commodities. In Romance languages, 'campo' is etymologically connected to rural areas, to the countryside. The Romance derivative 'camp', in the English translation, makes it possible for Levi to depart from the Lager as a linguistic construct alone among major Western European languages. In other words, 'Lager' stands apart, untranslated and untranslatable. My reading remarks on this separation by focusing on applicable significations in explicating 'Lager' and 'camp' in the context of the narrative.

The author-narrator's own recognition of a linguistic separation is exemplified in Chapter 3, 'The Greek', when Levi is searching for a particular soup-kitchen, the one 'behind the cathedral' (*RA*, p. 50). Not knowing which of the many churches in Cracow might be the cathedral, he asks for directions from a priest walking by. Their ensuing conversation is conducted in their only common language, Latin:

After the initial request for information (pater optime, ubi est menas pauperorum?), we began to speak confusedly of everything, of my being a Jew, of the Lager (*castra*? Better: Lager, only too likely to be understood by everybody) [...]. (*RA*, p. 51)

My point here, of course, is not to suggest an inherent linguistic signification that represents a fitting value judgement on German and Romance character (the etymological root of 'camp' at any rate is subject to dispute), nor do I propose that Levi makes use of such a signification. Rather, I am interested in the ways in which the (un)translatability of the Lager marks an emphatic, irreducible difference when travelling between the English and German translations and Levi's native language. That is to say, I recognize that retaining untranslatability signifies an historical determination (the Lager stands as an historical signifier) even as the moving away from it opens up conceptual understandings.

A camp is also the figurative site of political ideologies and alliances. In the context of military history, it is set up across the field of battle, sometimes entrenched in anticipation of war, but in times of peace, it is an abstracted site of political and cultural activism. This, however, need not minimize the stakes involved. In *La tregua*, the camp stands out as a locus that often refers back to the narrative's point of departure, the Lager, though decreasingly, as Levi moves east in the increasing hope of returning home. Levi and others have to unlearn the conditioning of the Lager while sleeping, eating, and staying at camps. So that, when Levi seeks shelter in a 'telegraph hut, packed with people' (*RA*, p. 40), he writes: 'I threw myself on the floor and fell asleep at once, as one learns to do in the Lager.' (*RA*, p. 41) Or in another example, at the Bogucice camp, both he and Leonardo are still 'subject to an uncontrollable hunger' (*RA*, p. 69) despite the generous rations. The tension between the author-narrator's increased appreciation of the camps as places to accommodate new solidarities and the memory of his experience of subjugation and deprivation in the Lager finds relief in the lengthening temporal and spatial distance between himself and Auschwitz, notwithstanding the concomitant hardships and uncertainties. The series of camps that make survival possible for Levi and others map out a European topography that creates possibilities of negotiations on a small scale. By this I mean that the mapping out of camps marks the course of a new Europe in the making, against the 'upturned [...] old Europe' (*RA*, p. 125). The camp emerges as a synecdoche of Europe. Levi's narrative focuses on numerous histories of individuals he meets in the course of repatriation, many of whom were also incarcerated at Auschwitz; yet, it is primarily the camps that enable the breadths and lengths of the multiple histories to be imagined. In the linearity of *La tregua*, these histories constitute moments when shifting, often unpredictable alliances and animosities break the diachronic pattern. These are internal, spatially expansive, synecdochal moments in the journey that moves along the narrative and takes Levi away from Auschwitz.

That the infinite chain of displacements that substitute for home not only moves forward, literally, but is contained within a particular camp, and extends to the subjectivity that constitutes an individual, becomes apparent right after the arrival of the Red Army, as Levi is still at Auschwitz. At first, however, he recognizes camps within the Lager. His transport from the smaller camp at Buna-Monowitz to '"the main camp" of Auschwitz proper' (*RA*, p. 22) ('del "Campo Grande", di Auschwitz propriamente detto', *T*, p. 18; 'vom "Großen Lager", das heißt genauer, von Auschwitz', *A*, p. 16) brings him face to face with the institutionalized scope of the nightmarish 'boundless metropolis' (*RA*, p. 22) ('una sterminata metropoli', *T*, p. 18; 'eine riesige Großstadt', *A*, p. 16). In the course of his repatriation, Levi will return to the subject of institutionalization over and over again: looking at the ways in which the camps after the Lager are organized, maintained and administered reflects serious criteria for his comfort and appreciation. Describing the Katowice camp, he writes:

> In practice, the organization of the camp was really left to individual or group initiative; but nominally the camp was under a Soviet Kommandantur [sic] which was the most picturesque example of gypsy encampment that one could imagine. (*RA*, p. 59)

Or, concerning the assembly camp at Slutsk, just before he reaches Starye Dorogi, he remarks: 'The Russian administration took no care at all of the camp, so that one wondered if it really existed; but it must have existed, since we ate every day. In other words, it was a good administration.' (*RA*, p. 127) One is deeply struck by Levi's reading of potentially authoritarian signs in view of a camp's provisionality, because his quest to go home is also a quest for stability, for the structural integrity of his house. Therefore, always already with hindsight to Levi's difficult life as a Holocaust survivor that ended in his suicide in 1987,[12] the tension between institutionalized fascism and camp provisionality produces an insurmountable anxiety.

II. THE TRUCE: FROM NATION TO NARRATION

It is only in the first moments of liberation, once the Lager is no longer a fascist institution governed by the Germans, that Levi's unexpected interaction with Thylle, a German political prisoner, lets him re-write the significance of Thylle's identity from the framework of nationality to one of transnational ideology. In other words, Thylle no longer signifies the privileged site of German-ness within the hierarchy of the inmates at Auschwitz, but rather in this transformative historical moment, comes to represent the abstracted camp, or site, of Marxism. Perhaps for Levi the significance of this shift rests in his understanding of Thylle not as Other (German, antisemitic) but in the suppressed story of his own antifascist, political struggle, that is, in a history of the Self.

> It was not easy to understand each other; not only because of linguistic difficulties, but also because the thoughts that weighed upon us in that long night were immense, marvellous and terrible, but above all confused. I told him that I was suffering from nostalgia; and he exclaimed, after he had stopped crying, 'ten years, ten years'; and after ten years of silence, in a low stridulous voice, grotesque and solemn at the same time, he began to sing the *Internationale*, leaving me perturbed, diffident and moved. (*RA*, p. 19)

Levi never retracted from this experience and perception of the hierarchies among the incarcerated at Auschwitz, to the contention of his East-German translator of *Se questo e un uomo*.[13] Levi's translator, Heinz Riedt, had himself been a partisan during the war in Padova; his brother-in-law had been an Auschwitz inmate. Gilliland writes:

> At one point, the translator, aware of the translation's intended audience, wrote to Levi to challenge a section in the text that appeared to say that the German inmates of the camp suffered less than those from other countries, or that even during their suffering they took certain comfort from the crazy idea that they were somehow separate from the others because they were still, after all, Germans.[14]

Levi however insisted on the validity of his perception. Not without discomfort, one reads Levi and Thylle's interaction as an anticipation of the later establishment of a post-war order in which the German Democratic Republic anchors its origin in Hitler's victimization of political dissidents, largely at the expense of coming to terms with, that is to say, quite literally addressing, an antecedent cultural formation steeped in anti-Semitic discourses. Anyone, ironically, who visited the concentration camp Buchenwald before the collapse of the German Democratic Republic can attest to this, for it was dedicated – discursively and artistically – primarily to German political prisoners, foremost Ernst Thälmann, the leader of the German Communist Party.[15] Levi perceives with a similar diffident regard people who are marked by their political battle against fascism in other places as well. For example, in the Bogucice camp (Chapter 4), he describes, as he does so many times throughout the book, the ways in which the camp is set up, organized, and bound by rules and regulations:

> The infirmary kitchen was run by two Parisian *maquisardes*, working-class women no longer young, also survivors from the Lager, where they had lost their husbands; they were taciturn and mournful women, whose past and recent sufferings appeared to be mastered and kept within limits on their precociously aged faces by the sharp moral consciousness of political fighters. (*RA*, p. 69)

Levi himself knows no political ideology that might support his own exhausted existence, though his voice assumes a humanist leadership position amid the anarchical truce. Consequently his notations of those for whom political (anti-fascist) ideologies comprise the basis of their distinct presence mark them as belonging to a different camp. His own partisan activities are not mentioned in *La tregua*, though they led to his deportation to Auschwitz.[16] I want to suggest here that the truce itself emerges as the only model that can, however precariously, stabilize the author-narrator and his narrative. As I move between the three titles of Levi's book, *La tregua*, *The Reawakening*, and *Die Atempause*, the relevance of each builds on a fundamental notion of the in-between space and time that separates enemy from enemy, consciousness from unconsciousness, the dead from the living. There is in *La tregua* an unfathomable range of ideologically founded, mobilizing strategies and tactics. They extend from the Soviet Army's victorious battle against fascism, over the Greek's economic conviction that the war can never be over, to Cesare's good-natured, unprincipled ruses; from the Soviet Union's blatant, bureaucratic inefficiencies, perceived by Levi to be antithetical to the German blueprints for maximum effectiveness, over the Greek's principally autonomous dealings, to Cesare's charitable generosity as a consequence of his deceptions. An exhausting sentence that tries to do justice to Levi's overwhelmingly complex linearity, in which he moves in-between war and peace, observant but afflicted.

III. CRISES AND PLEASURES OF TRANSLATION

It is not an easy task to conceptualize a construct as formidable as 'Europe' may sound, because it emerges from a narrative that does not explicitly set out to make it a formative subject. I argue, however, that that is because Levi picks it up, as it were, in the course of his journey from Auschwitz to Starye Dorogy, 'the mysterious camp' (*RA*, p. 135), that becomes, narratively speaking, the turning-point of *La tregua*. There is a map in the book that outlines Levi's course. In *La tregua* it is a fold-out page at the beginning of the final chapter, 'Il risveglio'; in *The Reawakening* the map precedes the narrative; and in *Die Atempause* it follows the entire written text on the very last page. The German and US publishers' decision to take the map from its site on the second page in the book's final chapter seems inappropriate within the context of my own argument. The itinerary across Central and Eastern Europe is precisely a cumulative result of Levi's repatriation that comes to a halt upon his return to Turin: it is not yet to be taken as though it were an established route, as its prefacing would suggest, nor is it a mere afterthought. Its textual incorporation in the brief, last chapter shows the reader where she or he has been taken via Levi's repatriation and what he has brought back, namely a new conception of Europe.

Elucidating this point, I want to pursue further the (un)translatability of the Lager. There, the act of translation in the process of liberation initially is a desperate attempt to decipher the voiceless. Eventually, it gives way to an improvisational understanding between people brought together under adverse circumstances conditioned by the truce. To put it differently, between people who do not understand one another, language increasingly necessitates performance to make survival possible in an unstructured time, or timelessness, wedged in Levi's memory as the truce: somewhere between the old order and the one to be established, or as the author writing in 1961 puts it:

> The war was about to finish, the long war that had devastated their country [Poland]; for them it was already over. It was the great truce; for the other harsh season which was to follow had not yet begun, nor as yet had the ill-omened name of Cold War been pronounced. (*RA*, pp. 59–60)

In order to pursue how Levi amasses a European community, it is necessary, once again, to start at the narrative beginning: in the Lager after the arrival of the Soviets. Two among many whose want of language stands out are a man and a child. The man's body has lost all elasticity and remains in a permanent fetal position that impedes the efforts of the Russians who want to bathe him. 'None of us knew who he was,' writes Levi, 'because he was in no condition to speak.' (*RA*, p. 23) The tattooed number on his arm replaces speech, identifying him as a Frenchman. The child, Hurbinek, a three year old, 'a nobody, a child of death, a child of Auschwitz' (*RA*, p. 25), has not learned to speak, but before his death, and under the care of an older child, for the first time, he enunciates a word: 'something like "mass-klo", "matisklo"' (*RA*, p. 26).

> Hurbinek continued in his stubborn experiments for as long as he lived. In the following days everybody listened to him in silence, anxious to understand, and among us there were speakers of all the languages of Europe; but Hurbinek's word remained secret [...] Nothing remains of him: he bears witness through these words of mine. (*RA*, p. 26)

In Levi's first reference to Europe here, it emerges as the place where many languages are spoken. Levi returns to this idea of the languages in Europe again in a later chapter. Describing how he met Cesare, he remembers the dysentery ward in which dying men 'were calling out names, praying, swearing, begging for help in all the languages of Europe' (*RA*, p. 71). Subsequently, and in the course of Levi's detour home to Turin, language, once it is recovered as a part of their agency by those fortunate enough to have survived its strategic dispossession in the Lager, slowly becomes a means of pleasure.[17] The already cited encounter with the priest conducted in a dead language (Latin) is an, albeit fragile, example of this. In the same chapter, Levi accumulates 'a fair number of disordered philological oddments' (*RA*, p. 49) ('un buon numero di nozioni filologiche sgangherate', *T*, p. 54; 'einige etwas wirre philologische Begriffe', *A*, p. 50) as he is sent out by the Greek to scout out the local market. His delight in discovering the meaning of the Polish genitive ending and the repeated recognition of common roots, words, and sounds among speakers of different languages establishes an odd kinship, as though all languages of Europe were in fact related. Thus Frau Vitta becomes the embodiment of life itself (la vita), and Primo Levi related to Marya Fyodorovna Prima.

If Europe has to do with a lot of languages, then somebody who speaks a lot of languages must be European. In other words, all the divided people whose subjectivity is founded partly on their ability to enunciate more than one language are then European. Subjectivity becomes European even as Levi gives voice to those who, like the Moor, can only speak through curses. (Un)translatability lies in the shifting margins of the less than perfect match of a signifier from one language to another; in the deliberated retention of a word as an historical signifier; and in the simple fact that people do not speak each other's languages, in which case speech has to be enacted and performance becomes translation. European identity in *La tregua* is performed through the act of translation. A case in point is the story of 'The Little Hen', to which Levi dedicates a chapter, and in which his friend Cesare plays the role of the translator. Out in the middle of the country, now almost accustomed to the often remarked-upon vastness of the Eastern European landscape, Levi, Cesare and fellow travellers are on their way to Starye Dorogi. Cesare becomes impetuously determined to eat chicken for dinner. A small village provides them with the opportunity to pursue the desired meat. But, alas, conveying to the initially suspicious villagers that they have come in search of a chicken proves to be a laborious, yet amusing task. Levi writes:

> I was in a pickle. Russian, they say, is an Indo-European language, and chickens must have been known to our common ancestors in an epoch certainly previous to their subdivision into the various modern ethnic families. '*His fretus*', that is to say, on these fine foundations, I tried to say 'chicken' and 'bird' in all the ways known to me, but without any visible result. (*RA*, p. 133)

Cesare begins to perform the chicken's various meanings: as the thing that lays eggs, makes certain sounds, and so on, but to no avail. Finally, Levi draws a picture of a chicken on the ground and gets the desired recognition. This episode points to the limitations of translation in performance as it shows, that is, literally depicts, them by seeking recourse to the visual image of the word.

IV. THEATRICAL SPACES OF EUROPE

Performance is linked to theatre and it is no coincidence then that as Levi moves east on his detour home, theatres and camps merge in peculiar ways. What I have suggested so far is that European identity is linked to the fragmentary, linguistic remainders of a distant common past. This past is constructed in the tongue-in-cheek, survivalist act of translation when meanings are conveniently transferred between similar words to establish commonality and kinship. But European identity in *La tregua* is constructed even more elaborately through theatrical performances. The author-narrator's transport to a camp, Starye Dorogi, 'not to be found on any map' (*RA*, p. 126) expands his continental horizon and thus re-draws the borders of Europe that had previously excluded the remoteness of Eastern Europe from the point of view of a Western European. The peripheral proves central in the quest to return to the centre of Levi's pre-war life. The horizon, the receding liminal image that leads on Levi's displacements, brings them to a halt at Starye Dorogi and opens itself up, like a curtain, to performance after performance.

It is as if a group of actors were touring the Soviet Union and just for such an occasion, the administration in charge erected a building that is soon called 'The Red House', in which an oversized theatre provided the troupe with a special incentive to pass through Starye Dorogi, the as yet unmarked place. The theme of mad architecture that has accompanied Levi's observations of foreign structures reaches the camp at the Red House where old roads meet in a 'truly singular building, which had grown without order in all directions like a volcanic flow' (*RA*, p. 138). It comes at no surprise then that one of the chapters telling about Levi's time in Starye Dorogi is titled 'Holidays'. Here the act of translation necessitated by the desire to communicate with the other receives a mixed narrative reaction. On the one hand, the frustration that comes with not being able to develop sufficiently a relationship between self and other is apparent in Levi's complaint that 'the difficulties of language reduced us [Russians and Italians] to stunted and primordial relationships' (*RA*, p. 157). On the other hand, the performative events that occur daily as well as on formally staged, special occasions create a representational space which pulls the marginal other, Russia, into a European relationship. Many of the performances are directly linked to war events. For example, a young Russian soldier re-enacts his attack on sleeping German soldiers. Levi writes:

> He is 'narrating' an episode of war; and because he knows that the language is not understood, he expresses himself as best as he can, in a manner which for him is nearly as spontaneous as, if not more so than, words: he expresses himself with all his muscles, with the precocious furrows on his face, with flashing eyes and teeth, with leaps and gestures; and from this is born a *pas seul*, full of fascination and force. (*RA*, pp. 158–9)

At Starye Dorogi the act of translation becomes the single common language between self and other, between Russians and Italians with war as a major referent. Levi narrates at length two events that pass the unchecked time, two months spent on the eastern periphery of Europe. The first one is the screening of three films, one Austrian, the other two Russian and American, on consecutive evenings. Implicit in the audience's reaction to the films is a recognition of the structural antagonisms that drive narrative plots. Especially in the case of the Italians who see themselves as villains in an Austrian film, point of view as taken by Self and Other becomes a discernible subject of the screenings. Levi writes:

> We Italians, so little accustomed to seeing ourselves cast as the 'enemy', odious by definition, and so dismayed at being hated by anybody, derived a complex pleasure from watching the film – a pleasure not without disquiet, a source of salutary meditations. (*RA*, pp. 164–5)

To be cast as the villain is to occupy the position of the Other. The Italian audience is sensitive to the recognition that narratives that hinge on this kind of dialectical animosity are most applauded when they provide the spectator with conveniently sympathetic points of identification.

The second event is the performance of a revue in which two acts stand out. One is a satire called 'The Shipwreck of the Spiritless' in which a group of sea-travellers who represent the Italians, is held hostage by cannibals – the Russians – on an island. At the end of one of the repeat performances, the actual notification that the following day the Italians would go home puts a final end to the act. The other is an eerie enactment of the '"Three-Cornered Hat" song' in which death-like figures slowly and systematically substitute the words of the refrain with motions until the complete loss of language results in 'the accumulation of gaps replaced by uncertain gestures' (*RA*, p. 173). 'The final repetition, with absolute silence from orchestra', writes Levi, 'was an excruciating agony, a death throe.' (ibid.)

CONCLUSION

In conclusion, I want to return to the question which began this essay by establishing the context for the quote that precedes it. Departing from the camp at Zhmerinka, unfamiliar sights lead Levi to the makeshift map of Europe: oddly shaped structures, 'low, unequal houses, built with a curious and amusing contempt for geometry and uniformity' (*RA*, p. 118); and a crossroad at which 'a gigantic, white-haired, barefoot storyteller recited' (*RA*, p. 118). Europe enters Levi's awareness amid the unknown, yet the familiar anatomical shapes are known well enough even 'when painted from memory, as if seen at a great distance' in this, for Levi, unfamiliar territory. Through his narrative, Levi includes a nation whose membership in the European community continues to be contested. I venture to say that the desire to include, not merely by naming, but by situating more specifically a place through narration, gave the German translators the same impetus. Since Piedmont played an important historical role in the unification of Italy, they took the peripheral liberty to designate Dronero 'the tiny village in Piedmont'.

In a recent essay 'Can Russia Return to Europe',[18] Michael Ignatieff writes: 'The Europe Russia returns to, after seventy years, is at a loss to know how to welcome her and her former Eastern European satellites.'[19] Furthermore,

> [t]he irony is that the people who believe most fervently in the European ideal are those currently excluded from EC membership. 'Being a good European' means much more in Tallinn, Riga, or Prague than it does in Paris or London.[20]

While I do not wish to heap on *La tregua* over half a century of European history with the establishment of the European Community, the division of Western and Eastern Europe and its concomitant developments, Levi's account of the repatriative process in the truce re-opens from a current political and cultural perspective the question of inclusion and exclusion, and the ways in which translation and performance operate in the remapping of geographical certainties. Levi himself wrote the book in the early 1960s after the founding of the European Common Market, and was not unaware of the distance in time and place that separated him as the author from the narrator of *La tregua*, as his reference to 'the harsh season', that is, the Cold War, suggests.[21] In the dystopian aftermath of World War II, Levi's experience of Europe constitutes a small, but utopian-coloured frame that injects a landscape with character-driven nations and narrations. The tension between the hopefulness that accompanies the protagonist through the camps and soup-kitchens of Europe and the storyteller's memory of his experiences as he remembers setting 'out on foot in the problematic search for human kind' (*RA*, p. 42) underpins the narrative with a double nostalgia: that for home at the time of the events and that for the utopian possibilities of a Europe made up of camps in which the getting away from history is the mobilizing force even as the task to preserve a history not to be repeated motivates the author.[22]

NOTES

1. Primo Levi, *The Reawakening*, trans. Stuart Woolf (New York: Simon & Schuster, 1965), p. 118. Quotations in the text are referred to by *RA* and page number.
2. Primo Levi, *La tregua* (Torino: Einaudi, 1965), p. 140. Quotations in the text are referred to by *T* and page number.
3. Primo Levi, *Die Atempause*, trans. Barbara and Robert Picht (Munich: Deutscher Taschenbuch Verlag, 1994), pp. 135–6. Quotations in the text are referred to by *A* and page number.
4. JoAnn Cannon, 'Cannon-Formation and Reception in Contemporary Italy: The Case of Primo Levi', *Italica* 69.1 (1992): pp. 30–1.
5. Georges van den Abbeele, *Travel as Metaphor from Montaigne to Rousseau* (Minneapolis: University of Minnesota Press, 1992), p. xxx.
6. Van den Abbeele, p. xxx.
7. A prominent Italian football club.
8. Homi K. Bhabha, 'Introduction: Narrating the Nation', *Nation and Narration* (London: Routledge, 1990), pp. 2–3.

9. 'But soon, from the very first hours of the journey, we were to realize that the hour of impatience had not yet sounded; the happy journey promised to be long and laborious and not without surprise; a small railroad Odyssey within our greater Odyssey.' (p. 182).
10. Van den Abbeele, p. xviii.
11. Van den Abbeele, p. xvii.
12. For a provocative essay on Primo Levi's suicide see Cynthia Ozick, 'Primo Levi's Suicide Note', *Metaphor and Memory* (New York: Alfred Knopf, 1989).
13. Gail Gilliland, 'Self and Other: Christa Wolf's *Patterns of Childhood* and Primo Levi's *Se questo e un uomo* as Dialogic Texts', *Comparative Literature Studies* 29.2 (1992): pp. 182–210, here p. 198.
14. Gilliland, p. 198.
15. For two articles that treat recent administrative politics of and towards Buchenwald see John Rodden, 'Memories from Hell', *America* 172.13 (15 April 1995): pp. 20–24 and John Rodden, 'Liberation from Lies', *Commonweal* 122.7 (7 April 1995): pp. 5–7.
16. For an essay on Levi's partisan activities see Claudio G. Segre, 'Italian Jews and the Resistance: the Case of Primo Levi', *Reason and Light: Essays on Primo Levi* (Ithaca: Cornell UP, 1990).
17. For an essay that treats Levi's relationship to languages in the Lager see Sander Gilman, 'The Special Language of the Camps and After', *Reason and Light: Essays on Primo Levi* (Ithaca: Cornell UP, 1990).
18. Michal Ignatieff, 'Can Russia Return to Europe?', *Harper's Magazine* 284.1703 (April 1992): pp. 15–18.
19. Ignatieff, p. 17.
20. Ignatieff, p. 18.
21. Mirna Cicioni suggests that Levi may have been partly inspired to write *La tregua* by 'the beginning of the gradual "thawing" of relations between the capitalist and the socialist blocs at the beginning of the 1960s', see Mirna Cicioni, *Primo Levi: Bridges of Knowledge* (Oxford: Berg Publishers, 1995), p. 40.
22. I want to thank Melissa Crabbe and Kate Elder whose help went into writing this essay.

Part II
Inner/Outer Perspectives in Comparison

5 World Fiction: the Transformation of the English/Western Literature Canon

Marion Frank-Wilson

INTRODUCTION

Within the last decade, the established canon of European and Western literatures has undergone a dramatic change with the emergence of a world fiction or transcultural literature that has transformed the traditionally Eurocentric western canon. This phenomenon can be seen in connection with the cultural, political and economical developments prior to and following the collapse of communism.

For the first time in the history of capitalism, the capitalist mode of production, divorced from its historically specific origins in Europe, appears as an authentically global abstraction. Production is constantly changing its location in search of profit and cheap labour as well as freedom from social and political interference. The scholar Alfred Dirlik points out that the narrative of capitalism is no longer a narrative of the history of Europe; non-European capitalist societies now make their own claims on the history of capitalism.[1] It is in this context that transcultural literature/world fiction has emerged. This essay discusses two representative works of world fiction: *The Buddha of Suburbia* by Hanif Kureishi,[2] and *The English Patient* by Michael Ondaatje;[3] both works can be seen as reflective of the emergence of global capitalism and its accompanying economic, social and cultural homogenization, as well as the simultaneous process of fragmentation in the disappearance of a centre to capitalism. By examining the concepts of identity and nationality in the two novels, I will explore some characteristics of world fiction.

WORLD FICTION

The expansion of the English literature canon during the last several decades has recently taken on dimensions that some scholars have described as a 'cultural revolution';[4] the reasons are numerous and can be seen from various perspectives. Owing to today's ease of mass communication and mass transportation, our world has become a 'global village'.[5] Since World War II, English has developed into the major *lingua franca* of our time: roughly 700 million people speak English – a total that represents more than a seventh of the world's population.[6] This, in conjunction with the breakdown of national barriers, has greatly contributed to the rise of the 'New Literatures in English'. For the English literature canon, this means that it must concern itself not just with British and North American literature, but also with that of Canada, Australia, New Zealand, Malaysia, Singapore, Hong Kong, the Philippines, and other countries.[7] In the following, I examine how this development came about, as well as its manifestations and practical consequences.

It is difficult to find a term to describe the phenomenon. Throughout English departments and the scholarly world, a variety of names is used: 'Literature(s) in English' referring to the problem of whether we should emphasize the features common to the whole body of 'Literature in English', or the diversity in the different 'Literatures in English'. Other terms used to describe the same subject matter are 'World Literature written in English' and 'International English Literature'. Still other titles – equally problematic – are: 'Literature(s) in English outside of England and the United States' – implicitly claiming superiority for the literature of Britain and the United States; 'Commonwealth Literature(s)' – excluding literatures from non-commonwealth countries; 'Post-colonial Literature(s)' – excluding literature from non-colonized countries; and the term 'New Literature in English' ignores the fact that some of those literatures are quite old.[8] While acknowledging the problems inherent in the term, in this essay I will refer to the subject matter as post-colonial literature, since it is my impression that this is the term most widely used these days by English departments and in scholarly publications.

Post-colonial literature today is proliferating and changing. In her outline of recent significant developments of post-colonial literature, Elleke Boehmer remarks that the so-called migrant writers among post-colonial authors demand particular attention, as their situation is increasingly regarded as representative of post-colonial writing.[9] Consequently, the focus of this essay is on two of the migrant writers, Hanif Kureishi and Michael Ondaatje. Since I contend that this type of writing is the result of a globalization of culture, in the following, the terms migrant writing, world fiction, and transcultural fiction are used interchangeably.

Whereas early post-independence writers tend to identify with nationalist causes and endorse the need for communal solidarity, in the 1980s and early 1990s many writers' geographic and cultural affiliations became more divided and uncertain. This is due to unprecedented demographic shifts during the late twentieth century which are brought about by numerous forces: anti-imperialist conflict, the claims of rival nationalisms, economic hardship, state repression, to name but a few.[10] Boehmer reflects that in post-independence literature, the result has been that the cosmopolitan rootlessness which developed in urban pockets at the time of early twentieth-century modernism has 'gone global'.

This globalization of ideas is also reflected in the publications of Fredric Jameson and Alfred Dirlik. Dirlik argues there is a parallel between the rise of the idea of post-coloniality in cultural criticism and an emergent consciousness of global capitalism in the 1980s. According to him, the themes now claimed for post-colonial criticism 'resonate with concerns and orientations that have their origins in a new world situation that has also become part of consciousness globally over the last decade'.[11] Post-colonial authors and critics therefore respond to the needs of the social, political and cultural problems created by this new world situation.

Under global capitalism, a new international division of labour arose: the transnationalization of production, where the production process is globalized. With the concept of global capitalism goes the decentralizing of capitalism nationally – it is becoming increasingly difficult to point to any nation or region as the centre of global capitalism. It is this transnationalization of production that is the cause of, on the one hand, the homogenization of the globe economically, socially and culturally, while on the other, the parallel process of fragmentation, in the disappearance of a centre to capitalism – and the resulting fragmentation into subnational regions. I agree with Dirlik when he points out that the narrative of capitalism is no longer the narrative of the history of Europe. For the first time, non-European societies are making claims on the history of capitalism. Consequently, together with economic fragmentation, comes cultural fragmentation, that is, multiculturalism.

It is within this context that transcultural literature, or world fiction, has emerged. Increasingly authors whose first language is not English have transformed the established canon of English literature by writing in English. As Pico Iyer in an article on the topic observed, whereas not long ago a student of the modern English novel would probably have studied Graham Greene, Evelyn Waugh and Aldous Huxley, today s/he will more likely be taught Salman Rushdie, Ben Okri or Timothy Mo.[12] The movement started in 1981 with Salman Rushdie's *Midnight's Children* and now has an ever rising following, including such names as Kazuo Ishiguro, Barry Unsworth, Michael Ondaatje, Hanif Kureishi, Timothy Mo, Derek Walcott, Keri Hulme and Ben Okri. The new transcultural writers are the result of an international culture which has emerged since the 1980s, and they write for an audience just as eclectic and uprooted as themselves: 'They are the creators, and creations, of a new post-imperial order in which English is the *lingua franca*, just about everywhere is a suburb of the same international youth culture, and all countries are part of a unified CNN and MTV circuit, with a common frame of reference in McDonald's, Madonna, and Magic Johnson'.[13] All of them express the view that we are living in a decentralized world, where not only the authors, but also the audience, through international cultural influences, have become less provincial. The rising number of multicultural studies and ethnic studies courses in universities has also contributed to the process.

Even though the field of world fiction is wide, and notwithstanding the fact that there are more differences than similarities between the writers, they all have something in common: all were born after the Second World War, they live and write in the cosmopolitan, multicultural centres – London, Toronto, New York – and they are all products of transculturalism themselves: Michael Ondaatje is a Sri Lankan of Indian, Dutch and English ancestry, was educated in Britain and now lives in Canada; Hanif Kureishi is the son of an English mother and a Pakistani father and grew up in London. Pico Iyer quite succinctly calls them 'amphibians who do not have an old home and a new home so much as two half-homes simultaneously': they are defined by being indefinable.[14]

Novels written by transcultural writers are invariably concerned with identity, and their major concern has been the protagonists' coming to terms with culturally and linguistically diverse and mixed origins.[15] By tracing the central theme of identity in the novels *The Buddha of Suburbia* and *The English Patient*, I will show that the

English literature canon, as indeed the European literature canon, has undergone a transformation which, rather than reflecting a Eurocentric perspective, is increasingly an expression of an emerging global culture.

CONFUSED IDENTITIES IN *THE BUDDHA OF SUBURBIA*

Hanif Kureishi's works include several screenplays and plays, *My Beautiful Laundrette & The Rainbow Sign, Sammy and Rosie Get Laid, Outskirts and Other Plays*; and two novels: *The Buddha of Suburbia* (1990) and, more recently, *The Black Album* (1995). He has also directed a movie, *London Kills Me*, which was released in 1991.

Despite Kureishi's mixed origins he maintains that he, unlike his father, is not 'caught between two cultures', and he insists that he is British and 'can make it in Britain'.[16] In his work, he deals with problems of acculturation among Asian immigrants in London. For him, the Asian immigrant experience is an aspect of the contemporary urban experience, rather than exclusively a race issue. Particularly in *The Buddha of Suburbia*, he shows that 'issues of politics, sex, and class transcend ethnic and racial divides'.[17]

The central character of the novel, Karim Amir, is, like Kureishi himself, the product of a marriage between an Indian man and a British woman. On one level, the novel can be read as a novel of initiation, as Karim struggles to grow up and find his own identity in the midst of his parents' failing marriage;[18] the novel begins when the family is intact and we first encounter Karim living in the suburbs of South London, together with his younger brother Allie, and his parents Haroon and Margaret. Very soon, however, his parents' marriage begins to disintegrate. Haroon discovers his interest in Oriental/Indian mysticism and sets himself up as the 'buddha' of the title.[19] He is assisted by Eva Kaye with whom he has an affair, and who is the reason why he eventually leaves his wife. Eva now manages Haroon's activities as the 'buddha of suburbia' and uses his success as an instrument to make their escape from the suburbs and move to London.

A sub-plot is constructed around the family of Anwar, Haroon's friend, who came with him from India. Anwar deals with the increasing pressure of racist attacks on his grocery store by rediscovering his Indian roots, and he turns to religion. He intends to follow his country's tradition of arranged marriage by forcing his daughter

Jamila to marry a man sent from India by Anwar's brother. Jamila at first refuses, but when Anwar goes on a hunger-strike she relents and marries Changez. Jamila has been one of Karim's best friends since childhood, and their friendship now turns into a brother–sister relationship as they try to come to terms with their lives as second-generation immigrants in the midst of their disintegrating families. Jamila turns to politics and feminism to find meaning in her life, and her strong opinions and political commitment form a strong contrast to Karim's own inability to take sides.

The Buddha of Suburbia goes beyond being simply a novel of initiation as it can be read as a novel that expresses a profound consciousness of alienation in a contemporary urban setting: all characters in the novel are in search of identity. Karim's father Haroon and his friend Anwar are only two of the 'in-betweens' mentioned by Pico Iyer: both are first-generation immigrants who, despite having spent most of their adult lives in England, still feel that they are basically Indian and do not feel at home in London. They are also aware, however, that the India they used to know no longer exists, and that they have no place to go back to. Haroon realizes that this condition of rootlessness is not limited to the immigrant experience but, rather is the result of developments in today's 'global village' that have left everybody alienated. Dissatisfied with his life as an office clerk, he turns to mysticism and teaches other people to find meaning in their lives. Anwar fails to transcend his alienation: he turns to religion and traditionalism which, in the end, kills him. Jamila is the one person in the book who is most successful in the construction of her identity. She comes to self-realization through a rigorous programme of self-education that leads her to feminism and a life of political commitment. Karim acknowledges the successful construction of her person when he comments:

> As I watched Jamila I thought what a terrific person she'd become [...] Her feminism, the sense of self and fight it engendered, the schemes and plans she had, the relationships – which she desired to take this form and not that form – the things she had made herself know, and all the understanding this gave, seemed to illuminate her tonight as she went forward, an Indian woman, to live a useful life in white England. (p. 216)

The protagonist whose struggle for identity we follow most closely throughout the novel is, of course, Karim. Like many other post-colonial characters, the character of Karim can be traced back to a much older literary work: *Kim*, by Rudyard Kipling,[20] which was written in 1901. It is ironical that the one archetype of all postcolonial writing is one of the most important works of colonialism. Iyer refers to Kim as a double agent, 'an Irish orphan who thinks in Hindi and can pass for almost any kind of local'.[21] His mentors are a Briton, a Muslim, a Hindu, and a Tibetan Buddhist, and the question we ask ourselves throughout the novel is 'who is Kim–Kim–Kim?' Iyers goes on to remark that many of the heroes of world fiction are Kims in disguise. This is certainly true for Karim in *The Buddha of Suburbia*, and the central question of the novel is 'who is Karim?' Karim is, in fact, more of a Kim in reverse, being the son of an Indian who can pass as an Englishman. In his introduction at the beginning of the novel, Karim himself comments on his ambivalent status:

> My name is Karim Amir, and I am an Englishman born and bred, almost. I am often considered to be a funny kind of Englishman, a new breed as it were, having emerged from two old histories. But I don't care – Englishman I am (though not proud of it), from the South London suburbs and going somewhere. Perhaps it is the odd mixture of continents and blood, of here and there, of belonging and not, that makes me restless and easily bored. (p. 3)

That sense of 'belonging and not' pervades much of Karim's life. In school, he does not feel he has much in common with the other students who harass him because of his dark skin; so he eventually stops attending. Unlike Jamila, where this same kind of racism triggered off a strong political commitment to a more equal society, Karim finds himself unable to form any close political ties. He sympathizes with his friend Terry, who is a member of the communist party. He even solicits money for the party. Still, he does not wholeheartedly commit himself to the party's agenda, realizing that their class war does not take into account race issues, and even Terry eventually concedes that Karim 'is not ready' to join just yet. Karim's inability to take sides and to commit to any form of relationship becomes particularly obvious in his attitude towards his family, especially after his parents' break-up, when he remarks that he now has several families to choose from: his father and Eva; his mother; Anwar and his wife; Jamila and Changez. All the time he is aware that he does not really belong to any of them, and he remains elusive. He drifts in and out of their lives, spending time living with all of them but never fully being a part of their lives.

The closest Karim comes to any form of commitment is his desire to become an actor. He readily accepts a role that is offered to him by one Eva's friends, the theatre director Jeremy Shadwell. Through his work as an actor, Karim finally develops a deeper understanding of himself and his place in society. In the small world of the theatre group, he is no longer able to ignore racial prejudice and just walk away from it. Instead, he now finds himself forced to react to it. At his first meeting with Shadwell, Karim encounters the familiar reaction of white Englishmen towards his dark skin when Shadwell speaks to him in Urdu, a language Karim does not understand. Shadwell comments:

> Everyone looks at you, I'm sure, and thinks: an Indian boy, how exotic, how interesting, what stories of aunties and elephants we'll hear now from him. And you're from Orpington.
> Yeah.
> Oh God, what a strange world. The immigrant is the Everyman of the twentieth century. Yes? (p. 141)

Karim is cast to play Mowgli in Kipling's *Jungle Book*. For Karim, this role represents the first step towards his acting career, and he is thrilled about the opportunity. He begins to have misgivings about the play when, during rehearsals, Shadwell makes him wear dark body-paint to look more authentically Indian, and imitate an exaggerated Indian accent. His ambition to become an actor, however, outweighs any pangs of conscience he might have. He does not acknowledge the fact that Shadwell merely exploits the Indian part of his personality, and he continues with the rehearsals. He ignores the significance of his part in the play until opening night, when he sees the shocked reaction of his friends and family. Jamila's reproaches that he had let himself be used to pander to prejudices against Indians finally makes him acknowledge that he feels ashamed of his role in the play.

Karim's second attempt at acting looks more promising initially, but turns out not to be much more successful. A radical left-wing producer, Matthew Pyke, offers him a part in another play. Karim's initial enthusiasm is crushed when he finds out that even the politically correct liberal Pyke fails to recognize Karim's mixed origins and asks him to create a character from his own background, 'someone black'. He ends up playing the comic character of an Indian immigrant who has just come to England – a character fashioned after Changez, Jamila's husband. It points to Karim's growing awareness of himself as being English with Indian origins – that, without being aware of it himself, he has filled the character with his own experiences and thoughts. And, significantly, on opening night, Changez does not recognize himself in the play and instead remarks that the character Karim had created was obviously based on autobiographical experiences.

Pyke not only uses Karim to perpetuate racial stereotypes, he also manipulates his sex-life. He first encourages one of the actresses, Eleanor, to start a love-affair with Karim, and later, when he desires her for himself, offers Karim his own wife, who is interested in Karim's exotic-looking body. As a result of Pyke's manipulations, Karim's and Eleanor's relationship breaks up, and Karim emerges hurt and disillusioned.

It is through these disillusionments that Karim comes to a better understanding of himself, society, and his place in it. He finally recognizes his Indian heritage:

> But I did feel, looking at these strange creatures now – the Indians – that in some way these were my people, and that I'd spent my life denying or avoiding that fact. I felt ashamed and incomplete at the same time, as if half of me were missing, and as if I'd been colluding with my enemies, those whites who wanted Indians to be like them. (p. 212)

He acknowledges the Indian in him while at the same time realizing he is English – notwithstanding the fact people try to deny him that part of his identity. In the last scene, when Karim takes his 'extended' family out for dinner to celebrate his new role in a soap opera, he sums it up:

> And so I sat in the centre of this old city that I loved, which itself sat at the bottom of a tiny island. I was surrounded by people I loved, and I felt happy and miserable at the same time. I thought of what a mess everything had been, but that it wouldn't always be that way. (p. 284)

This last paragraph, which shows how Karim painfully constructed his identity out of various fragments, is reflective of the political, economic and social developments that have contributed to the emergence of world fiction. The traditional nation-state has lost its meaning in the face of global migration. Rather than populations of clear national origins and loyalties, as before, we now have increasing numbers of 'in-betweens' like Karim. This diminshed significance of the concept of nationality is also the topic in *The English Patient* by Michael Ondaatje, which is a novel entirely about the 'new race of post-national souls'.[22]

CONFUSED NATIONALITIES IN *THE ENGLISH PATIENT* (1992)

Ondaatje's works cover a wide variety of topics, ranging from a book about *The Collected Works of Billy the Kid* (1970) to *In the Skin of a Lion* (1987), a novel about immigrant workers who contributed to the building of Toronto. He has also published three collections of poetry and a family memoir, *Running in the Family* (1982), about his parents' generation in Sri Lanka.[23] His best-known novel is *The English Patient*, for which he received the prestigious Booker Prize and which has recently been made into an award-winning movie.

Ondaatje is yet another example of the mixed heritage of expatriate writers. He was born in Sri Lanka and moved to Britain at the age of nine in 1952, and from there to Canada in 1962. He is of the opinion that all Canadians – and Australians other than Aboriginals – are immigrants and he consequently feels no less at home in Canada than any other Canadian.[24] Except for *Running in the Family*, Ondaatje avoids direct reference to Sri Lanka in his works. It could be argued, however, that he never stops writing about his own predicament as an expatriate writer.[25] This is certainly the case in *The English Patient*, a novel about a group of outsiders, 'about those for whom identity is elusive and home remains a site of conflict and uncertainty'.[26]

The novel is set in the abandoned Italian Villa San Girolamo during several weeks in the summer of 1945, following the end of World War II. San Girolamo is an abandoned monastery that had been occupied first by the German army during the war, and later by the Allied Forces, who used it as a field hospital. As the novel opens, the Americans have moved their hospital further north, leaving behind a young Canadian nurse, Hana, and her only patient, a severely burned Englishman, the 'English patient' of the title. Hana had been traumatized by the horrors of the war and chose to stay in San Girolamo to care for her patient. They are soon joined by Caravaggio, a friend of Hana's late father who had heard about her remaining in the villa, and who has come to protect her and help her recover from the traumas of the war. The fourth member of the group is Kirpal Singh, nicknamed Kip, a young Indian from the British army. Kip sleeps in a tent in the garden of the villa during those weeks, defusing bombs left by the German army in San Girolamo and the surrounding area. He and Hana have a brief affair before each of them moves back to their respective countries, Canada and India.

Like *The Buddha of Suburbia*, *The English Patient* is concerned with the construction of identity and the elusive nature of nationalism. Much of Italy had been destroyed during the war, leaving a desolate landscape behind, where every river they came to was bridgeless, 'as if its name had been erased, as if the sky was starless, homes doorless' (p. 129). All four characters in the novel, each in their own way, have lost their former identities during the war. They meet at a time of confusion and chaos, where the destruction of the outer world mirrors the protagonists' inner confusion. And now, 'with hardly a world around them, [...] they are forced back on themselves'. The term Ondaatje uses repeatedly throughout the novel to describe their struggle to re-establish their identities is to 're-assemble' the fragments of their personalities.

Caravaggio is the character about whom the reader gets to know least. He is introduced as a friend of Hana's late father who has seen her grow up and who, now that Hana's father has been killed in the war, tries to act as a substitute father for her. We are told that he used to be a gentleman-thief before the war and that he was used as a spy by the Allied armies. It was in connection with these activities that he lost the thumbs of both of his hands, and when he turns up at the villa, he, like Hana is 'in darkness'. His character, however, is less deeply developed than those of the other protagonists, and his role in the novel mainly is to help Hana and the English patient 're-assemble' themselves.

Hana had spent the last war years as a nurse working with severely injured soldiers, many of whom she watched die. This experience left her traumatized and was the reason for her 'disassembly'. Outwardly, she functioned in her work, but her mind went into a self-protective state of shock where emotions could not touch her. As an outward sign of her diminished state of existence she cut her hair short and lost interest in her appearance; her loss of identity seemed complete when, two years later, she caught her reflection in a mirror by accident and did not recognize herself:

> She watched the little portrait of herself as if within a clasped brooch. [...] Hi Buddy, she said. She peered into her look, trying to recognize herself. (p. 52)

During the weeks at San Girolamo, she slowly begins to put the pieces of her personality back together. As with Karim in *The Buddha of Suburbia*, Hana's fragmented identity leaves her unable to commit herself to any person or location: at night, she sleeps in a hammock off the ground, each night in a different room. Gradually, she relaxes and begins to take an interest in her surroundings and in her companions to the point where San Girolamo and its inhabitants represent a kind of durability and security, and she feels safe 'in the miniature world she had built' (p. 47). When Kip arrives at San Girolamo, she falls in love with him and eventually spends the nights with him; she is finally able to talk about her experiences. During those weeks at San Girolamo Hana slowly 're-assembles' her personality, so she can eventually write to her step-mother, for the first time in years, to tell her that she will be coming back home. She has emerged as a complete person, someone who will

> always have a serious face. She has moved from being a young woman into having the angular look of a queen, someone who has made her face with her desire to be a certain kind of person [...] she did not inherit that look or that beauty, but [...] it was something searched for and [...] it will always reflect a present stage of her character. (p. 300)

Unlike Hana, whose loss of identity was caused by the war, the English patient's 'disassembly' had started long before the war and was voluntary. It is Caravaggio who feels the need to restore his identity:

> He needs to know who this Englishman from the desert is, and reveal him for Hana's sake. Or perhaps invent a skin for him, the way tannic acid camouflages a burned man's rawness. (p. 117)

During long conversations with him Caravaggio discovers that the 'English' patient in fact is not English at all: he is Count Almasy, a Hungarian, who was a desert explorer and then, during the war, worked as a German spy in the North African deserts. When his plane crashed, his body was burned so badly that he was unrecognizable, so the British never had cause to question his nationality. During the years Almasy had spent as an explorer in the desert, he had systematically erased traces of his national origins; he had realized the absurdity and the fleeting nature of nationalism:

> The desert could not be claimed or owned – it was a piece of cloth carried by winds, never held down by stones, and given a hundred shifting names long before Canterbury existed, long before battles and treaties quilted Europe and the East [...] All of us, even those with European homes and children in the distance, wished to remove the clothing of our countries. [...] Erase the family name! Erase nations! I was taught such things by the desert. (p. 139)

It is ironical then that Almasy, who went to English schools, has no trouble passing himself off as an Englishman. It is also significant that his body is burned black – which makes him resemble the Indian Kip more than any Englishman. The idea of nationalism is made further ridiculous through the character of Kip himself. When he first arrived in England, he lived in the household of an English aristocrat, Lord Suffolk, who introduced Kip to British culture. Kip quickly grew fond of habits typically associated with England and the English, such as drinking tea, and he comes across as more English than the English patient. He spends many hours with him, and Almasy sees in Kip a younger version of himself, when he comments that 'Kip and I are both international bastards – born in one place and choosing to live elsewhere. Fighting to get back to or get away from our homelands all our lives.' (p. 176)

Kip, despite his English behaviour, remains the foreigner. Owing to his foreign looks, he was mostly ignored by the other soldiers, and 'he was accustomed to his invisibility'. He adopted the habit of keeping to himself and, consequently, Hana notices a 'self-sufficiency' and 'privacy' about him which was the result of his invisibility. It is significant that the job for which he applies in the army is that of a sapper; defusing bombs was an extremely dangerous occupation and most sappers died young – which is why, for example, they avoided forming deep friendships and became loners. His work, therefore, allows him to come to terms with and ignore the racial prejudice he encounters everywhere. Like Karim and Hana, he had learned the only way to protect himself is to not depend on any kind of human relationship. It comes as a shock to him, then, that he falls in love with Hana and consequently loses his self-reliance.

Even in his relationship with Hana he is aware that he is a foreigner to her Western culture, just as she feels out of her own culture when she is in his tent. Nonetheless, for a short time at least they are able to open up to each other during the nights they spend together 'in 1945, where their continents met in a hill town' (p. 225).

Their brief idyllic affair ends abruptly with the bombing of Nagasaki and Hiroshima. Suddenly, Kip sees 'all those around him, in a different light'. He is no longer able to regard Hana, Caravaggio or the English patient as individuals. For him, they are now representatives of Western civilization, which has oppressed other nations for centuries:

> American, French, I don't care. When you start bombing the brown races of the world, you're an Englishman. (p. 286)

Kip realizes that the outward expressions of English culture that he has adopted, as well as his nickname, Kip, which incidentally has been given to him by an Englishman, are signs of his own oppression. For, despite his conformist behaviour, the English have never allowed him to feel as part of their culture. The bombing of Nagasaki and Hiroshima forcefully make him see that '[h]is name is Kirpal Singh and he does not know what he is doing here'. (p. 287). Disillusioned, he leaves San Girolamo and returns to India where he becomes a doctor and marries an Indian woman with whom he has two children. The novel thus ends with Kip and Hana returning to their own countries.

This return to their national origins, however, is not offered as a solution. Even back in their own countries, Kip and Hana come across as cultural 'in-betweens'. Years after his return to India, Kip finds himself thinking about Hana, feeling an urge to be with her and talk with her, as he used to at San Girolamo. Similarly, Hana even at 34 'has not found her own company, the ones she wanted'.[27]

The reader is left with the impression that attachments to nationalities have lost their relevance. The feeling of 'in-between', of 'belonging and not' that is reflected in *The Buddha of Suburbia* and *The English Patient* is a state of mind that comes with living in a culture that is becoming increasingly global. Since the success of Salman Rushdie's *Midnight's Children*, which demonstrated that a novel about something as foreign as modern Indian history could indeed attract large audiences, publishing houses have started to bring out mass-market editions of international writing to cater to an increasingly cosmopolitan audience. They realized that these works of world fiction are, in the words of Carlos Fuentes, 'harbingers and heralds of what literature will be like in the 21st century', when we are going to live 'in a new century not only of instant communication but of instant migration'.[28] A meaningful and relevant literature canon ought to reflect such important social developments, and the transformation of the English literature canon from one with a traditionally Eurocentric orientation to one which reflects the recent developments in world fiction is a welcome and necessary development.

NOTES

1. Alfred Dirlik, 'The Postcolonial Aura: Third World Criticism in the Age of Global Capitalism', *Critical Inquiry* 20.2 (1994): pp. 328–56, here p. 350.
2. Hanif Kureishi, *The Buddha of Suburbia* (New York: Penguin, 1990).
3. Michael Ondaatje, *The English Patient* (New York: Vintage, 1992).
4. Ivo Vidan, 'Expanding Curricula: Global Literature in English', *Literature(s) in English: New Perspectives*, ed. Wolfgang Zach (Frankfurt: Peter Lang, 1990) p. 53.
5. Wolfgang Zach (ed.), *Literature(s) in English: New Perspectives* (Frankfurt: Peter Lang, 1990) 11. Pico Iyer, 'The Empire Writes Back', *Time* 8 Feb. 1993, p. 52.
6. Horst Priessnitz, 'The Dual Perspective of "Anglo-Colonial" Literatures and the Future of English Studies: a Modest Proposal,' *Literature(s) in English: New Perspectives*, ed. Wolfgang Zach (Frankfurt: Peter Lang, 1990) p. 31.
7. Ibid, p. 32 ff. Wolfgang Zach, 'Introduction' in *Literature(s) in English*. Vidan, pp. 47–52.
8. Zach, p. 12.
9. Elleke Boehmer, *Colonial & Post-colonial Literature* (Oxford: Oxford University Press, 1995).
10. Boehmer, p. 232.
11. Dirlik, p. 330.
12. Iyer, p. 50.
13. Iyer, p. 55.
14. Iyer, p. 52.
15. Iyer, p. 52 ff.
16. Hanif Kureishi, 'Interview' with Marcia Pally, *Film Comment* 22 (Sept.–Oct. 1986) p. 53.
17. Victor J. Ramraj, 'Diaspora and Multiculturalism', *New National and Postcolonial Literatures: an Introduction*, ed. Bruce King (Oxford: Clarendon Press, 1996) pp. 214–29, here p. 224.

18. Sylvia Mergenthal, 'Acculturation Processes and Family Structures: Timothy Mo, *Sour Sweet*, Hanif Kureishi, *The Buddha of Suburbia*, Kazuo Ishiguro, *A Pale View of Hills*,' forthcoming, p. 6.
19. Mergenthal, p. 7.
20. Rudyard Kipling, *Kim* (Harmondsworth: Penguin, 1987).
21. Iyer, p. 52.
22. Iyer, p. 50.
23. Ramraj, p. 227.
24. Ramraj, p. 227.
25. Chelva Kanaganayakam, 'Exiles and Expatriates', *New National and Postcolonial Literatures: an Introduction* (Oxford: Clarendon Press, 1996) pp. 201–13, here p. 207.
26. Kanaganayakam, p. 207.
27. Michael Ondaatje, *The English Patient*, p. 301.
28. Carlos Fuentes as quoted in Iyer, p. 55.

6 France and its DOM: the Ambivalence of European Identity
Ute Fendler

While discussing European identity, one is very often inclined to forget the French West Indies, which are geographically far away from France but whose inhabitants are French citizens. The ambivalence of the European identity of the French West Indian can only be understood in the historical context. The main events of West Indian history are genocide of the natives committed by the European discoverers and settlers and, consequently, the slave trade between Africa and the Caribbean Islands, which was started in order to ensure the supply of plantation workers. At the end of the nineteenth century, after the abolition of slavery, other waves of migration followed: Indian and Chinese workers were hired to continue the work after the freed African slaves had fled. Although slavery was abolished, the living and working conditions did not change. As a consequence, the French played an ambiguous role: as colonizers, they were committed to bringing European civilization and its ideals and values like liberty, equality, fraternity to other peoples so that they could 'profit' from the benefits of European civilization. At the same time, colonization in the Caribbean meant enslavement and oppression of the non-European people and, therefore, negated these European ideals to which the non-European peoples should have adhered.

Europe incorporated the oppressor and the liberator. This ambivalent position determined the question of identity for the French West Indian.[1] Two events turn the history of the French West Indies into a special one: first, in 1941, France declared the French Caribbean Islands the so-called 'Départements d'Outre-Mer' (DOM), and the French West Indians became French citizens. Legally, these descendants of African slaves and Asian immigrants had from then on the same status as those citizens born in France of French parents. Second, in 1957, the DOMs were integrated by law into the EEC.[2]

French citizenship is meant to be the realization of the ideal of equality, fraternity and liberty but the West Indians have continually experienced racial discrimination, as the historical constituents that predetermine the relationship between the French and the Caribbean French still seem to be valid. The ideals and values of European civilization are consequently called into question by the reality of the relationship between the French and the French West Indian. The French/European culture was presented as being superior to others, and it is this false superiority that justified the colonization. The French culture, being the culture of the colonizer, is the dominant one. The other cultural elements have been suppressed or neglected for centuries.

As a consequence of the continuing ambivalence of European ideals and their realization experienced by the French West Indian, the ideals and the self-representation of the French as the representatives of the European civilization are losing their absolute value. The French West Indian turned therefore to the non-European elements. The *Négritude* movement questioned the predominance of the European/White culture and identity. Other movements like *Antillanité*[3] and more recently *Créolité*[4] followed. The continuation of the movements expresses the vital necessity of finding and valorizing components of Caribbean history and identity other than the French one. This search finds its repercussions in literary works and has been a central question for literary critics.

My interest will be focused rather on how the French, the dominant group which predetermines the meaning of French citizenship or French – and later on, European – identity, is represented in literary texts of Francophone West Indian authors. It reflects the ambivalent image of what French/European identity is meant to be and how it is experienced by the French West Indian.

It is remarkable that French literary history is split into a French and a French West Indian one. So, even in literature, the separation of French from the Caribbean and French from France is obvious, and the line is drawn by members of both sides. The need to define oneself is very strong as the different ethnic identities are permanently called into question by confrontation with the other, the French, the ex-colonizer. The new literary history *Lettres Créoles*, edited by Patrick Chamoiseau and Raphaël Confiant,[5] is an alternative history of the literature that has been neglected by the French literary critics in the past. Thus, the editors include commentaries on the literature of Békés – white people born on the islands.

While reading Francophone novels of the West Indies, one's attention is called to the repetitive occurrence of two main subjects: first, the question of colour that persists from the days of slavery up to today, and secondly, the experience of the First and Second World Wars which was decisive because Caribbean men were recruited to defend France against Germany. Fighting for France became a test to show whether or not the Caribbean people 'merited' their only recently received citizenship. Their loyalty in those wars was, however, repaid with racial discrimination.[6] Topics dealing with racism can be found in most novels that choose to discuss socially or politically related subjects.[7]

The recurrence of these subjects illustrates the relationship between the French and the Caribbean French and sheds a light on how French/European identity is perceived by the Caribbean French. In the following, I would like to present a few examples taken from texts by some well-known Caribbean authors.

Patrick Chamoiseau is probably one of the best known and accepted authors from the French West Indies in France. This can be derived from the fact that he is the only French West Indian author to receive the Prix Goncourt, for his novel *Texaco*.[8] His first novel *Chronique des sept misères* (1986)[9] offers a good example for the ambivalence of this relationship between the French and the French West Indian by illustrating the status of the education system. On the one hand, the European pretends to civilize the other peoples by education; on the other hand, the system is euro-centred and represents therefore at the same time the superiority of the white man. School is the means to colonize and to assimilate the French West Indian: it is through education that he can hope to achieve the superior position of the white and, at the same time, it is through the same education that he learns about his inferiority.

> Contrairement à ses soeurs, elle put se rendre à l'école. Ce fut un monde nouveau, hors de la réalité même, où elle apprit à lire et à écrire en français, langue insolite qui surprenait ses parents. Fanotte exigea là même que sa fille l'utilise en s'adressant à elle, et le respect alors? Félix Soleil, par contre, ne semblait jamais pouvoir s'en accommoder. Cette langue lui était certes familière (c'était celle des gendarmes-à-cheval) mais il ne l'avait pas imaginée dans sa maison.[10]

This quotation illustrates the different aspects of the French school system and its significance for the colonized: it represents the access to another world which means more respect, that is the positive aspect, but at the same time it means an alienation of oneself from one's own world, that is the negative aspect. In addition to that, it also means control of the French West Indian by the French and their subordination to the French.

Additionally, Chamoiseau's novel reflects the influence of the Second World War on the relations between colonizer and colonized. One of the characters is involved in the war by taking the dissidents by boat to the next island from which they could join the army of the Allies. His interest though is not political but economic: he earns a lot of money during the war.

By choosing a character whose interest is not idealistic or political but purely economic, Chamoiseau is able to ridicule the ambitions of the French to use the Caribbean as cannon-fodder. Here, it is the Caribbean who profits from the war.

The islands becoming French *départements* is another point of sublime irony:

> Messieurs et dames de la compagnie, à mesure que passait le temps, les avions et bateaux de France augmentaient. [...] Les békés vendaient leurs terres agricoles aux organismes d'H.L.M., ou aux fonctionnaires amateurs de villas, et construisaient sur la jetée des entrepôts d'import-export. Bientôt, ils quadrillèrent le pays de libres-services, supermarchés, hypermarchés, auprès desquels les nôtres faisaient triste figure. Le peuple des établis, tout à la joie d'avoir été sacré membre du grand pays (Français par un coup de loi), était fier de ces vitrines étincelantes, ces rayons interminables débordant de beautés. [...] Nous fêtâmes cette loi au flambeau, avec la frénésie qu'ont généralement les orphelins quand une mère les recueille.[11]

It is not legal and political equality which is perceived as a direct consequence of the law, but the economic implications. The choice of images and words expresses irony, namely the relationship between the centre and periphery still exists, even after the islands have been assigned the same status as the other French *départements*. The paternalistic attitude continues and manifests itself in the economic relations: France is looking for new markets for its goods.[12] The DOM believe that they have reached equality due to the illusion of the same standard of living. In his latest novel *Texaco* (1992), the allusions to a critical attitude towards France are less pointed, but there are still the same subjects, namely colour, language, and war.

The following is just one example of the pervasiveness of the question of colour in society:[13]

> Mon Esternome apprit à titrer chaque personne selon son degré de blancheur ou la déveine de sa noirceur. Il apprit à se brosser la rondelle de ses cheveux huilés dans l'espoir qu'un jour de l'impossible année cannelle, ils lui flottent sur le front. Tout un chacun rêvait de se blanchir: les békés en se cherchant une chair-France à sang bleu pouvant dissoudre leur passé de flibuste roturière; les mulâtres en guignant plus mulâtre qu'eux ou même quelque béké déchu; enfin, la négraille affranchie, [...].[14]

In *Texaco* the hope of the French West Indian for assimilation finds its expression in the support of the French during the war.

> La guerre avait surgi sans raison, en dehors de nous et de nos élans pour pénétrer l'En-ville. Nous ne sûmes qu'une chose: la douce France, berceau de notre liberté, l'universelle si généreuse, était en grand danger. Il fallait tout lui rendre. Comme la campagne nous affamait et que l'En-ville nous refusait, nous trouvâmes dans l'armée une perspective offerte de devenir français, d'échapper aux békés. Malgré ceux qui fuyaient, nous fûmes des milliers à devancer les mobilisations. Les békés, voyant cela d'un oeil plus détaché, placèrent leurs marchandises du côté d'Amérique, et se mobilisèrent sur la patrie de leurs commerces.[15]

This time, Chamoiseau has chosen to present a character who supports the French. However, in the quotation above, indirect criticism can be perceived. As the protagonist points out, the freed slaves could no longer make their living on the plantations because they refused to work in the fields. Similarly, they were not welcome in the towns. Becoming a soldier in the French army was, therefore, one of the rare ways of making a decent living and of being respected. The French propagandistic slogans demanding help against a supposed common enemy became hollow if taken up by a person dependent on this same authority.

In addition to Chamoiseau, I would also like to mention the novels by Raphaël Confiant, the co-editor of the literary history *Lettres Créoles*. The plot of his novel *Le Nègre et l'Amiral*[16] takes place during the Second World War and concentrates on the living conditions of the Martiniquan people. Here again, we encounter the same subjects: language, colour and war.

In this novel a difference is made between the *Français-France*

(French spoken in France) and the *Français-Banane* (French spoken in the French West Indies)[17] which expresses different social status and education levels.

On the subject of war, the criticism is voiced again that this war is a war between whites[18] who try to involve other peoples. The positive attitude towards war, however, is also present: two thousand men join the army at once – but there is no white Martiniquan among them. The hope to gain respect by fighting the war with the French is alive, but the critical undertone is present at the same time: the white Martiniquan has no need to risk his life to prove to the French his value as a man and citizen.

These few examples show that due to the common history of slavery, the question of colour persists, and all other subjects like education, language, culture and war are closely connected with it.

It is interesting that the novels are always placed in a historical context. The criticism of the way the French/European ideals are realized in the Caribbean context is therefore not applied to any contemporary situation. That may be the reason why the criticism is possible and why novels containing this kind of criticism have been awarded French prizes. Chamoiseau's first novel *Chronique des sept misères* contains a number of ironical comments on the relationship between the French and the Caribbean French. In *Texaco*, the novel that won the award, the irony has considerably diminished.

I would now like to give some more examples from the novels of another well-known author, Maryse Condé, who has been awarded *Le Grand Prix Littéraire de la Femme, le Prix Anaïs Nin,* and the *Puterbaugh prize*,[19] but who, however, unlike Patrick Chamoiseau, has not been awarded the most significant prize in France, the *Prix Goncourt*.

In her short story 'Pays Mêlé' of 1985,[20] she goes further than Chamoiseau and Confiant. In addition to the subjects of war and colour, she chooses to write about the events of the 1960s and the 1980s, transgressing the border between historical and political subjects. Apart from a few comments, the short story has been neglected by literary critics. However, the book entitled *Pays Mêlé* consists of two short stories 'Pays Mêlé' and 'Nanna-ya', and it marks a turning point in the work of Maryse Condé: her novels published before 1985 deal *grosso modo* with the relationship between the Caribbean islands and Africa. The novels after *Pays Mêlé* concentrate on the Caribbean or the Americas.

'Pays Mêlé' covers almost 200 years of Guadeloupean history.

Racial, social and economic discrimination ends up in manifestations such as the events of May 1967,[21] in the founding of the GONG (Groupe d'Organisation Nationale Guadeloupéenne), and the ARC (Alliance Révolutionnaire Caraïbe).[22]

The narrator, a doctor, trying to reconstitute the biography of a young victim of a bomb attack, finds out that the victim has been an activist himself in the Independence Movement. The experiences of the activist and the commentaries of the narrator give a survey of the history of Guadeloupe: the economic influence of France brings about the destruction and the loss of traditional working modes, while tourism adds to the alienation without offering employment. The revolt of the young man is presented as an unavoidable reaction against a world that is controlled by foreigners. The narrator tells these events in a sympathetic tone.

The plot, referring to real events in the early 1980s, ends in 1983 with a narrative account of bomb attacks. The neglecting of the short story by the reviewers may be due to its position towards contemporary political events, as Maryse Condé published the short story in 1985, only two years after these acts of terrorism by the Independence Movement.

In 1989 she published her novel *Traversée de la Mangrove*[23] which was a success, although the story alludes again to contemporary history. The anti-colonial discourse of the years of the independence wars finds its expression in the following quotation:

> Dans l'ombre, des gens traçaient sur les murs des lettres étranges qui sonnaient comme des tocsins. Des inscriptions injurieuses, 'De Gaulle assassin', 'A bas le colonialisme' – un mot nouveau!.[24]

The criticism is not very harsh as it is a politically innocent and ignorant figure who remembers the slogans. It reflects the fact, though, that at a certain time anti-colonial ideas were under discussion.

A second quotation referring to the 1980s shows the actual state of the DOM:

> Quand Lucien s'embarquait dans ses envolées idéologiques, Carmélien le ramenait sur terre d'un moqueur:
> – Ouvre les yeux, mon cher! Nous sommes déjà européens! L'Indépendance est une belle endormie qu'aucun Prince ne réveillera plus.[25]

The Afro-Caribbean discusses with the Indo-Caribbean the problems of the islands. While the African still dreams of social change, the Indian reminds him of the reality they live in: the islands are members of the European Community. In comparison with the neighbouring islands, the economy of the French islands seems to be the only one functioning. That is the reason why nobody seriously thinks about independence any more: the people of the French islands prefer economic wealth to political independence.[26]

The quotation above marks the end of an evolution that has started with the *départementalisation* of the islands. There have been two main positions: the option of independence from France and the option of full integration with France. The author calls attention to the fact that the criticism of the political and economic influence of France on the islands slowly disappears.[27]

The examples given above should illustrate that the question of French identity in the Caribbean context has multiple facets. There is first of all the ideal concept of the French/European identity based on such values as liberty, equality, fraternity and democracy. These ideals are contested by the history of colonizing and enslaving non-European peoples. The French West Indian would have to bring together these extremes in his personality. He lives the contradictions while the French from France can forget about the negative historical events and identify only with the ideal concept. The criticism and questions raised by the French West Indians also call into question the basis of the French/European identity.

My thesis is that in the choice of subjects and language, Francophone West Indian literature reflects not only the non-existence of *one* French identity for all French citizens, but it also shows that the mechanisms of cultural and political dominance are still working.

Criticism is only accepted if it concerns historical subjects that can no longer be of political interest. Political subjects, though, are taken up rarely and in an inoffensive way: otherwise, this kind of criticism would question the relationship between the DOM and France.

As the novels quoted above respect these principles – apart from *Pays Mêlé* which is in consequence neglected – they are read, reviewed and they have even received awards. In order to support my thesis, I would like to give an example of a novel that ignores these boundaries and is also completely neglected by literary critics: *La chasse au Racoon*, by Max Jeanne, published in 1980 by Karthala.[28]

The novel takes up the subject of war. The Caribbean French soldiers have to go through the same experiences as their fathers and grandfathers – but this time in the Algerian war. The new aspect is that the Caribbean is fighting in the army of the ex-colonizer in order to oppress another colonized people.

> Et, du jour au lendemain, Bolo s'était retrouvé en Algérie, brute galonnée faisant le coup de feu contre bicots et fellaghas... au nom du droit des peuples à disposer d'eux-mêmes.
> De nombreux amis à lui qui se trouvaient dans la même situation avaient préféré passer carrément du côté des Algériens. D'autres encore s'étaient réfugiés dans certains pays de l'Est. Par peur ou simplement par indécision ou encore pour ne pas peiner davantage son notable de père, Bolo était resté dans l'Armée française pour y apprendre ce qu'il savait déjà, que la déclaration des droits de l'homme ne concernait ni le Nègre ni l'Arabe.[29]

The criticism is direct: the French claim to be the representatives of the idea of equality and fraternity. In the name of these ideals of the European enlightenment, the French justify the civilization of non-European peoples or rather their colonization. The French Caribbean, having been assimilated by the French to the extent that he identifies himself completely with French culture, has taken over the 'civilizing work' of the French. However, reality is the opposite to the ideal. Human rights are neglected by the French. The confrontation with this new experience sheds new light on Caribbean history. History is usually written by the dominating group. Caribbean history is therefore to be seen as the history of civilization brought from Europe. The criticism in this novel challenges this interpretation and asks for a revision.

Jeanne's novel touches another subject of conflict. Tourism on the Caribbean Islands is revealed to be another sort of colonization.[30]

> Drapeaux français. Canadien. Suisse. Yankee. Hollandais. Tous enfin rassemblés dans la même partouze. Finies les gueguerres de la coloniale. Finis les p'tits jeux de gendarmes et de voleurs. Poussez pas! Désormais y'a de la place pour tous. N'est-y pas beau le progrès? Ça gêne plus personne maintenant que l'île soit D.O.M. ou DOMINION, l'essentiel étant qu'elle reste nobiscum. Le fric, c'est bien connu, abolit les frontières entre philantropes. Ici on accepte toutes les monnaies. Et en avant la zizique![31] Viva y viva le carnaval carambolesque des chaînes bordelières.[32]

Jeanne plays with words and concepts in a very satirical and ironical way. He draws attention to the fact that DOM, which is originally meant to convey the idea of equal status, could also be interpreted as an abbreviation for dominion. It becomes evident that the islands are still being exploited in the interests of France: the Caribbeans supply the land, the sea and the workers to fix the ideal arrangements according to the concepts of the colonizer. The beauty of the landscape and the possibility of becoming rich attracts also the former colonizing nations.

The illusion that tourism could be a profitable industry not only for the investors but also for the population is destroyed:

> Il était plutôt rare en effet que les constructions d'écoles ou d'hôpitaux aillent au-delà de la première pierre posée par tel ou tel minhistrion de passage. Il est vrai qu'ils ne présentaient pas le même caractère d'utilité publique que le 'complexe hôtelier' de Saint-François. Après tout, ça servait surtout aux nègres et aux coolies, les hostos.[33]

Again the narrator lays bare the context and the nature of tourism on the island. Hotels are built because they are profitable for the French investor, projects of public interest are usually initiated by the French minister who doesn't live on the island and is not really concerned about their development. The argument for the official support for tourism is that tourism would create employment for the Caribbean population. But the comment of the narrator is merciless and one is left in no doubt that the Caribbean does not profit at all, as the following quotation proves:

> Quant aux zozotochtones, y gagnent pas grand-chose à l'affaire, mais y sont tout fiers de voir figurer leur commune en bonne place au hit-parade des hôtels les plus chics.[34]

Once again, the French are shown not as fellow-citizens but as colonizers and profiteers. The advantages of being a French *département* are challenged.

Jeanne goes even further in referring to the events of May 1967. Those are central to the plot whereby demonstrations were quelled by special police troops coming from France.[35] The government gained advantage from the events by arresting the leaders of the organization fighting for the independence of Guadeloupe. Jeanne adds some historical authenticity by giving the sources in footnotes when quoting from declarations made by witnesses during the trial against the presumed leaders of the movement.[36]

Again, the language the narrator uses is eloquent. The French are characterized as the oppressors who try to hide behind a philanthropic vocabulary.

> Les mercenaires du commissaire Bamou qui prenaient un peu d'exercice s'en donnaient à coeur-joie. Enfin un petit match d'entraînement. Carte blanche. Vous avez carte blanche, avait dit le patron. On va faire un carton de tous ces fauteurs de trouble. Pointe-à-Pitre, stand de tir au pigeon. Ouais. Pas de demi-mesure. Une seule méthode: le nettoyage par le vide...[37]

and further on:

> Ça commençait plutôt mal pour l'Etat français qui, en dépit de tous ses efforts en ce sens, n'avait pas réussi à étouffer ce qui, à l'instar de bien d'autres procès (...) ne manquerait pas d'éclabousser l'image de marque d'une France prétendûment pays des droits de l'homme et de la liberté.
> [...] dans ce combat de Goliath contre David la situation risquait d'évoluer au désavantage de ceux qui avaient imaginé le scénario et que d'accusatrice la France se retrouvât finalement accusée DOMICIDE VOLONTAIRE.[38]

The ambivalent image of France can well be seen in the last quotation. France presents itself as the defender of human rights. But the Caribbean experience with the French government reveals another aspect of the French character: colonial and racist elements still influence the relationship with their DOM.

The three examples taken from Jeanne's novel should show that there are other elements in the relationship between French and French Caribbean peoples besides the question of colour and such historical occurrences as slavery and the Second World War. The events Jeanne has chosen to write about could also be considered as a kind of continuation of the earlier events. All of them have the same tenor: the French West Indians have become fellow-citizens by law, but nevertheless they still do not have the same freedom and possibilities as the French.

Another example evoking the problems of the French West Indies being French is one of the more recent novels of Raphaël Confiant, *L'Allée des Soupirs*.[39] In 1959 and 1961 Martinique experienced demonstrations comparable to those in Guadeloupe in 1967. The demonstrations against unemployment, impoverishment, and social injustice were put down by French police.[40]

(...) au quatrième ou cinquième jour du couvre-feu, le lycéen Janon fut abattu sans sommation à la mitraillette par une horde de C.R.S. déchaînés. On l'entendit voltiger un à-moué-à-moué déchirant dans la noirceur de la nuit: 'L'esclavage a été aboli en 1848, bande de chiens-de-fer!'[41]

This kind of description appears in multiple reports of different individual experiences: the unpolitical and innocent Ancinelle who has a rendezvous with her lover happens to get involved in the demonstrations; the lover, a teacher and representative of French knowledge, of the written word, and the *quimboiseur*,[42] the representative of the Caribbean knowledge, of the oral word, do meet by chance at the very moment when a group of demonstrators clashes with a group of policemen. However, the core of the events, the brutal suppression of the revolt by the French police, is not altered by the different perspectives. The language used for the descriptions of these scenes is military, and the procedure of the French government towards French citizens is criticized.

Special attention is drawn to the ambivalence of French citizenship in the West Indian context. In the quotation above, the West Indian French citizen reminds his French co-citizens of the fact that slavery has been abolished, meaning implicitly that the French government treats the Caribbeans as slaves who can be shot without any justification.

The question of citizenship is also raised by introducing the subject of education. The following quotation will show the meaning of education and knowledge:

J'ai vu Grans Z'Ongles, oui, le manieur d'herbes maléfiques, affronter une bande de C.R.S. déchaînés et les tourner en dérision: 'Où la Seine prend-elle sa source?' a-t-il demandé et aucun des soudards n'a pu répondre.
'Au plateau de Langres, sacrés couillons! Et à quelle date Jeanne d'Arc a-t-elle brûlée vive, hein?... En l'an 1431! Ha-Ha-Ha! Voyez-moi ça, n'êtes-vous pas de bons Français? Des Français bien français?'[43]

The French West Indian has been educated in the same way as the French born in France. Knowledge of French history serves to prove their indebtedness to the French community, their Frenchness. Ironically, the French themselves don't know their own history. If knowledge about history and culture were the criterion of gaining admittance to the French community, many French would not obtain

French citizenship. The novel shows that there exist two sorts of French citizenships and calls into question the ideal of equality.

This novel by Confiant has been awarded the *Prix Carbet* in spite of his harsh criticisms. This may be due to the fact that Confiant manages to insert his criticism in a variety of versions of stories and of histories. By this means of inserting political elements into Creole storytelling, the dig at the French government is softened.

However, Condé's short story and Jeanne's novel present the conflicts of the French government with its DOM without any techniques of veiling or minimizing the negative impact on the DOM.

The question remains of why the criticism in more recent novels like *Allée des Soupirs* by Confiant and *Traversée de la Mangrove* by Condé has not prevented their critical discussion as seems to have been the case for their books published in the 1980s. Condé has softened her criticisms, but Confiant has added and enforced criticizing elements. Thus, it might also be the increasing popularity and international success of West Indian literature that has influenced and eventually changed its reception in France. In addition, the growing distance in time to the events of the 1960s and the 1980s may also play a role.

Nevertheless, novels of French Caribbean authors are still mainly published by French publishing houses (most of them in Paris) which is a means of controlling the intellectual life in all of the French territories. A kind of non-institutionalized censorship can ensure the preservation of the positive humanitarian and egalitarian image of France which is vital to justify the dominance of the concept of French/European identity based on White/European values that would not yet allow non-European elements to be integrated, as the examples taken from the French Caribbean novels have shown. So far, the European identity or European integration in the context of the French West Indies remains ambivalent.

The Guadeloupean, Georges Trésor, who analysed the relationship between the DOM and France at the period when they were facing the opening up of the EU in 1993, took political, economic and cultural aspects into consideration. He stated, in giving some interim results of his analysis, that the French West Indian, in spite of his belonging to France and to Europe, defined himself in terms of differences to the French/European.

> Consciemment ou inconsciemment, ils sentent en effet qu'à travers le problème de l'intégration de la Guadeloupe à l'Europe de 1993, c'est toute la question de la définition de leur identité dans

l'ensemble européen qui se trouve posée. Quelles que soient en effet les appréciations optimistes ou pessimistes que les Guadeloupéens portent sur les éventuelles conséquences économiques et sociales de l'intégration de notre pays au Marché unique, dans leur manière de se représenter les enjeux de cette intégration, ils réagissent en tant que membres d'une communauté distincte de la communauté française.[44]

So far, I can only conclude along with Trésor that the process of political and economic integration seems to proceed but the question of cultural identity or even integration is still open.

NOTES

1. See, for example, Jacques Fredj, 'Le Maillon Colonial', *Autrement. Antilles: Espoirs et Déchirements de l'âme créole* 41 (1989): pp. 21–6. Patrick Chamoiseau, Raphaël Confiant, *Lettres Créoles: Tracées antillaises et continentales de la littérature 1635–1975* (Paris: Hatier, 1991) pp. 104–6.
2. See Georges Trésor, 'Le Syndrome Européen', *Etudes Guadeloupéennes* 4 (1991): pp. 82–101.
3. Edouard Glissant, *Le Discours Antillais* (Paris: Editions du Seuil, 1981).
4. Jean Bernabé, Patrick Chamoiseau and Raphaël Confiant, *Eloge de la Créolité* (Paris: Gallimard, 1989).
5. Patrick Chamoiseau, Raphaël Confiant, *Lettres Créoles* (Paris: Hatier, 1991).
6. See Henri Bangou, *La Guadeloupe: La nécessaire décolonisation. 1939 à nos jours,* tome 3 (Paris: L'Harmattan, 1987).
7. See, for example, Roger Toumson, *La Transgression des couleurs: Littérature et langage des Antilles. XVIIIe, XIXe, XXe siècles*, Tomes 1 et 2 (Paris: Editions Caribéennes, 1989).
8. Patrick Chamoiseau, *Texaco* (Paris: Gallimard, 1992).
9. Patrick Chamoiseau, *Chronique des sept misères*, Collection folio (Paris: Gallimard, 1986).
10. Ibid., 27: 'Contrary to her sisters, she could go to school. This was a new world, even outside of reality, where she learned reading and writing in French, this extraordinary language that surprised her parents. Fanotte demanded at once that her daughter should use it when addressing her, it's a question of respect. Félix Soleil, on the contrary, never seemed to be able to come to terms with it. This language was certainly familiar to him (it was the language of the policemen on horseback), but he had never imagined it coming into his house.' [All translations are my own.]

11. Ibid., 133/4: 'Ladies and gentlemen, as time passes, the number of planes and ships from France is increasing. The "Békés" sold their land to the institution "HLM" or to the clerks interested in villas, and built warehousing for import-export next to the wharf. Soon afterwards, they covered the country with a net of shops, supermarkets and shopping-centres, in comparison with which ours came off badly. The established people being happy to be sacred members of this great country (being French by law), were proud of those shining shop-windows, those never-ending rows of shelves overflowing with beautiful things. We celebrated this law with that kind of passion that orphans usually show when a mother adopts them.'
12. See, for example, Eve Dessarre, *Cauchemar Antillais* (Paris: François Maspero, 1965).
13. See, for example, Michel Giraud, 'Les Masques de la Couleur,' *Autrement. Antilles* 1 (1989): pp. 88–95.
14. Chamoiseau, *Texaco*, 83: 'Mon Esternome learned to classify every person according to the degree of his whiteness or of the misery of his blackness. He learned to brush the disc of his oiled hair hoping that one day in the impossible cinnamon year, they would hang down to his forehead. Everybody dreamed of becoming white: the "békés" were looking for blue-blooded "French flesh" who could dissolve their past of non-aristocratic pirates; the mulattos were squinting at persons that are whiter than themselves or even at some degenerated "béké"; finally, the liberated Negroes, [. . .]'.
15. Ibid., 210: 'The war had come without reason, it had come without our contribution and without our vigour to penetrate the town. We knew only one thing: sweet France, the cradle of our freedom, the universal and so generous one, was in danger. We had to give back everything to her. As the countryside starved us and the town turned us back, the army offered us the chance to become French and to escape the békés. In spite of those who ran away, there were thousands of us who anticipated the mobilization. The békés, considering the situation in a more indifferent way, did their business in America and mobilized for the fatherland of their markets.'
16. Raphaël Confiant, *Le Nègre et l'Amiral* (Paris: Grasset, 1988).
17. Ibid., see pp. 34, 39, 40.
18. Ibid., see p. 111.
19. She received the Grand Prix Littéraire de la Femme in 1986 for *Moi, Tituba, Sorcière*, the Prix Anaïs Nin of the Académie française in 1988 for *La Vie Scélérate* and the Puterbaugh prize for her work in general.
20. Maryse Condé, *Pays Mêlé suivi de Nanna-ya*, Collection Monde Noir Poche (Paris: Hatier, 1985).
21. See Henri Bangou, *La Guadeloupe* (Paris: L'Harmattan, 1987) pp. 172–3. Racial riots had been put down by French police. Several dozen persons were injured or killed. In consequence, the French government arrested the leaders of the communist party and of the Independence Movement as being responsible for the confrontations.
22. See Jacques Canneval, 'La Guadeloupe en première ligne', *Autrement. Antilles* 41 (1989): pp. 67–77.

23. Maryse Condé, *Traversée de la Mangrove* (Paris: Mercure de France, 1989).
24. Ibid., 219: 'In the dark, some people drew strange letters on the walls which sounded like alarms. Insulting inscriptions, "De Gaulle, murderer", "Down with colonization" – a new word!'
25. Ibid., 230: 'When Lucien got stuck on his ideological tangents, Carmélien brought him back to earth with a mocking tone. "Open your eyes, my dear! We are already Europeans! Independence is a Sleeping Beauty that no prince will ever wake up any more".'
26. See Dessarre, *Cauchemar Antillais*. See also Georges Trésor, 'Le syndrome européen,' *Etudes Guadeloupéennes* 4 (1991): pp. 82–101.
27. Georges Trésor calls attention to this fact in his article already quoted above and he gives the following explanation: 'Le PIB par habitant en Guadeloupe représente peut-être moins de la moitié de celui de la Métropole, mais il est, et quelque fois de loin, plus élévé que le PIB par habitant de la plupart des pays voisins de la Caraïbe dont les activités de production ne sont pas forcément moins performantes que les nôtres.

'C'est connu, ce sont les aides et les transferts publics en tout genre en provenance de la Métropôle et de l'Europe qui rendent supportable le déficit de notre balance commerciale et nous assurent un niveau de vie relativement élevé. C'est là la raison fondamentale de la réussite non pas économique, mais politique d'un système auquel les Guadeloupéens expriment leur attachement, de manière parfois ostentatoire mais également de manière confuse et indirecte'. Trésor, ibid., p. 86.

'The gross national product per person in Guadeloupe represents maybe less than half of that of the metropolis, but it is higher – and sometimes considerably higher – than the GNP of most of the neighbouring Caribbean countries whose capacities of production are not necessarily less efficient than ours. It is well known that the financial aids and the transferring of public funds coming from the Metropolis and from Europe make the deficit of our commercial balance supportable and they assure the relatively high standard of living. That is the fundamental reason of the – not economic but political – success of this system to which Guadeloupeans affiliate sometimes in an ostentatious, but also in a confused and indirect, manner.'
28. Max Jeanne, *La chasse au Racoon* (Paris: Karthala, 1980).
29. Ibid., p. 26: 'From one day to the next, Bolo had found himself in Algeria as a brute in uniform shooting at "bicots" [North-Africans] and "fellaghas" [partisans] in the name of the people's right of self-determination. Many of his friends who were in the same situation had preferred to change sides and join the Algerians. Others escaped to certain Eastern countries. Bolo stayed in the French army, because of fear, or just because of indecision or again in order not to cause more pain to his notable father. He stayed to learn what he already knew; that the declaration of the human rights didn't concern either the Negro nor the Arab.'
30. This point of view is also present in *Pays Mêlé*.

31. 'Zizique' might be a blend of the words 'musique' and 'zizi', of 'music' and 'prick'.
32. Jeanne, p. 55: 'French flags. Canadian. Swiss. Yankee. Dutch. All are finally united in the same party of debauchery. The colonial squabbles are over. The playing of cops and robbers is over. Don't push! From now on, there's room for everybody. Isn't progress wonderful? The fact that this island may be DOM or DOMINION doesn't disturb anybody. It is essential that it is "nobiscum". Money, everybody knows that, abolishes borders between philanthropists. All currencies are accepted. And ahead, the prick! Long live the carnivalesque chains of whorehouses.'
33. Ibid., p. 53: 'It was rather rare indeed that the construction of schools and hospitals went beyond the laying of the foundation stone by this or that histrionic minister on his way through. It is true that they don't represent the same character of public usefulness as the hotels of Saint-François. After all, the hotels were – above all – useful for the Negroes and the Coolies.'
34. Ibid., p. 55: 'The silly natives don't gain a lot in this affair, but they are very proud to see that their home town occupies a good position in the hit-parade of the most elegant hotels.'
35. See Henri Bangou, *La Guadeloupe*, 173/4.
36. See, for example, 168. The footnote refers to the following testimony: *Le procès des Guadeloupéens. 18 Patriotes devant la Cour de Sûreté de l'Etat français* (CO.GA.SO.D., 1969). See also: Félix Rodes, *Liberté pour la Guadeloupe. 169 jours de prison* (Paris: Editions Témoignages Chrétiens, 1972).
37. Jeanne, p. 136: 'The mercenaries of the superintendent Bamou who needed some practice profited to their heart's content. Finally, a small practice match. Free hand. You have carte blanche, the boss had told them. We are going to shoot all those troublemakers. Pointe-à-Pitre, a pigeon rifle-range. Yeah. Not half-hearted. There's only one method: making a clean sweep.'
38. Ibid., pp. 161–2: 'The beginning was rather negative for the French state which had not managed – in spite of all its efforts in this sense – to suppress, as in many other processes, all the elements which would damage the positive image of France as the self-styled representative of human rights and the right of freedom.
    [...] in this battle of Goliath against David, the situation risked taking a disadvantageous turn for those who had set the scenario. France would turn from the position of the prosecutor to the one of the accused of "volontary domicide".'
39. Raphaël Confiant, *L'Allée des Soupirs* (Paris: Grasset, 1994).
40. See Bangou, p. 158 and Dessarre, p. 76.
41. Confiant, *Soupirs*, p. 36: '[...] on the fourth or fifth day of the armistice, the high-school pupil Janon was shot without warning by the machine gun of a mob of CRS who had gone mad. One could hear a cry for help piercing the dark of the night: "Slavery was abolished in 1848, you mob of iron dogs!"'
42. *Quimboiseur* is a kind of sorcerer.

43. Confiant, *Soupirs*, p. 371: 'I have seen how Grans Z'Ongles [Big Nail], yeah, the expert of malefic herbs faced a mob of CRS who had gone mad and made fun of them. "Where is the source of the 'Seine'", he asked and none of those tough guys could answer. "On the plateau of Langres, you fools! When was Jeanne d'Arc burned alive, huh? In 1431! Ha-Ha-Ha! Look at that, aren't you good Frenchmen? Some real French?"'
44. Ibid., p. 93: 'Consciously or unconsciously, they feel, indeed, that through the problem of integration of Guadeloupe into Europe in 1993, the whole question of how to define their identity in the European community is asked again. Whatever optimistic or pessimistic appreciations the Guadeloupeans do make in respect to eventual economic and social consequences of the integration of our country in the Common Market, their manner of presenting to themselves the advantages and the risks of this integration reflects that they react as members of a community that is different from the French one.'

7 Immigrants in Britain: National Identities and Stereotypes
Susanne Fendler

Images of Europe as a whole have been imposed from the outside and they have been constructed from the inside. However, Europe is not always being presented as a unified front, but rather it falls into regions about which myths have been formed of what is typical of them. Malcolm Bradbury, for example, has investigated the myths of Europe that have been created by Americans, some of which are still influential today. He states that '[t]he Europe [the Americans] imagined was not so much a nation, or even a complex of nations. It was an idea, an opposite, a polar contrast'.[1] Seen from the outside and used as 'the other' to the concept of a unified America, Europe is also being presented as a unity. The Americans offered 'a generalised spirit of "Europe" as one place, to develop in the European imagination'.[2]

Later on he adds:

> Europe was a continent that lacked any fixed or comprehensible borders or limits, a firm eastern perimeter. It had no acknowledged common existence, and no single nation could ever achieve mastery of this continent. Hence Europe was an idea less of peoples than of élites, monarchs and archbishops, theologians and humanists [...].[3]

Washington Irving, in his travel accounts of Europe, sent home accounts of 'quaint regional habits'. 'Each nation Irving visited and "sketched" felt he had somehow done them quite a favour.'[4] For England, Irving contributed towards the 'myth' of the English countryside which looms so large in the tourist and 'heritage' industry. In order to present an unspoilt image Irving ignored the fact that the Industrial Revolution had changed most of the country.[5] However, his images have remained until today and are in fact being cultivated. As one example of how a myth is being perpetuated and/or destroyed I am going to choose that of the English gentleman, presented to perfection, for example, by Richardson in Sir Charles Grandison. Shirley Robin Letwin, in her discussion of the history of the term 'gentleman' up to the nineteenth century, summarizes the qualities of a gentleman as simplicity, courage, courtesy, truthfulness, polish, calmness, collectedness. Additional qualities are naturalness, self-respect and a readiness to stand fast.[6] Looking at this list of characteristics one can understand why the best examples **must be** fictitious.

The two texts which are going to be discussed here present, among other topics, views of the English gentleman. A discussion of the two texts will show how the myths of a nation are being analysed and questioned – from the inside and from the outside.

The two novels I have chosen for discussion offer points for comparison in different ways. Nigel Williams's novel *East of Wimbledon*,[7] is written by an English author and describes an English anti-hero – a degenerate version of the English gentleman. In this novel the main character, Robert Wilson, is confronted with another culture, which Williams describes as as proud of itself as the English culture (used to be), which makes the English appear weak and undetermined, just like their representative in the novel.

In contrast, Kazno Ishiguro's acclaimed novel, *The Remains of the Day*,[8] presents the picture of an English butler, who embodies the idea of an English gentleman to perfection.

Ishiguro's cultural background is characterized by hybridity: born in Japan, he grew up in England from the age of five and never returned until 1989. However, as his parents never intended to stay in England for such a long time they took care to keep him in touch with the Japanese culture. The issue of Ishiguro being placed and raised between two worlds – particularly regarding the question of his European or English identity – is addressed by a Japanese novelist, Kenzaburo. Kenzaburo states that Ishiguro seems to most Japanese to be a Japanese author, as he is described as quiet and peaceful; Kenzaburo, however, assesses him as an English author as he sees him as possessing a tough intelligence.[9] Thus, Ishiguro himself has been a target for the kind of cultural stereotypes that exist and that influence assessment of any author. His ambivalence also becomes obvious when Ishiguro describes himself as homeless. Including himself in this position he argues later on from an English author's point of view that '[t]here is a sense among younger writers in England that England is not an important enough country anymore'.[10] Europe is now, he claims, the larger frame of reference which allows a greater scope for writers from small countries and directs the interest towards larger political issues such as 'the great intellectual battles between liberty and authoritarian regimes'.[11]

On the other hand, for Ishiguro living in Europe means living far away from the main events.[12] Ishiguro obviously holds the position that political and intellectual issues determine the importance of literature, conveying a 'natural authority' on those who come from politically unstable countries, and automatically dismissing those who write from the relative security of western Europe.

In his introduction to the special issue of the *PMLA* on literature and the idea of Europe, Timothy Reiss states that 'much of European culture is caught up as well in imperialism and colonialism, matters that have received far more theoretical attention in recent years than have the internal conflicts'.[13] Thus, Reiss supports Ishiguro's assessment. Matters 'at home', be it Europe generally or the western part of it, are considered to be minor affairs, the great events taking place elsewhere. This emphasizes another aspect the two novels have in common. They both examine what happened to England's concept of herself as an empire once imperialism had declined or was at least waning. Ishiguro's main character, the butler Stevens, also relates the story of Britain's involvement in European politics before World War II, whereas Williams's Robert Wilson takes up the story after nothing has been left of the Empire and Britain finds itself confronted with the nationalism and chauvinism of other cultures being displayed within its own boundaries. However, their interrogation of these views is in the one case bordering on satire (*East of Wimbledon*) and in the other case an almost depressing view of what this nation holds up as one of its representative stereotypes (*The Remains of the Day*).

NIGEL WILLIAMS, *EAST OF WIMBLEDON*

The main character (hero definitely not being the appropriate term) is an unambitious 24-year-old Englishman, who is unable to keep a job and has definite problems when it comes to distinguishing between reality and his own version of it. He is still living with his parents, who believe that somebody will finally discover his talents – even though all of Robert's jobs only ever lead to disasters for his employers (*EW*, p. 22).

The novel starts in the middle of Robert's interview for a job at the 'Islamic Boys' Day Independent School, Wimbledon' (though the name changes several times throughout the novel, shuffling the words around and thereby demonstrating to the reader, if not to Robert, that this school is a doubtful affair).

Robert pretends to have studied classics at Oxford and to have converted to Islam and the novel begins with a discussion of the kind of English literature Robert will have to teach:

> [Malik, the headmaster:] 'You, of course, among your other duties, will be teaching Islamic English literature.'
> Robert nodded keenly [...] 'In that context,' he said, 'do you see Islamic English literature as being literature by English, or Welsh or Scottish Muslims?'
> They both looked at each other in consternation. Perhaps, like him, Mr Malik was unable to think of a single Muslim writer who fitted that description.
> 'Or,' went on Robert, struggling somewhat, 'do you see it as work that has a Muslim dimension? Such as ... *Paradise Lost* for example.'
> What was the Muslim dimension in *Paradise Lost*? Robert became aware that the room had suddenly become very hot.
> 'Or,' he went on swiftly, 'simply English literature viewed from a Muslim perspective?'
> 'You will view English literature from a Muslim perspective,' said Malik with a broad, affable grin, 'because you are a Muslim!'
> 'I am,' said Robert – 'I am indeed!'
> He kept forgetting he was a Muslim. If he was going to last any time at all at the Islamic Independent Boys' Day School Wimbledon, he was going to have to keep a pretty close grip on that fact.
> (*EW*, pp. 3–4)

The English literary canon, especially with *Paradise Lost* as an **English** epic, represents certainly one part of English culture that has been taught (and is being taught) all over the world as part of and affording access to Englishness. National identity is supposed to express itself in literature, as the introductory part on the comments of Kazeburo regarding Ishiguro's cultural background makes clear. Nowadays, the traditional canon especially is under attack from all sides – meaning all those who have been considered as not representing the majority (that is, white, male, English). One way of dealing with the traditional canon is to view it from the 'outside' and this is what Malik, the future headmaster of the school, is taking for granted. The whole concept is ridiculed, however, as Robert tends to overlook the fact that he has introduced himself as a Muslim. Malik proclaims the aim of the new school to be that the pupils are supposed to '"become part of British society and yet to retain their Muslim identity"'. (*EW*, p. 6) To this Robert answers:

> 'I must say,' said Robert, with the unusual conviction that he was speaking the truth, 'that I don't really feel part of British society!' (*EW*, p. 6)

The temptation is great to quote in full the first two chapters as immediately the whole (mild) satire and the problems that are likely to befall Robert become obvious. Not believing in the truth himself, Robert does not recognize how little has yet been planned at this school. For example, being shown around the place, Robert is supposed to imagine the chemistry labs of which there is so far no sign. Consequently, the narrative voice comments: 'This sounded like something out of the *Arabian Nights* – a command for the chemistry labs to appear.' (*EW*, p. 7) Robert is well-suited for this insecure situation as he has no conception of reality, no idea of what is going on in the world, seeing it as one of his achievements that he does not remember who the leader of the Labour Party is (*EW*, p. 4).

The doubtful affair of the school is one plotline of Robert's story, the second line is introduced in the next chapter when he is being approached by two men whom Robert terms as Yasser Arafat and Saddam Hussein, the men with and without, respectively, tea towel on their heads (*EW*, p. 18). The two men threaten Robert and everybody else connected with this school that they will die and 'burn in hell-fire when the day comes'. (*EW*, p. 21) For a long time Robert is left entirely in the dark as to what all this is about. Everybody whom he tries to ask about these occurrences treats his lack of knowledge as a joke. All the answers he gets mystify him (and the reader) even more. Robert is being followed by people who only wear one proper shoe; he is told about the Wimbledon Dharjees, the Occultation of the Nizari Ismailis but nobody ever explains what all this is about – and obviously to this part of society, of which Robert becomes a part when he claims to be a Muslim, the names and events are well-known and they expect **everybody** simply to know.[14] Slowly, Robert (and the reader) gathers that a blind boy, Hasan, who is placed in Robert's care, is considered to be a descendant of Hasan, the second Imam, and may finally succeed his ancestor ('return with hell fire', *EW*, p. 172) on a certain day. How little Robert understands what is going on around him is shown when he reflects:

> If he had had any decency he would have talked to Mr Malik about what was going to happen. He would have warned him. He was the only one to know that today was the day when Hasan was going to wreak his revenge. (*EW*, p. 168)

But of course, all but Robert know what is going on. This rather weird story about Islamic fundamentalism provides the interest and 'the action' of the novel.

With the exaggerated story Williams stresses how little the representatives of the two cultures understand each other. Robert is a weak version of the English gentleman, at least in some respects. He is ever polite, tries to do his best, tries to be gallant – and ends up being caught up in a catastrophe the one time he is honest. His pupils regard Robert as 'an exotic form of entertainment' (*EW*, p. 67). Robert constantly tries to show his familiarity with Islam. Having only read *Morals and Manners in Islam*, however, he comes up with rather weird rules which nobody around him cares about, his pupils belonging to 'the latest recruits to the mysterious section of English society known as the lower upper middle class' (*EW*, p. 67). They are being sent there to 'grow up English' (*EW*, p. 68). So, in fact, Robert, trying to fit his own view of what Islam is about and unable to fit into his own society, is the odd one out.

In contrast, the organizer of the school, Mr Malik, is suave and visionary. He is also involved in dubious businesses but he always remains in control. Malik emphasizes that modern Islam is tolerant.[15] Describing Malik to his parents Robert states: '"I'm not sure what he is [...] He's not English, that's for sure." Except that there was something quite incredibly English about Malik.' (*EW*, p. 32)

The difference between the English culture – at least as Williams presents it – and the immigrants' hold on their culture is given voice when Robert demands to know: 'Why do you all think you're right? [...] What makes you so certain?' (*EW*, p. 210) This is Robert's problem. He does not know what the truth is, his inability ever to tell the truth being a symptom of that. This other culture and Islam appeal to him because Muslims seem to him to have convictions which he completely lacks.

Being asked what makes them so certain about their convictions Malik answers.

Mr Malik begged for silence, and got it. He appealed to Robert Wilson as an English gentleman. He appealed to his sense of honour and fair play. He mentioned the British royal family and the ancient universities of Oxford and Cambridge, to which, he reminded him, he belonged, and he spoke, movingly, of the game of cricket. 'Try and play a straight bat, Wilson!' he said.
Robert said he was not an English gentleman and he was incapable of playing a straight bat. [...]
He went on to talk about Wimbledon. He put forward the view that almost everyone in Wimbledon was, like him, completely lacking in convictions, principles or indeed anything that makes human beings tolerable. (*EW*, pp. 210–11)

Mr Malik refers Robert to the idea of the English gentleman – having himself rather more of a resemblance to one than Robert. The royal family, Oxbridge, cricket and the ideal of the gentleman are icons of Englishness. But Robert rejects them all, for himself and for his neighbourhood. Not knowing, not being sure is to him the new essence of the English culture. In fact, though presented in this sarcastic way, Williams thus holds up for inspection a widely held (postmodern) idea – that nothing is certain and nothing concrete exists which one can hold on to. This, we have been told by Lyotard among others, is the sign of a post-modern, post-industrial, post-colonial society; whereas the ability to hold (in comparison) simple beliefs and follow them without questioning is the due of a pre-modern society.

Williams presents England as run-down, uncertain and unsure of its value. He has chosen a particularly incompetent representative, as the final comment emphasizes:

> Robert Wilson recovered from his encounter with the lorry [...].
> He has a set of symptoms – listlessness, lack of interest in the world, and a tendency to sleep more than twelve to fifteen hours out of the twenty-four – that make him unfit for any kind of regular employment, but at least now he has a doctor's note to explain the fact to the authorities. (*EW*, p. 215)

Another example of incompetence is Robert's parents who blindly believed in their son in spite of his obvious incompetence. Wilson senior is shown to suffer from a cultural shock, just by being confronted with Islam inside his own house. In the beginning he had been portrayed as a liberal, asking his son to address him by his first name and dismissing qualifications (*EW*, pp. 22–3). But as the narrator points out:

> A lot of Mr Wilson senior's liberal attitudes had not stood the test of having two converted Muslims living in the house. He was often to be found slumped in front of the television, muttering about nig-nogs. At Christmas he had insisted on hanging up Robert's stocking on the end of his bed, and had suggested the two of them visit the Cranborne school carol service. (*EW*, p. 128)

Being confronted with a different culture Wilson senior reverts to icons of Englishness and Christianity. Mrs Wilson takes a different approach and reverts to praying after meals:

> It was not clear whether this remark was addressed to Allah, Jehovah or the London Muffin Company. She had taken, this spring, to a sort of generalized reverence that looked as if it was planned to accommodate any new religion to which her son or his girl-friend might have become attached. (*EW*, p. 128)

Some of the Muslim characters are ridiculed (such as those with only one proper shoe and the other teachers, one of whom sentences Robert to death). But this group also includes the positive examples such as Malik, or a Mr Shah who resembles, as Robert thinks, the Duke of Edinburgh, and one of his pupils, Sheikh, who goes to Oxford at the age of 15.

Robert is introduced by Malik as 'the future – the first sign that British society is going to throw off the shackles of racism and colonialism and produce something genuinely multicultural, like ... er ... him!' (*EW*, p. 112) Only this 'er', the hesitation and his remark that Robert 'is, although this may seem incredible, the kind of man who used to rule the world' (*EW*, p. 112) are hints that Robert might not be as positive an example. To the reader, however, the irony of the narrator at least is clear. Malik seems to see Robert as the ideal version of the English gentleman, but he does not truly seem to see him as what he is: an incompetent figure and a fraud. Thus, both sides seem to admire each other, but in fact they do not see each other as individuals but as embodiments of the other culture. Robert naively admires what he believes to have understood about Islam and Malik obviously admires some features of Englishness, but he also sees Britain as 'a melting pot' (*EW*, p. 190). Robert sees Malik as a 'strong man, and his word – like the Prophet's – was law.' Malik can convince people and he is the one who presents to others the 'truth'. 'Truth [...] is whatever is confidently asserted and plausibly maintained', (*EW*, p. 201) which underlines the view of the postmodern society. In the comparison invited between the English (mostly ridiculous types) and the Muslims the Muslims win – win the narrator's and the reader's support and a possible future. In what seems to be Robert's one moment of truth and clairvoyance he makes a speech on the danger of too much tolerance and the insignificance of Britain:

> 'Oh, then that's fine, isn't it?' said Robert. 'I'll swap you the Garden of Gethsemane for the Night of Power, you know? You'll let us believe something clearly insane, and we can allow you to do the same.'
> [...]
> 'I'm nothing,' he said. 'Don't you understand? England is full of people who are nothing. You're living in a country that doesn't exist. A country where people go to church, and try and help their neighbours, and bicycle to work down country lanes, and believe in....' Here he brandished the armour and its painted cross in the faces of the crowd. '... all this!'
> [...]
> What finally broke him was the realization that here was yet another person who, like his parents, thought him a stronger, nobler person than he actually was. Why did the world assume that you must be interested in any kind of truth, let alone the fundamental variety? Why did people always want you to have aspirations?
> 'England,' went on Robert, 'is no longer anything to *do* with the country that carved up India or shipped out whole generations of Africans as slaves. It's a squalid little place, full of people who don't believe in anything.' (*EW*, pp. 204–5)

Accepting his own emptiness, Robert here for once appears as a serious person. In this moment he actually denounces both sides: Malik because he did not recognize the truth about Robert and is taken in by his admiration of England, and England as a now empty and unimportant place. He denounces the necessity to hold opinions because neither side takes its religion seriously, but at the same time he claims that nobody does hold an opinion in this society, thus pointing at his own dilemma. In the end, he is 'saved' because the accident allows him to show his flaws openly. The message is not clear, however. Neither side is completely sympathetic or engaging and the reader is left alone to puzzle out Robert's dilemma.

The influence stereotypes have on our ability to judge and assess each other is clearly presented. Malik 'has fallen' for the ideal of the English gentleman and is unable to meet Robert on his own terms, or England herself for that matter. England is in the clutches of postmodernism, post-colonialism and probably post-industrialism, and all those 'post-isms' indicate that nobody knows what is going to happen next. From the 'outside', though within the country, England still seems to hold some of its former glamour and importance – represented in the icons of Englishness. But from the 'inside' those stereotypes are perceived as empty and old-fashioned.

KAZUO ISHIGURO, *THE REMAINS OF THE DAY*

In contrast to Williams's novel, Ishiguro's received some critical attention, and assessments range from seeing it as 'the funniest new novel I've read in ages'[16] to a novel on the myth of the English butler which is being destroyed.[17] Caroline Patey starts her article with the following words:

> One of Ishiguro's press-favoured personae is the Japanese-writer-more-English-than-the-English; one of the current clichés about his highly acclaimed third novel, *The Remains of the Day*, is the English-butler-more-English-butler-than-any-English-butler. The reviewers' opinion, of course, is never completely unfounded, and there is undoubtedly a certain amount of 'Englishness' in various features of the book, such as its main character's extreme verbal and emotional restraint as well as many a moment of cold humour. But stereotypes are never entirely satisfying and one is often tempted to question them (and run the risk of elaborating counter-clichés!) [...].[18]

Reviewers and critics, however, are divided in their opinion whether *The Remains of the Day* is a novel *about* Englishness, working *with* a concept of Englishness or *destroying* the concept while looking at it from the outside. Ishiguro comments on this point:

> I think it's almost impossible now to write a kind of traditional British novel without being aware of the various ironies. The kind of England that I create in *The Remains of the Day* is not an England that I believe ever existed. [...] it is used as a political tool [...].[19]

Here, Ishiguro is arguing along the same lines as Bradbury. He takes up the myth and holds it up for inspection. Though Ishiguro claims that he is not interested in 'saying things about specific societies'[20] I will nevertheless take up the question of how he deals with this particular myth.

Williams approached the myth of the perfect English gentleman-like behaviour from the ironical side and in addition transferred these qualities to the immigrant Malik. Ishiguro in contrast presents us with a 'real English butler'. As Mr Farraday, the new American owner of Darlington Hall, demands to know and have confirmed:

> 'I mean to say, Stevens, this *is* a genuine grand old English house, isn't it? That's what I paid for. And you're a genuine old-fashioned English butler, not just some waiter pretending to be one. You're the real thing, aren't you? That's what I wanted, isn't that what I have?' (*RD*, p. 124)

Stevens, the butler, answers in the affirmative.

The Americans are looking for Englishness, in two cases (in this novel) buying great houses as they are interested in English traditions – or what they think they are. The narrator, Stevens, conveys what the 'outsiders', the Americans, think of Britain: namely that grand old houses and butlers are genuinely English and Stevens himself shows no doubt that he is in fact this 'genuine article'. Another incident takes place when another American, Mr Lewis, takes part in the secret conference at Darlington Hall, which is held to discuss the treatment of Germany. Mr Lewis criticizes English values when he criticizes the 'English gentleman'. Lewis points out that a gentleman is an amateur meddling in affairs which are none of his business. He sees this as a particularly European problem:

> 'He [that is, Lord Darlington, Stevens's former employer] is a gentleman. No one here, I trust, would care to disagree. A classic English gentleman. Decent, honest, well-meaning. But his lordship here is *an amateur.*' [...] 'He is an amateur and international affairs today are no longer for gentlemen amateurs. The sooner you here in Europe realize that the better. All you decent, well-meaning gentlemen, let me ask you, have you any idea what sort of place the world is becoming all around you? The days when you could act out of your noble instincts are over. Except of course, you here in Europe don't yet seem to know it.' (*RD*, p. 102)

At this point the narrator, Stevens, who tells us all this whilst driving through the West Country incidentally, as it turns out, taking account of his life, places this comment in such a context that the reader is invited to look down upon the rudeness of this Mr Lewis, who has been established as a mean, scheming character. Towards the end, however, when Stevens begins to doubt Lord Darlington's achievements and acts, the same argument is repeated by the son of one of Lord Darlington's friends:

> 'His lordship is a gentleman. That's what's at the root of it. He's a gentleman, and he fought a war with the Germans, and it's his instinct to offer generosity and friendship to a defeated foe. It's his instinct. Because he's a gentleman, a true old English gentleman. And you must have seen it, Stevens. How could you not have seen it? The way they've used it, manipulated it, turned something fine and noble into something else – something they can use for their own foul ends? You must have seen it, Stevens.' (*RD*, p. 223)

That, however, is in fact the point (and the tragedy) of the narrative. Stevens did not see it. Having been taken in by his ideal of the English butler ('The Gentleman's Gentleman' is the title of the professional journal) he mistakes what the ideal of the English gentleman is all about. Let us return, however, to this conference and the other guests' reaction to Mr Lewis's statement.

Lord Darlington equates professionalism with cheating and manipulating (*RD*, p. 103), and Mr Lewis and Lord Darlington have indeed the ideal of the gentleman in mind as it is also drawn by Letwin. A gentleman is exactly a gentleman because he is no professional. Any professionalism is contradictory to this idea.[21] Originally, a gentleman does not have to follow any kind of profession to make his living. Any tasks a gentleman takes on he assumes because he wants to do something for the sake of others. The narrator's allegiance is at this point still clear. The reader is drawn into the narrative and is expected to feel as upset and as disapproving about this rude behaviour as are all the Europeans present.[22] Mr Lewis has been discredited by his own behaviour which Stevens happened to witness more than once. The French guest, M. Dupont, also criticizes Mr Lewis's behaviour. He mentions his 'most clumsy technique, the audacity and crudeness' (*RD*, p. 101). Mr Lewis is dismissed further as the narrator notes that Mr Lewis is apparently drunk (*RD*, p. 102).

The Americans are thus contrasted with the Europeans in general, and the English more specifically. Mr Lewis represents the negative side, no honour and no manners. Mr Farraday represents a more positive side, easy-going, considerate and fond of 'bantering' as Stevens calls it. In contrast, the Europeans have good manners, even if former enemies are together in one house, and honour, as Darlington tells Mr Lewis (*RD*, p. 103). This honour and the good behaviour due between gentlemen are also what motivate Lord Darlington's involvement in politics:

> 'He was my enemy,' he was saying, 'but he always behaved like a gentleman. We treated each other decently over six months of shelling each other. He was a gentleman doing his job and I bore him no malice. I said to him: "Look here, we're enemies now and I'll fight you with all I've got. But when this wretched business is over, we shan't have to be enemies any more and we'll have a drink together." Wretched thing is, this treaty is making a liar out of me. I mean to say, I told him we wouldn't be enemies once it was all over. But how can I look him in the face and tell him that's turned out to be true?' (*RD*, p. 73)

This German friend Lord Darlington refers to later commits suicide and this is Lord Darlington's true motivation for his involvement in politics, as Stevens tells us to defend him (*RD*, p. 73). His honour and 'a desire to see "justice in this world" lay at the heart of all his actions'. (*RD*, p. 73)

In one of the first discussions preceeding the conference, Mr Lewis explains that Americans are puzzled by the different reactions of the French and the English to the Germans. Although both have lost a lot in the war, the French hate the Germans but the English do not (*RD*, p. 87). Mr Lewis puts it down to temperamental differences, but for Lord Darlington it comes down to a question of honour and civilization:

> '[...] I venture we are talking about something rather more. It is unbecoming to go on hating an enemy like this once a conflict is over. Once you've got a man on the canvas, that ought to be the end of it. You don't then proceed to kick him. To us, the French behaviour has become increasingly barbarous.' (*RD*, p. 87)

Similarly, to Stevens the key terms are dignity (*RD*, p. 42) and duty. His particular misunderstanding about the role of the 'gentleman's gentleman' is that to fit the ideal he has to efface his own individuality, for a butler should never allow himself to be 'off duty' in the presence of others. [...] A butler of any quality must be seen to *inhabit* his role, utterly and fully; he cannot be seen casting it aside one moment simply to don it again the next as though it were nothing more than a pantomime costume. (*RD*, p. 169)

Only alone can he be 'himself' – but Stevens does not realize that a sense of oneself needs an 'other' against which to establish the self. He, therefore, gives up his individuality and his personal needs and defines this as his professional abilities. To him this is essentially English. Stevens sees those qualities which make a good butler as inherent only in the English:

It is sometimes said that butlers only truly exist in England. Other countries, whatever title is actually used, have only manservants. I tend to believe this is true. Continentals are unable to be butlers because they are as a breed incapable of the emotional restraint which only the English race are capable of. Continentals – and by and large the Celts, as you will no doubt agree – are as a rule unable to control themselves in moments of strong emotion, and are thus unable to maintain a professional demeanour other than in the least challenging of situations. If I may return to my earlier metaphor – you will excuse my putting it so coarsely – they are like a man who will, at the slightest provocation, tear off his suit and his shirt and run about screaming. In a word, 'dignity' is beyond such persons. We English have an important advantage over foreigners in this respect and it is for this reason that when you think of a great butler, he is bound, almost by definition, to be an Englishman. (*RD*, p. 43)

To Stevens, national stereotypes are not stereotypes but a question of race. One stereotype he employs here is that of the Celts who were used in the nineteenth century as 'the other' against which Englishness was defined – for example, by Matthew Arnold. Stevens repeats old arguments that were used for self-definition such as rationality (English) against emotionalism (Celts) and focuses them on his own position, without ever showing a hint that he is aware of the way he is using these stereotypes. Like his employer Lord Darlington, Stevens is taken in by the code of the gentleman. For Stevens the key term is 'dignity', but the examples Stevens gives of dignity may also be interpreted as lack of emotion. Stevens remembers a story, for example, about a butler in India who does not show any emotional reactions when he discovers a tiger in the dining room but he merely announces a delay and shoots it. In this example we cannot necessarily attribute the behaviour to a repression of emotions in any negative sense. However, this kind of story about typically English behaviour abroad, namely keeping one's nerve while everybody else panics has been connected with images of creating an empire. The English are fit to rule, the implication is, because they are emotionally suited to it, whereas other more emotional 'races' (Celts and Indians, for example) are not.

The episode that Stevens presents as his own triumph (*RD*, p. 110) clearly shows a repression of feelings. On the evening of the conference already mentioned Stevens's father dies, but Stevens goes on about his duties as usual. Similarly, he hides behind his façade as a butler when Miss Kenton obviously tries to attract him and when she finally gives up and accepts somebody else's offer of marriage. In this context David Gurewich comments that 'once you take his professionalism, his *dignity*, out of the picture, not much is left'.[23] A great butler is to Stevens someone who is 'attached to a distinguished household' (*RD*, p. 113), distinguished not in terms of rank and social station but in terms of 'utility' for 'the progress of humanity' (*RD*, p. 114). Stevens sees his generation as more idealistic (*RD*, p. 114) than former generations. His life, he explains, has been well spent in serving someone who works for the benefit of all people. So far the narrator displays no doubts. However, when it becomes obvious that this demands a complete self-effacement, the terms seem to be dubious. Even more doubts arise when it becomes clear that Stevens withholds all judgement. When Lord Darlington is taken in by the Nazis and dismisses two German Jewish servants, Miss Kenton threatens to leave, but later admits that she stayed out of cowardice, because she had nowhere to go (*RD*, p. 152). On the same occasion, Stevens merely obeys orders and when challenged on this point by Miss Kenton later on he claims that '[n]aturally, one disapproved of the dismissals. One would have thought that quite self-evident.' (*RD*, p. 154)[24] Stevens's whole behaviour in this episode makes it obvious that this was not the case, however, neither in the original episode nor now when he is being challenged.

Stevens gives up his feelings, his private life and his own views for his idea of the perfect butler. He allows himself to be shown off in a discussion among Lord Darlington's guests as a representative of common people, who in a democracy should voice their own opinions but cannot have any, so the argument goes (*RD*, p. 199). Lord Darlington suits Stevens for he also longs for a strong leadership and envies Italy and Germany for their authoritarian regimes (*RD*, pp. 198–9). Stevens defends his views, remembering those episodes, and repeats for the sake of the reader that 'such as you and I' (*RD*, p. 199) cannot understand enough about the world to be allowed to interfere. If the employer represents all that is worthy then the butler should stop formulating his own ideas (*RD*, p. 200). Thus, Stevens justifies his own life, but the doubts shine through when he writes:

> How can one possibly be held to blame in any sense because, say, the passage of time has shown that Lord Darlington's efforts were misguided, even foolish? Throughout the years I served him, it was he and he alone who weighed up evidence and judged it best to proceed in the way he did, while I simply confined myself, quite properly, to affairs within my own professional realm. And as far as I am concerned, I carried out my duties to the best of my abilities, indeed to a standard which many may consider 'first rate'. It is hardly my fault if his lordship's life and work have turned out today to look, at best, a sad waste – and it is quite illogical that I should feel any regret or shame on my own account. (*RD*, p. 201)

These justifications of his life and recollections show him getting more doubts the more he encounters 'normal' people on his journey through the West Country. Again he denies having had anything to do with Darlington Hall and its disreputable history. And then he encounters somebody who defines dignity in quite different terms. Dignity in this definition is also a mark of the 'true gentleman' (*RD*, p. 185) and this man claims that '[d]ignity's something every man and woman in this country can strive for and get'. (*RD*, p. 186)

And he continues:

> 'That's what we fought Hitler for, after all. If Hitler had had things his way, we'd just be slaves now. The whole world would be a few masters and millions upon millions of slaves. And I don't need to remind anyone here, there's no dignity to be had in being a slave. That's what we fought for and that's what we won. We won the right to be free citizens. And it's one of the privileges of being born English that no matter who you are, no matter if you're rich or poor, you're born free and you're born

so that you can express your opinion freely, and vote in your member of parliament or vote him out. That's what dignity's really about, if you'll excuse me, sir.' (*RD*, p. 186)

The speaker also relates this to 'being born English'. A different tradition of Englishness, therefore, is introduced here. Stevens refutes this point, however, until his doubts surface at the end of his journey and he almost admits that he has chosen wrongly. His interview with Miss Kenton had taken place, and having been told that she considered a life with him Stevens realizes:

> [...] as you might appreciate, their implications [that is, her confessions] were such as to provoke a certain degree of sorrow within me. Indeed – why should I not admit it? – at that moment, my heart was breaking. (*RD*, p. 239)

To a complete stranger he later admits that '[...] I gave my best to Lord Darlington. I gave him the very best I had to give, and now – well – I find I do not have a great deal more left to give.' (*RD*, p. 242) He continues his self-justification:

> 'Lord Darlington wasn't a bad man [...] at all. And at least he had the privilege of being able to say at the end of his life that he made his own mistakes. His lordship was a courageous man. He chose a certain path in life, it proved to be a misguided one, but there, he chose it, he can say that at least. As for myself, I cannot even claim that. You see, I *trusted*. I trusted in his lordship's wisdom. All those years I served him, I trusted I was doing something worthwhile. I can't even say I made my own mistakes. Really – one has to ask oneself – what dignity is there in that?' (*RD*, p. 243)

Still in a tragically understated style Stevens allows the reader a glimpse of his feeling that he has failed in his life. His further plans include only that he may adopt bantering, 'particularly if it is the case that in bantering lies the key to human warmth.' (*RD*, p. 245) However, he still regards this as a duty.

Stevens turns out to be a sad imitation of the English butler and those elements of Englishness that he represents. Having mistaken the ideal and reduced himself to fit it he has wasted most of his life.

Looking at the ideal from a distance, Ishiguro presents us with a view of what can happen if you lead your life in accordance with a particular role-model. It is also clear that Stevens misunderstood some of the elements. However, the misunderstandings are inherent in the model. The myth turns out to be a restriction, such as it is for the Americans in the novel, who demand the 'real thing', which is in fact the myth as conveyed to them by Irving.

The novel may thus be 'only' about England on one level. On another level it is more generally about the restrictions people (as individuals and as nations) impose on themselves and on others by dealing with each other in terms of stereotypes.

Though looking on the situation from 'inside England' Williams demonstrates the same point. An understanding is not possible if you are not ready to look beyond your own range and your own picture of the world. 'The other' is necessary to define yourself against. Thereby you restrict the 'other' but also yourself. In different ways Williams and Ishiguro have demonstrated this with the example of the concept of 'the English'. Both authors show the limitations which are inherent in stereotypes. Williams focuses on the effect stereotypes have on the understanding between people belonging to different nationalities. Though the contrast is European and extra-European this can be applied to all international relations, on a personal as well as on a political level. In contrast, Ishiguro displays the effects stereotypes and myths can have on one's self-perception. In both cases they are highly restrictive, not leaving any room for true understanding – of each other or of oneself. Thus, while stereotypes and myths are necessary to create a sense of a nation, of a common identity, they also incorporate the danger of hindering further development.

Ishiguro pointed out that nowadays important events take place elsewhere. In this case, however, England and Englishness can stand for any nation and any nation's mythical self-image. Neither of them specifically addresses the idea of Europe. However, especially within Europe, several of these self-images clash. Added to this is the myth of Europe as a whole – as the 'cradle of Western Civilization'. Though barely hinting at a wider perspective, both demonstrate the problems that have arisen and will continue to do so.

NOTES

1. Malcolm Bradbury, *Dangerous Pilgrimages: Trans-Atlantic Mythologies and the Novel* (London: Penguin, 1995), p. 7.
2. Bradbury, p. 475.
3. Bradbury, p. 476.
4. Bradbury, p. 475.
5. Bradbury, pp. 66–7.
6. Shirley Robin Letwin, *The Gentleman in Trollope: Individuality and Moral Conduct* (London: Macmillan, 1982), pp. 16–19.
7. I use the edition published by Faber, London, 1993. After quotations the novel is referred to as *EW*, followed by the page number.
8. I use the edition published by Faber, London, 1989. After quotations the novel is referred to as *RD*, followed by the page number.
9. See Kazuo Ishiguro and Oe Kenzaburo, 'The Novelist in Today's World: a Conversation', *Boundary* 18.3 (1991): pp. 109–122.
10. Ishiguro/Kenzaburo, p. 119.
11. Ishiguro/Kenzaburo, p. 120.
12. Ishiguro/Kenzaburo, p. 121.
13. Timothy J. Reiss, 'Introduction: Literature and the Idea of Europe', *PMLA* 108.1 (1993): pp. 14–29, here p. 18.
14. See for example *EW*, pp. 82–3.
15. For example *EW*, p. 210.
16. *The Guardian*, as quoted on the back of the paperback edition.
17. Anne Luyat, 'Myth and Metafiction: Is Peaceful Co-Existence Possible? Destruction of the Myth of the English Butler in Kazuo Ishiguro's *The Remains of the Day*,' *Historicité et Métafiction dans le roman contemporain des iles britanniques*, ed. Max Duperray (Aix-en-Provence: Université de Provence, 1994), pp. 183–96.
18. Caroline Patey, 'When Ishiguro Visits the West Country', *Acme* 44.2 (1991): pp. 135–55, here p. 135.
19. Kazuo Ishiguro/Allan Vorda (Interview with Kazuo Ishiguro), *Face to Face: Interviews with Contemporary Novelists*, ed. Allan Vorda (Houston: Rice University Press, 1993), pp. 3–35, here pp. 14–15.
20. Ishiguro/Vorda, p. 16.
21. At least on this social level. It is slightly different of course from Stevens's point of view. On the other hand, he takes pride in that part of his profession that imitates the idea of the gentleman and sees this as going beyond the mere professional demands as we will see further down.
22. On the reliability of Stevens as narrator see Kathleen Wall's '*The Remains of the Day* and its Challenges to Theories of Unreliable Narration', *The Journal of Narrative Technique* 24.1 (1994): pp. 18–42.
23. David Gurewich, 'Upstairs, Downstairs', *The New Criterion* 8.4 (1989): pp. 77–80, here p. 78.
24. For a detailed discussion of this point, see Wall.

8 A Never Closer Union? The Idea of the European Union in Selected Works of Malcolm Bradbury
Paul G. Nixon

This essay examines selected works of Malcolm Bradbury which incorporate representations of the European Community (EC) or the European Union (EU), as it is now known. The works that form the basis of this analysis are primarily two 'television novels', *The Gravy Train*[1] and *The Gravy Train Goes East*,[2] produced by Portman Productions, London, for Channel 4 Television in 1990 and 1991 respectively. Supplementary references are also made to two of Bradbury's books. One is a novel, *Rates of Exchange*[3] and the other, *Why Come to Slaka?*[4], a fictional guidebook to the land of Slaka created in *Rates of Exchange* and which resurfaces as the prime location for *The Gravy Train Goes East*.

Slaka is a fictitious state somewhere in eastern Europe where real socialism is said to exist.[5] Slaka, as Bradbury explains, is 'a land of noble achievements' (*Slaka*, p. 9) and is

> [k]nown in all the history books as the bloody battlefield of central and eastern Europe. [...] it is a land that has frequently flourished, prospered, been a centre of trade and barter, art and culture, but has yet more frequently been pummelled, fought over, raped, pillaged, conquered and oppressed by the endless invaders who, from every direction, have swept and jostled through this all too accessible landscape [...] almost every tribe or race specialist in pillage and rape, have been here, as to some necessary destination, and left behind their imprint, their customs, their faiths, their architecture, their genes. This is a country that has been now big, now small, now virtually non-existent. Its inhabitants have seen its borders expand, contract and on occasion disappear from sight, and so confused is its past that the country could

now be in a place quite different from that in which it started. (*Exchange*, pp. 1–2)

The decision to examine Bradbury's television work in greater depth than his books may irritate traditionalists but it is an exciting opportunity to discuss the way in which Bradbury's work, acclaimed in the literary field, transfers to the small screen. It is this difference that, coupled with the dearth of critical comment concerning these particular elements of his work, makes it of such interest, thus facilitating an examination of the way in which Bradbury has been able to adapt to a different medium with its immediacy and wider popular audience, its unforgivingly focused lens which – when combined with that immediacy – negates the ability to interact in stages but both demands and needs the viewer's full attention. Bradbury has found television to be not only an interesting medium with which to collaborate, whilst making money in the process presumably, but also an intriguing enough subject for a book.[6]

Whilst some may argue the Reithian line that 'broadcasting is in no sense to be regarded as a substitute for the reading of good books or the study of good music',[7] as Richard Hoggart notes, 'it can be argued that some of what people now see on television is better nourishment than most of the reading that they are presumed to have discarded'.[8] Unfortunately, there is no space here for a modernist/postmodernist spat about the notion of cultural orthodoxy and the hegemony of traditional values as 'high art'. Such a philosophical balloon full of hot air has, for the purposes of this work at least, been well and truly pricked. Intertextuality exists and any interpretation must be fluid. Quattro Stagioni could be Vivaldi or pizza, each is of equal merit depending upon the situation.

In the broadest sense Bradbury's work, to date, has been based upon the examination of 'the problems of liberalism, humanism and moral responsibility in the later 20th century world'.[9] What has this to do with the EU? As we shall see below, Bradbury, whilst in one sense shoring up and accepting the popular prejudices of the Euro-myths (rampant bureaucracy, large and complex frauds, faceless government by dictat or directive), injects characters into the scenario who illustrate human weakness (both their own and that of others) and who hope to sweep away such indifference to their fellow man and reorientate the organization towards humanistic liberal values.

The Gravy Train and *The Gravy Train Goes East* both reflect and ridicule English interactions within the European Union and the wider Europe. It is upon this quintessentially stereotypical English (not British) view of Europe that Bradbury's works are based. The stereotypes portrayed reflect those held by the English to be true and whilst some of them may be shared by other nations, particularly those relating to the English themselves, they are most specifically an English view. As Sheridan Morley commented in a review of *The Gravy Train*: 'It manages to make of the Common Market an even greater satire than has already been achieved by its own functionaries.'[10]

Nicholas Fraser, in a recent book review,[11] argued that

> books about Europe fall into two categories: the plumber's manual, filled with meaningless diagrams purporting to explain recent refinements of the Brussels bureaucracy, and the slender essay, usually the work of a French savant, in which the progress of the European idea, or lack of it, is elegantly adumbrated.

This classification poses a few problems for the committed scholar of the EU or what Bradbury terms 'the Bloody Belgium Empire'.[12] First, that of definition: the English, whoever they may turn out to be, have long had difficulty separating the notion of Europe from that of the EC or the EU.

The generalized English ambivalence to the EU appears to stem from the archetypal English view of their inherent superiority over foreigners and all things foreign, an unquestioning belief in monarch and country (no need to ask which monarch, which country, for the English there can be only one) as being the defining gift of God to the English nation (or is it the reverse?). This confers a status and consequential arrogance on the land and its inhabitants which is perhaps best displayed by recourse to that oft-quoted newspaper headline: 'Fog in Channel. Continent Cut Off.' The insularity that this viewpoint exemplifies still exists amongst many of the English. For them, an affection for 'Europe' or 'matters European' equates to, at best, stupidity and a misunderstanding of one's special place in the hierarchy of the world's population or, at worst, outright treason.

Secondly, whilst one could dispute whether text books on the EU really are a 'plumber's manual' or an attempt, admittedly often a failed one, to demystify the workings of a labyrinthine governmental and multi-functional organization, Fraser neglects to mention a third type of book/narrative, that of the fictional representation of Europe in general and the EU in particular which is the focus of this study.

This could lead on to the question of what indeed the EU actually is, but that topic requires a much greater effort of analysis and explanation than can be attempted in this short space and is the matter of some debate amongst academics and political commentators. Suffice to say that the architectural composition of the institutions of the EU can be, broadly, agreed upon although it may be subject to sporadic revision. It is the direction, the goals and the aspirations of the EU, as a vibrant and changing political entity, that cause problems. Just as there are many readings of 'Europe', there are differing interpretations of the EU, what it is and what it should become. This is evidenced in the various discussions at the recent Intergovernmental Conference, concluded at Amsterdam, where there were deliberations upon issues such as economic and monetary union, trying to eradicate the democratic deficit and widening the union. This widening would be achieved by admitting central and eastern European countries that have only recently emerged from communist control. All of these issues have implications in a wider sense for the future structure and operation of the EU. The examples of Bradbury's work that form the subject of this chapter, amongst the other sub-plots and literary devices, use humour as a means of investigation, in order to try to address some of the issues of import in the modern EU and the moral debates (or the lack of such debate) behind them. This is particularly the case in *The Gravy Train Goes East*. Let us now examine them in more detail.

THE GRAVY TRAIN

The Gravy Train is constructed around the experiences of an initially innocent German, Hans-Joachim Dorfmann, first seen boarding a train at the typical small German town of Bad Zweikirchen.[13] Perhaps this may be interpreted as a reference to Bradbury's own upbringing, and the experiences that may well have conditioned his writing, to the time that Bradbury spent with his grandparents, as a war-time refugee, in Macclesfield, a small northern English town best known for its silk-weaving industry.[14] Dorfmann arrives in Brussels to take up a junior position in the Directorate of Information and Culture: Sub-Section, Books. Right from the start Bradbury's narrative focuses on the problems facing Dorfmann and, perhaps on a wider scale, the EU itself. In the car, on the way to Berleymont from the station, his idealism receives its first blow. On telling his driver, Gustav, that 'I would like to make the world a better place. The market is better than a European war'[15] he elicits the immediate somewhat world-weary reply from the seasoned old campaigner 'Monsieur, it [the market] is a European war.'[16] The internecine warring of member states is demonstrated as being nonetheless vicious in the very institution that was originally designed to offer an end to conflict in Western Europe. Conflicts still erupt between member states over issues such as trade or economic development. Ever-shifting policy coalitions ebb and flow as compromises are thrashed out. The EU is occasionally criticized for its decision-making processes which often produce outcomes based on the lowest common denominator, although the former Yugoslavia acts as a telling reminder of the alternatives. The EU has not yet managed to break down the barriers of nationalism, as envisaged by one of its founding fathers, Jean Monnet. What it has done, most successfully, is to shift the conflict to another potentially less damaging arena. Member states' differences are settled at the conference table or more likely in private meeting rooms, not on the battlefield.

From the moment Dorfmann arrives at the Berleymont building in Brussels, there are problems of entry. Arriving without the correct credentials he is denied entry by the staff. This could well be viewed as a metaphor for the problems that the former communist states of central and eastern Europe face in their attempts to join the club that is the modern EU.[17] This theme is dealt with more fully below in the discussion on *The Gravy Train Goes East*. Bradbury also immediately emphasizes the linguistic tensions inherent within Europe and could also be parodying the phenomenal confusion and costs, in both time and money, of translation borne by the EU. This is achieved by having the receptionists and security guards fail to understand Dorfmann's (correct) English pronunciation of his new superior's name. Dutch, French and German-sounding renditions of the name are given until it is eventually agreed that the person sought is the Englishman, Spearpoint. Each of the characters, including Dorfmann, speak their lines using their own idiosyncratic interpretation of 'proper English'. Occasionally, their linguistic shortcomings add to the overall confusion by having their intended message received in a different way to that which was intended by the sender. Such misinterpretation and an occasional lack of clarity add to the humour.

Bradbury thus explores the potential misunderstandings and false interpretations that the misuse of language can cause. Bradbury in this vignette at the Berleymont reception is also re-introducing 'the painful, broken but meaningful English Slakans speak'[18] which he himself identifies as being 'the technique of using English spoken by non-native speakers as its [the novel's] tone of voice',[19] as previously portrayed in *Rates of Exchange*. Indeed James Acheson argues that the novel is one with 'humour deriving largely from the Slakans' inept use of English'.[20] Through this Bradbury is both acknowledging and exploiting the fact that English as a language no longer belongs to the English but is a world language and as such undergoes a constant re-interpretation and revision. Bradbury in his characterization of the old-guard English addresses the conflict that exists between the conservatives, such as Spearpoint, who wish to freeze their one 'true' language (and the values that they deem it to represent) in Anglo-centric aspic as the last remaining outpost of the British Empire and those who wish for a language that could be described as following the lines of Maoist political doctrine in that it accepts, happily, the notion of permanent revolution. Spearpoint's constant irritation at having to correct 'improper usages' of English is evidence of this. As Dorfmann recounts his difficulty of entry to the Berleymont building saying: 'They didn't seem to know you at the desk',[21] Spearpoint replies: 'Bloody typical! Foreigners you see.'[22] Every error is capable of being explained by birthright.

Dorfmann represents a portrayal of longing on Bradbury's part: a naive longing for the world to be other than the nasty, devious place that we have found it to be. Harking back to the rebellious teenage days that we all endured, of wishing, nay intending, to change the world only to find that the harsh economic realities of the late twentieth century induce a conformity that saps that spirit in so many of us that we are barely able to interpret it without considerable help – let alone follow the themes of liberal humanism that Bradbury seems to wish us to do.

Within many of Bradbury's works[23] the literary world is often portrayed in glowing, almost heroic, terms. One example of this is the way in which Bradbury elevates Katya Princip, the people's novelist in *Rates of Exchange*, who is later installed as the President of Slaka in *The Gravy Train Goes East*. The relationship between writer and character is further morphed by Dorfmann's love of books. The unworldly Dorfmann is, of course, the very same Dorfmann who in his previous job at the United Nations brought Nietzsche to Zaire with such apparent success.[24] Dorfmann's idealism regarding books is brought down to earth by the following conversation with Spearpoint:

> [Spearpoint] This commission has 22 directorates, Agriculture, Education, Industry, anything you like. Of them the dullest, darkest, dumbest and daftest is Information and Culture. Even worse is the sub-section books. Which you are joining.
> [Dorfmann] But books are very important, I love books. That's why I'm here.
> [Spearpoint] I love them too. I have a whole pile of them on my bedside table. When I am old I'll probably read some of them but can you get milk from them? Beef? Grain? Oil seed or more importantly subsidy? And how do you feel about measuring them? Weighing them? Making them all the same size? Putting VAT on them? Translating them into Fresian? Banning them? Is that your kind of thing?[25]

Spearpoint is the archetypal self-seeking bureaucrat with little or no interest in his work outside that of his own self aggrandisement. Married to Hilda, 'the daughter of an Earl', but unhappy with his station in life, he complains to Dorfmann:

> My secretary is Spanish. My desk has only got three drawers. My office is on the dark side of the building. In the city with the world's best restaurants I get second best. This is the bottom directorate. I want the top one ... Agriculture.[26]

The pace of the plot now moves on and at a champagne reception, given by the Belgian Royal family, Dorfmann is quickly embroiled, however unintentionally, in the schemes of various nefarious characters to defraud the EU of a substantial amount of cash via a scam involving plum production and distribution. These characters include the Director General of Agriculture, the Frenchman, and thus to British eyes not to be trusted, Jean-Luc Villeneuve.

Temporarily escaping from the clutches of the arch-villain Milcic with the help of Nadine Principal, journalist and spy, Dorfmann's first day in Brussels spirals out of control in the best traditions of farce. Dorfmann completes his inaugural evening in the Belgian capital by being seduced by the beautiful Nadine (a plot-line which must have done wonders for male recruitment to administrative posts at the EU). Dorfmann's seduction is by no means the last time sex is seen as being used to provide leverage in the political intrigues that follow. Relationships ebb and flow as the narrative unfolds. Spearpoint and the Italian Commissioner of Agriculture, Gianna Melchiori, Villeneuve and Delise – presented as his daughter but later revealed not to be – and Dorfmann, who seems to fall prey to the guiles of almost every woman that he encounters, with the exception of his politically Green, hometown girlfriend Christa, are all depicted using sex and sexual innuendo as a manipulative tool. Dorfmann's innocence and liberalism are further exposed through his post-coital conversations. These, somewhat unusually perhaps, regard solving the third-world famine crisis by moving EU surpluses there and advocating the use of environmentally friendly wind-power. As these sentiments are advocated by, and attributed to, Christa but addressed to Nadine, it is yet another example of the honest stupidity of Dorfmann.

As *The Gravy Train* is 'a story which requires so much suspension of disbelief'[27] and 'most of the viewers' credulity is exhausted by the end of the first part',[28] it comes as no real surprise when, rather than waking up, *Dallas*-style, to find that the previous evening's events had been only a dream, Dorfmann arrives at Berleymont to find he has been promoted and transferred, along with Spearpoint. Both are now moved to DG VI, Agriculture. 'Dorfmann who brought Nietzsche to Zaire'[29] is now 'Dorfmann of Soft Fruits'.[30] Dorfmann's first task is to deal with trainloads of rotting plums. Unbeknown to him he is caught up in a massive attempt at fraud. In a complicated and fast-moving chain of events Dorfmann is eventually 'persuaded' to accompany the plums, which have been loaded onto trucks owned by Milcic and which are bound for Bulgaria. He discovers that the trucks are being used to smuggle so-called Star Wars computer technology to the east. He is later told by Alexei, a spy of indeterminate affiliation, that he is 'riding a Trojan horse'.[31] This is a simile that Bradbury has used before in his novel *Eating People is Wrong*,[32] again an example of Bradbury's re-use of ideas.

Prior to crossing into Bulgaria the trucks are re-badged. Whilst presented on the surface as a ruse to facilitate the smuggling of the computer technology, this reincarnation could be viewed as an allegory for the way in which western companies re-design or segment their image to meet the perceived differing needs and attitudes of western and eastern European customers. When the trucks eventually arrive in Bulgaria, Dorfmann and the 'plums' are greeted by Gregor Personip, a Bulgarian Government Trade Official:

> My Friend, the peoples of my country send you their greetings. They ask only that you look around you and wonder at the triumphs of our modernisations. We wish you peace and friendship, amity and concorde. We greet you with warm hearts and open loins hoping for a wonderful intercourse.[33]

One can't help but wonder just who is actually screwing whom, given the nature of the way eastern Europe is being developed, or exploited depending upon one's viewpoint, by western companies and the trade being undertaken, albeit unknowingly by Dorfmann. The ideological war is being won not on the battleground of high political values, as Bradbury perhaps wishes were the case, but on conspicuous consumption. The acquisition of money replaces Marxism as the icon of success, western values supplanting indigenous ones. Thus when being dined by Personip, Dorfmann is surreptitiously given a briefcase that he later finds to contain millions of US dollars and is toasted with the words: 'Still, there is money. Do we drink to it? To Dollar and Mark, to Pound and Yen and one sip yet even for Rouble',[34] exemplifying the negation of past values and illustrating that there are, following the fall of the Iron Curtain, to use Bradbury's own phrase, new and more appealing 'rates of exchange' in the modern Europe. Dorfmann, more by luck than good judgement, manages to extricate himself from the situation and in the process thwart the plan of large-scale fraud. He returns triumphant, much to the dismay of Villeneuve.

THE GRAVY TRAIN GOES EAST

'Tempus fugit' and thus in *The Gravy Train Goes East* we find Dorfmann, originator of the policy of 'Glasnost with plums',[35] working for yet another global organization, the World Bank. He is working on location in India, sitting high up, reminiscent of a Prince of the Raj, astride an elephant. This acts as a metaphor for the rise in Dorfmann's status and reputation following his exploits in *The Gravy Train*. He is soon to return to the familiar territory of Eastern Europe and the EU.

The opening shots of episode one of *The Gravy Train Goes East* give us a pictorial tour of the land of Slaka[36] first created in *Rates of Exchange.* We see contrasting shots of socialist progress, Transylvanian-style castles and food queues with a woman emerging clutching, and indeed caressing, an amalgam of two of Slaka's main exports, a tin of beetroot.[37] There is a voice-over, quoted below, to introduce us both to the land and to the idiom of English used as 'a language deeply changed by its modern role as a lingua franca':[38]

> Welki, welki. Welcome to lovely Slaka. Happy land from fairy tale and modern workers' paradise.
> Who does not relish the chance to visit our so happy land? Yes! Come for our remarkable shoppings. Slaka is a truly modern Marxist state and really a street walkers' paradise. Why not enjoy our famous foods and eat a typical meal beneath a bird-filled tree? Come and drink the medicinal waters in our parks. Of course in Slaka we admit that not everything is perfect ... yet. But here we have a saying. In Slaka there is always a saying never a doing. You cannot build socialism in a day or produce a baby in a week. How lucky we have brave leaders who have the courage to try.

At this point General Vulcani's government undergoes what is described as a peaceful revolution, although we later hear that akin to the former Romanian dictators, the Ceauçescus, they are arrested trying to flee the country and shot after a mock trial. Galina Vitali, yet another woman who finds Dorfmann irresistible and who turns out to be Vulcani's daughter, explains the shifting political sands of post-revolutionary Slaka. She describes the political retrenchment of the Slakan people as being, 'on Friday ex-Marxists. On Saturday Social Democrats. On Sunday, Christian Democrats.'[39]

Slaka now needs a new president for new times, enter stage left (quite literally) the writer Katya Princip. In her opening words to an opera-audience in the Slakan capital she emphasizes the one-sided nature of the relationship, the rate of exchange, between her country and the west, especially in cultural and linguistic terms: 'Excuse me, I speak English, western cameras are here.'[40] Slaka and everything in it are to be subjugated to the need to embrace western values to gain the prize of EU membership.

Again, as in *The Gravy Train*, there is an explicit difference of emphasis, opinion and definition between the Weltanschauung, perhaps it should be 'Europaanschauung', of the British (or should that be English?) and that of the rest of the EU member states' governments. The federalist Euro-vision is put forward with vigour by Villeneuve but naturally with France at the forefront:

Madames, Messieurs, mes cher Eurocrats. How good of you to take time from your busy desks to hear your new Deputy President. You know, we in Berleymont are sometimes called faceless bureaucrats. What a pleasure for me to look around and see so many fine faces here... They tell us we are unelected officials, very well. When I hear that I think of our great European Cathedrals, Chartres, Rouen, Notre Dame de Paris.... To build a great vision you choose only the best. That is what we have done in Berleymont.... It is sometimes said that in every Frenchman there is somewhere a little Napoleon. And why not?! Don't we live again in a great age of destiny. Once more the star of Europe rises, the spirit of fortune beckons, the door to the east swings open. Mes amis, cher amis, I love Europe like a mistress. Now comes Super Europe! Soon we will be not 12[41] but 15, 20, 30![42]

The British, in contrast, ensnared in their pre-fall of empire attitudes, display an almost total disregard for the opinion of other, supposedly partner, nations. Spearpoint illustrates this when responding to the question 'Aren't we the odd one out?' he replies: 'Not from our point of view. From our standpoint the other eleven are the odd one out.'[43] After a later meeting there is another example of the small-minded British attitudes as Penhurst is interviewed for television:

[Penhurst] Britain has made substantial gains at this meeting.
[Interviewer] A few language labs and an improved beef quota? Is that really enough?
[Penhurst] And Swindon as European City of Culture 1998! This meeting, Mr. Rogerson, has been a triumph for British diplomacy.[44]

Only when they are forced to do so by harsh economic reality intruding into their quaint Rapunzel-like slumbers do the British seem in tune with their European partners, the British, as ever, looking backwards towards times of former glories and not forwards to future relationships yet to be forged. Bradbury captures this superbly, depicting Spearpoint making references to Britain's part in saving Belgium from the Nazis during World War II whilst being questioned at Zaventem Airport in Brussels by a customs officer who ignores any diplomatic status that Spearpoint may or may not have. Detained like an ordinary traveller, his anger is further increased as he sees Dorfmann being waved through unchallenged. Spearpoint is apprised of his revised class status when the new geo-political reality is spelt out to him by the customs officer who gleefully points out: 'you're just from Britain, he is World Bank'.[45] This theme of tension between the British and their partners runs as a thread throughout the story and one can almost detect a note of sympathy from Bradbury as the British experience the anguish engendered by the changing world, a constant changing geo-political environment, a foreign intruder in their ordered world. As Penhurst, a British Foreign and Commonwealth Office minister, bemoans:

> Why don't I understand the map of Europe anymore? I suppose because they keep changing the bloody thing everyday. That's why! Give me the cold war, at least we knew where we were and where the other bastards were too![46]

The scenarios adequately represent the distrust, confusion and misunderstandings that characterized relations between Britain and her partners throughout the last quarter of a century and perhaps beyond. Irrespective of which government is in power, much of the British public are sometimes mistrustful of the ways in which 'Brussels' can interfere in their traditional British way of life, although there are occasions such as the issuing of the recent Directive on Working Hours whereby EU decisions are gleefully accepted.

Following the collapse of communism one could view the new ideological tension in Europe as being that between integrationists or federalists (France and Germany) and intergovernmentalists (the British and to a lesser extent the Danes). Whilst shifts of power following recent elections in Britain, France and Germany may lead to moves towards a more convergent policy agenda being developed and agreed between the nations, there does seem to be a fundamental divergence upon the track that the EU train should follow. The British are shown supporting Slakan entry in order that the Slakan economic situation will 'drain the EU dry'.[47] As Penhurst comments on being asked about the British policy on Slakan entry, 'Oh, absolutely. Cornerstone of our policy. Bring in Eastern Europeans and mess up the whole issue of European Federalism.'[48] Just as in real life, widening the EU can be seen as a brake on the deepening tendencies of the Federalists.

Thus Dorfmann, once thought idiotic but after his successes in Bradbury's earlier story now a man to be listened to, is invited to

Brussels by the also upwardly mobile Villeneuve. His mission, should he choose to accept it, is to act on behalf of the EU as an adviser and consultant upon the Slakan economy and therefore upon Slaka's suitability for entry to the EU. He is thus charged with powers not just to determine Slaka's inclusion or exclusion from the European club that is the EU but in Slakan eyes to include Slaka into Europe, for as the British Ambassador to Slaka comments: 'Here Europe stops and nothingness begins.'[49] For the Slakans, and many others, the EU is Europe.

As Dorfmann checks in for his flight on the Slakan state airline, Comflug, he experiences the dual principles that operate in much of eastern Europe, whereby locals often receive preferential treatment. Dorfmann must therefore deposit all his bags, including his briefcase, into the hold, whilst Slakan passengers breeze past carrying large items of hand luggage, unchecked, onto the plane. This duality is also evident in the economic sphere where the Slakan currency has 17 different exchange values.[50] The Slakan case for entry to the EU is, in pure economic terms, weak. As Parson, Villeneuve's Danish *aide-de-camp*, points out:

> [Parson] The member states would never agree. Slaka has no democracy, no economy, the inflation is appalling. Their government is mismanaged, the industry has collapsed. No-one would admit them like that.
> [Villeneuve] They admitted Britain like that.[51]

The reply illustrates nicely both the antipathy towards Britain due to the way it has operated in Europe, demonizing EU institutions and bureaucracy in order to score domestic political advantage and often delaying the proposed actions of the other member states, and the way that the EU has sought to move beyond purely economic considerations in considering its future shape and strategy. Thus the drive to integrate the former communist states of central and eastern Europe into the EU has been powered not just by economics but by concepts such as security, democracy and equity. These are the very concepts that contribute towards the liberal democratic model that Bradbury holds so high in his works. As a sub-plot the battleground of the ongoing fight between Britain and the rest of the EU is depicted as being one that centres upon trade but which for the British at least is hinged upon language and the doors that it can open. As Penhurst explains the advantages for trade to Spearpoint, 'Get them young with *Janet and John Go to the Zoo*, then before you know it they're buying their knickers from Knickerbox and their guns from Vickers.'[52] Bradbury, in a device that so eloquently pokes fun at the pettiness and class basis of traditional English values, scripts it as allowing Slaka and the wider eastern Europe a choice between two beverages. The Europeans have COFFEE ('*C*ommunity *O*peration for *F*reeing *F*unds for *E*astern *E*urope'),[53] an aid-based economic answer to the problems of the region, whilst the British scheme puts a greater focus upon cultural identification leading to a type of national brand-recognition and higher sales, particularly of arms, via the use of TEATIME (*T*eaching *E*nglish *A*broad *T*o *I*ncorporate *M*iddle *E*urope).[54]

The depiction of Slaka is one of depression, not just economic but in other spheres also. As noted in a review of the series: 'its [Slaka's] romance turned out to be bogus, its culture primitive and cheap'.[55] The country is pictured as chaotic and disorganized. Many Slakans have embraced capitalism, indeed they are shown as embracing it all too well for western tastes. This is particularly true of those Slakans involved in the seemingly burgeoning exchange of capital for coitus. Slakans are portrayed, almost to a person, as devious, scheming, hard-drinking individuals who are not to be trusted. Ivo Tankic, for example, now of the Ministry of Economic Affairs and formerly a member of Vulcani's nomenklatura, is a back-slapping, happy-go-lucky type involved heavily in various criminal practices, with extensive links to the secret police. His welcoming toasts on offering Dorfmann a glass of 'rot'vitti',[56] the local fire-water: 'I do not drink. I do not smoke. I do not go with women, except when you are here. May you come here very often'[57] exemplifies the duplicitous characters by which eastern Europe is portrayed and personified. The eastern European post-communist thirst for freedom is shown as having run out of moral steam and is in the process of being replaced by capital accumulation and consumerism, a situation lamented by President Princip as she considers the withering of her own hopes and aspirations for change in Slaka that led her to assume the Presidency:

> You know why I did this. For 40 years there was suffering and many people suffered with courage and with dignity. Then came our miracle of freedom and now my dear you know what has happened? My people talk only of BMW's, of Sony videos, the fast buck, the trip to the west. I cannot bear to believe that only repression keeps people good. But I see we must be careful for

when we make a miracle we have to live a long time inside it. Marxism was a miracle once.[58]

Again the plot of Bradbury's script intertwines numerous characters such as Doctor Plitplov, who is described by Bradbury as 'a leading mental figure',[59] the Steadimans (the British Ambassador and his wife) and Professor Rom Rum, all of whom are reincarnated from *Rates of Exchange,* with religious icons, saintly (and subsequently economic) miracles, brutal and repressive state policemen and lots more besides. British policy on Slakan entry oscillates as the plot twists and weaves a tale of greed, sex, treachery, blackmail, literature and philosophy, double-dealing, diplomacy and duplicity. In other words, an everyday tale of political folk in the modern European Union.

Meanwhile, our hero, Dorfmann, accidentally stumbles upon two miracles that can provide a future for Slaka. The first miracle is the discovery of the existence of Vulcani's foreign bank-accounts in which one hundred million dollars have been salted away. This is also, not quite so coincidentally, the very sum that Villeneuve has promised for the COFFEE project. It is hoped that this can be returned to Slaka. The second miracle is of a wheelchair-bound child who is 'cured' by St Valdopin as a statue of the saint threatens to crush her in the cathedral. This is the miracle that Dorfmann has sought which can be turned to economic advantage à la Lourdes and Medjugore. Through miracle-inspired tourism, neatly taking Slaka into a service-based economy, Dorfmann allows the door of Slakan entry to be pushed, if not open, then ajar. It is, however, soon slammed shut again by a new coup. Dismayed at the delays in their entry and the obstacles placed in their way, Slaka reverts to its Marxist roots, emphasizing the cyclical nature of politics and history with the self-effacing and clearly incompetent Rom Rum becoming the next president. As Galina comments: 'Karl Marx was right. History is everything. You cannot evade the time you live in, the place you come from. It's a prison, a box with you inside.'[60] The constant factor of all the three Slakan regimes that we witness is Tankic, wielding power from the sidelines but seemingly destined to be ever the bridesmaid and never the bride.

One could argue that Bradbury and Dorfmann might like to be the main characters in David Lodge's novel *Changing Places*.[61] In essence they would each like to be the other – Dorfmann to lose himself in philosophy and literature whilst Bradbury perhaps wishes that rather than being a writer he could have had a more direct influence on politics, to play a greater part in the creation of liberal democracies that he so clearly admires. In one sense Bradbury seems to imply the similarity between the two professions in the words of Katya Princip:

> You know what is a politician? It is someone who invents a fiction and tries to tell the world it is a reality. And you know what is a writer? It is someone who invents a reality and tries to tell the world it is a fiction.[62]

NOTES

1. Malcolm Bradbury, *The Gravy Train*, produced by Portman Productions, London for Channel 4 Television, 1990.
2. Malcolm Bradbury, *The Gravy Train Goes East*, produced by Portman Productions, London for Channel 4 Television, 1991.
3. Malcolm Bradbury, *Rates of Exchange* (London: Secker & Warburg, 1983).
4. Malcolm Bradbury, *Why Come to Slaka?* (London: Penguin, 1986).
5. Erhard Reckwitz, 'Literaturprofessoren als Romanciers – die Romane von David Lodge und Malcolm Bradbury', *Germanisch-Romanische-Monatsschrift* 37.2 (1987): pp. 199–217, here p. 212.
6. Malcolm Bradbury, *Cuts: a Very Short Novel* (London: Hutchinson, 1987).
7. John Reith, *Broadcast over Britain* (London: Hodder and Stoughton, 1924).
8. *Daily Telegraph*, 1 November 1986.
9. Malcolm Bradbury in Susan Windisch Brown, *Contemporary Novelists* (New York: St James's Press, 1990), p. 128.
10. Sheridan Morley, 'Ripe Comedy Sprouts in Brussels', *The Times*, 28 June 1990: p. 18.
11. *Observer*, 20 July 1997: p. 16.
12. Malcolm Bradbury, *The Gravy Train Goes East*, Episode 1.
13. Malcolm Bradbury, *The Gravy Train*, Episode 1.
14. *The Times, Magazine*, 28 June 1997: p. 62.
15. Malcolm Bradbury, *The Gravy Train*, Episode 1.
16. Ibid.
17. For a description of the most recent attempts to accede to the EU see John Eatwell and Mats Karlsson, 'If ever the twain are to meet', *Observer*, 20 July 1997: p. 2.
18. Maria Suárez-Lafuente, 'Rates of Exchange: Language, Love and Politics', *Dutch Quarterly Review of Anglo-American Letters* 17.1 (1987): pp. 23–37, here p. 26.

19. Malcolm Bradbury in Windisch Brown, p. 129.
20. James Acheson, 'The Small Worlds of Malcolm Bradbury and David Lodge', *The British and Irish Novel since 1960*, ed. James Acheson (New York: St. Martin's Press, 1991), pp. 78–92, here p. 84.
21. Malcolm Bradbury, *The Gravy Train*, Episode 1.
22. Ibid.
23. See *Cuts, Dr. Criminale* and *Rates of Exchange*.
24. Dorfmann is depicted as a career diplomat who enjoys eventual success without ever quite understanding how or why it was achieved.
25. Malcolm Bradbury, *The Gravy Train*, Episode 1.
26. Ibid.
27. John Turner, 'Exploiting the Euro-Joke', *Times Literary Supplement*, 20–26 July 1990: p. 776.
28. Ibid.
29. Malcolm Bradbury, *The Gravy Train*, Episode 1.
30. Ibid.
31. Malcolm Bradbury, *The Gravy Train*, Episode 3.
32. Malcolm Bradbury, *Eating People is Wrong* (London: Secker and Warburg 1959), p. 197.
33. Malcolm Bradbury, *The Gravy Train*, Episode 3.
34. Ibid.
35. Malcolm Bradbury, *The Gravy Train Goes East*, Episode 1.
36. For a fuller explanation of everything that you might wish to know about Slaka, see Malcolm Bradbury, *Why Come To Slaka?*
37. For those wrestling with this apparent conundrum the two resources are tin and beetroot.
38. Malcolm Bradbury in Windisch Brown, p. 129.
39. Malcolm Bradbury, *The Gravy Train Goes East*, Episode 1.
40. Ibid.
41. At the time Bradbury wrote *The Gravy Train Goes East* there were only 12 members of the then European Community.
42. Malcolm Bradbury, *The Gravy Train Goes East*, Episode 1.
43. Malcolm Bradbury, *The Gravy Train Goes East*, Episode 2.
44. Malcolm Bradbury, *The Gravy Train Goes East*, Episode 3.
45. Malcolm Bradbury, *The Gravy Train Goes East*, Episode 1.
46. Ibid.
47. Ibid.
48. Malcolm Bradbury, *The Gravy Train Goes East*, Episode 4.
49. Malcolm Bradbury, *The Gravy Train Goes East*, Episode 3.
50. Again, this idea of fluid exchange rates is a device which can be traced back to Slaka's previous appearance in *Rates of Exchange*, p. 148.
51. Malcolm Bradbury, *The Gravy Train Goes East*, Episode 1.
52. Ibid.
53. Ibid.
54. Ibid.
55. Lynne Truss, 'The Great Escape to Abroad', *The Times*, 23 November 1991, Weekend Section, p. 3.
56. The Slakan for Plum Brandy. For a fuller explanation of the Slakan language, see *Why Come to Slaka?*

57. Malcolm Bradbury, *The Gravy Train Goes East*, Episode 1.
58. Malcolm Bradbury, *The Gravy Train Goes East*, Episode 3.
59. Ibid.
60. Malcolm Bradbury, *The Gravy Train Goes East*, Episode 4.
61. David Lodge, *Changing Places* (London: Secker and Warburg, 1975).
62. Malcolm Bradbury, *The Gravy Train Goes East*, Episode 4.

Part III
The Idea of Europe and National Identity

9 A Romanian View of Europe: George Uscatescu
Liliana Mihut

As George Uscatescu asserted in 'Autopresentazione', a self-presentation requested by the Italian journal *Filosofia Oggi* on his 70th birthday, his life was conducted in the name of unity between profession and calling.[1] Inspired by Max Weber's view, expressed in his *Politik als Beruf*, professor and writer George Uscatescu understood this unity in a different way: as referring not to politics, but to philosophy, that is to the 'practice of "logos" in the most profound possible sense'. The best expressions of his concern with the 'vitality' of logos, especially of the cultural logos, are his ten books and many papers, written in various languages, dedicated to the theme of Europe. Well-known as a European humanist, he never forgot his roots; he wrote a few books, many essays, and almost all of his poetry in Romanian. He pleaded and worked for the integration of his native country's culture in Europe, with the condition that its own identity be preserved.

This essay is an attempt to highlight Uscatescu's encyclopaedic approach to the idea of Europe and also his particular interest in defining the identity of Romanian culture and its opening to Europe. Although this contribution is not mainly about his works of fiction, his poetry is presented as a demonstration of the coexistence of European and national identity. His biography also illustrates the European itinerary of his life which deeply influenced his work.

WHO WAS GEORGE USCATESCU?

George Uscatescu (1919–1995) was born in Romania, near Targu Jiu, a town which is widely known thanks to the genius of the sculptor Brancusi, to whom he dedicated several books and essays.

Growing up in an atmosphere of love for culture and passion

for reading, he soon discovered such fundamental writers as Shakespeare, Goethe, Plato and Kant. He graduated from the Faculty of Philosophy and Letters, and also from the Faculty of Law of the University of Bucharest; afterwards he got his PhD in the same fields at the University of Rome.

At the end of the war he left Italy for Spain and, in the next decades, became an outstanding academic and cultural figure not only in his new country, but at the European level as well. He was professor at various European and American universities and, for many years, Professor of the Philosophy of Culture and Aesthetics at Complutense University of Madrid. He held the offices of President of the Iberian-American Society of Philosophy in Madrid, and President of the International Society of Humanistic Studies 'Giovanni Gentile' in Rome; he was a member of numerous academies, writers' associations, and boards of prestigious journals.

George Uscatescu wrote in Spanish, Italian and French, as well as Romanian, and authored about one hundred books and a few thousand essays and papers. He was awarded the Prize of Latin Union (Paris) for *La mort de l'Europe?* (1957), the Prize of European Unity (Rome) for *Profetas de Europa* (1962), and the National Prize for Literature (Madrid) for *Erasmo* (1969).

His works belong to the philosophy of culture and aesthetics, to the history of philosophy, the philosophy of history and political philosophy and, last but not least, to literature. Although his favourite subject could be considered as culture in general, he actually focused on the human condition, more exactly the existence of man as a cultural species.

No doubt a *leitmotif* of Uscatescu's work is humanism. In 1968, during the great student upheavals, he made a 'case' against contemporary humanism which was open to conflicts and crises. In his *Proceso al humanismo*, he identified various kinds of humanism in the contemporary world, almost all of them in conflict with each other. Transcending this crisis meant for him to reach a single viable humanism, which has the real man at its centre: 'the humanism of liberty and truth'.[2]

Through these ideas, he met Martin Heidegger, to whom he dedicated many writings, including a 'Romanian homage' published in *Destin* on the 80th birthday of the German philosopher. As seen by Uscatescu, the main message of Heidegger is: 'in the middle of all degradations of the century man continues to be a rational animal'.[3] Supporting this premise, Uscatescu pleads for a restoration of humanism which would assimilate the new technological world.

As a follower of the great European humanists Uscatescu believed that the fundamental problem for a viable humanism is European unity.

THE IDEA OF EUROPE

When Uscatescu reached the age of 65 a group of outstanding European professors and scholars published a book paying homage to him. Among them was Constantin Noica, the Romanian philosopher who had studied in Germany and, then, translated European classics into Romanian as well as developing his own philosophical school. Noica characterized Uscatescu thus: 'He is not an author, he is a map. Reading him you see rising, little by little, the contours of a new continent which he in an inspired way calls a "mental continent" and which seems to us [...] an *elaborate* version of Europe.'[4]

Uscatescu began his series of books on the theme of Europe with *El problema de Europa* (1949), a work which had a major impact on the debate in Spain and, later, in France under the title *La mort de l'Europe?* (1957). The book is a confession of a generation which had come to maturity during the war and then became very concerned with the future of their world. What is the actual problem of Europe? In Uscatescu's view it is: how will the old continent pass through the period of crisis? Will it be a winner or a loser? Answering these questions he did not share the existing wide-spread scepticism, rather he expressed 'the belief that the generation of to-morrow will be a much more unitary generation than the preceding ones'.[5] In support of his belief he invoked the force of a renewed European conscience.

But Uscatescu warns that a new definition of this conscience has to take into account the reality of a divided continent; it must restore the contribution of Eastern Europe to European culture and civilization. This is the main theme of *Europa ausente* (1953), which focused on the problem of that part of Europe which was absent from the new developments of the continent. In a time of East–West confrontations, Uscatescu asserted: 'the spirit of European unity cannot be separated into zones of political and economic influence'.[6]

In 1969 Uscatescu published two books, about two key figures of the Renaissance, who played an essential role in the development of modern Europe: Machiavelli[7] and Erasmus.[8] Uscatescu's choice was not accidental; he selected them because the problem that they faced had much in common with contemporary European problems.

Uscatescu treats their ideas and activities not only as a scholar, but as a writer as well. He comes close to them not only rationally, but also with affection and empathy, connecting them to the present although they lived a long time ago. He calls them 'characters'; the book on Machiavelli starts with the assertion: 'Machiavelli has become a kind of a key-character of our epoch'; and the book on Erasmus begins: 'Erasmus is an actual character.'

Although the two characters were similar in their genius and love of culture, they expressed two different ideas of Europe. Agreeing with other scholars, Uscatescu considers Machiavelli to be contemporary thanks to two aspects: 'desacralization of politics' and 'real humanism'. On the one hand, Machiavelli provided a political and a-religious meaning of Europe; on the other hand, in his view, man is 'complex and contradictory, struggling in a frame offered by concrete historical conditions'.[9]

Unlike Machiavelli, Erasmus assumed the unity of Christendom as a basis for European unity. This view is seen by Uscatescu in its entire complexity, not just as a religious one. Erasmus is called 'a modern European in the largest sense of the word' because he preserves from the Middle Ages the idea of a unique Europe understood in a modern way: as a profound and diversified cultural unity, characterized by humanist ideas, freedom of thought, human rationality and dignity.[10] Uscatescu's volume on Erasmus was recognized not only as philosophical and political writing, but also as a literary work, and was awarded the Spanish National Prize for Literature.

Comparing both views Uscatescu concludes that modern European countries did not live under the idealistic Erasmian message of peace; instead they followed the Machiavellian pragmatic approach supporting a powerful state. But in the 'European republic of the spirit' the message of the 'citizen of the world', as Erasmus had wanted to be, is still alive. He is a 'symbolic presence' in contemporary crises which also have religious bases characterized by fanaticism and intolerance:

> His time much resembles our time, but we are lacking a spirit as high as his. A spirit that deeply loves freedom, peace, conciliation, tolerance, humanity, the common sense of things, and that despises

and moves away from dogmas, prejudices and the force of instincts.[11]

The cultural dimension of European unity was one of the key theses expressed by Uscatescu in all the books he dedicated to this theme. At the end of the 1970s he published *Europa, nuestra utopia*,[12] a book so entitled because the Old Continent, always subject to unfulfilled community projects, could become a Utopia. But, in spite of all complex developments and difficulties, he believed that the European Community remains 'an idea in the making' and expressed concern and bitterness at what he considered the failures of this process:

> Grave actual tensions, a certain anarchy in the realm of ideas turn Europe into a Community that tends to be more and more accepted as an economic reality, leaving on a back seat the possibilities of becoming again a strong political entity, and pushing aside its prerogatives of cultural guide and leader of the world on a field dominated by the dialectics of negation.[13]

This far from reassuring diagnosis raises such dramatic questions as: Which Europe? Where is Europe? What is Europe and where is it going?'[14] These questions have often been asked by both scholars and politicians in the last decades. Uscatescu is under no illusion that there are simple answers, and he is fully aware of the interfering alternative solutions. He is opposed to a technocratic Europe and in favour of the development of a consciousness of a European homeland. This homeland is seen as contributing its own to the concept of unity in diversity; each national state is a holder of the European cultural inheritance and is able to make a contribution to projects of European unification. Uscatescu pleads again for what he named the 'absent Europe' some years earlier: during the height of the Cold War he stated that it was time for a new relationship between East and West.

His plea was not only for a genuine European unity but also for real integration of his Romanian homeland into the new Europe.

THE IDENTITY OF ROMANIAN CULTURE

Uscatescu strongly believed that Romanian culture is entitled to be recognized at both the European and international levels, and he worked hard for it. He belonged to that generation of intellectuals who grew up in the enthusiastic atmosphere following the Great Union of Romania (1919) and who shared a feeling of responsibility for the future of their country. After World War II, when Romania was included in the Soviet Union's sphere of influence, many of these remarkable people went into exile. Uscatescu characterized his generation in 'Autopresentazione': 'it was the generation of the century, marked more than any other [...] by the singular adventure of the liberty induced by different forms of internal and external exile' (*Filosofia Oggi*, p. 399).

Although he was living at the other side of Europe, Uscatescu did not remain a simple spectator of Romanian culture; he considered that he belonged to it, and he was concerned for its destiny and for his own place in this destiny. Significantly, in 1951, he became the founder and director of a publishing house, collection and journal called *Destin* (Destiny), which published many books, papers, essays, and poems written by expatriates from the *Pontus Euxinus* (the ancient name of the Black Sea) almost all of them in Romanian. During a period of more than 20 years the journal provided longevity and continuity despite the unfavourable material conditions of exile. The publishing house operated for more than 40 years, and printed about a hundred books.

The 'Foreword' of the first issue of the journal defined the attitude which guided this cultural act of Romanians in exile. They consider 'the phenomenon of emigration as a process of historical and spiritual disintegration, and, as such, the mentality of the emigrant as a spiritually fruitless attitude'; consequently, the intellectual elites operating in freedom have to be 'a fruitful extension, in an ongoing alert state of mind regarding the Homeland'.[15]

Supporting this goal of cultural continuity with the homeland, *Destin* published remarkable papers and essays on cultural, artistic, historical, political, judicial and philological topics, as well as poetry. *Destin* did not politicize: in other words, it was not involved in political disputes among various groups, but engaged in political work in the name of freedom, by denouncing totalitarian practices, and supporting revaluation of Romania's place in Europe. Although marked by sporadic links with the motherland, the journal and the collection emphasized those aspects and dimensions of Romanian spirituality which appeared to be more favourable to its openness to the world.

Mircea Eliade, the great historian of religion who left Romania for France and then for the United States, endorsed George Uscatescu's universalistic approach to Romanian culture. Eliade published most of his own prose, parts of his diary, and many essays written in the first decades after the war in *Destin*. On the fifteenth anniversary of the journal he wrote: 'There is no doubt that this admirable work of George Uscatescu and his associates of Madrid represents one of the most significant Romanian cultural victories in exile.'[16]

It was particularly important that at the height of 'proletarian' culture (1950–60) a journal published abroad promoted authentic Romanian culture. In the last issue, in 1972, the question was posed: is it possible to turn back in Romania? Uscatescu warned that, in spite of the promising opening of the last decade, the new ideological bombardment' could be a sign of a return to Stalinism.[17]

Most of Uscatescu's writings about his native country in *Destin* were compiled in a book, published first in Romanian,[18] and then in Spanish.[19] The volume is a review of the work carried on by Romanians in exile, and an attempt to draw the coordinates for a 'new itinerary': an ontology of Romanian culture. This new synthesis is considered necessary for the universal projection of Romanian culture, especially since Western culture itself is at a crossroads: contemporary man is more and more unsatisfied with it and, consequently, more open to revaluation of ancestral, exotic or folk expressions of spirituality. In Uscatescu's view, there are two permanent elements of Romanian spirituality throughout history: one is what the ancient Greeks designated *Nemesis*, or the limits of human power; the other one is *Freedom*. These two ideas stimulated the 'miracle' of Romanian creativity. In search of a new definition of the main characteristics of his homeland's culture Uscatescu states:

> This new and actual definition would have to recognize an objective base in Romanian culture, beyond the folk perspective, and to trace an ontology of this culture inspired from a *Romanian humanism*, a supreme and rich fruit of a profound sense of balance, measure and moderation, a happy blend of serenity and lyricism.[20]

Equally concerned with the future of his homeland and that of the Continent as a unified entity, Uscatescu defines the relationship of Romania with Europe in an apparent paradox: 'a strengthened idea of Romanian community' will increase its possibilities of integration 'with its own personality' in 'an authentic European community'.[21]

This approach is consistent with the way in which he analyses the nationalist phenomenon. Written at a time when the necessity for continental political unity had just been placed on the agenda and, on the other hand, at a time when communism threatened the existence of nations, this paper was an attempt to articulate a balanced analysis of the problems of nation and nationalism. The 'extremist deviations' and the 'excesses' of nationalism were rejected, but the preservation of national cultural tradition was defended: in Uscatescu's view, only a 'guilty' intellectual and political 'short-sightedness' can see 'the possibility of constituting a superior European force in the disappearance of national values and of the patrimony of sentimental and emotional forces created by the long experience of living together as part of a nation, in the course of the centuries'.[22]

In order to prove the potential of Romanian culture to enter universal culture Uscatescu invokes those figures who are considered to be the best expressions of its creativity: philosophers, historians, writers, poets and artists. But 'the best possibility of major integration into national culture' lies with Mihai Eminescu, the Romanian national poet. As he always did when approaching historical 'characters', Uscatescu focuses on Eminescu's quality of being our contemporary:

> There is an Eminescu which we always carry with us, a noble embodiment of all that can be highest in our never-ending rediscoverings. But there is another Eminescu as well, a supreme synthesis of Romanian essences, our absolute explanation. In this second Eminescu the rediscovering of all of us, as people and as a nation is possible.[23]

More proof of the universal opening of the Romanian culture invoked by Uscatescu is provided by the works of Constantin Brancusi, 'my genius countryman', as he is called in 'Autopresentazione'. In the volume dedicated to the 'rebel' who was one of the great founders of modern art Uscatescu stresses the idea that behind Brancusi's work is a two-fold history: of Western art and of his own people. Inspired by a new vision of space, an obsession with flying, and a utopian aspiration for the infinite, Brancusi created, among other valuable works, the famous Column of the Infinite, Gate of the Kiss, and Table of the Silence, through which he 'made contact points of his native town, Targu Jiu, with the universe'.[24] More particularly, the Endless Column has been interpreted as a symbol of the continuous ascension of generations, and of the eternity of the human condition expressed in a modern manner.

POETRY – AN ILLUSTRATION OF THE COEXISTENCE OF EUROPEAN AND NATIONAL IDENTITY

Like Heidegger, Uscatescu believed that poetry is the best means of expressing the essence of human being and of humanism. Consequently, poetical spirit is present in all his writings, which are imbued with suggestive expressions and metaphors. At the same time, as he declared in 'Autopresentazione', all his work is integrated in his poetry, which is not philosophical, but is rather in a complex relationship with metaphysics. It is a 'pure poetical catharsis', a product of maturity which accesses a 'new expressive language'. According to its author, this poetical work reflects a double inheritance: it continues the work of the great Romanian poets of the inter-war period, particularly Lucian Blaga, George Bacovia, Ion Barbu, and Emil Botta; it also expresses admiration for the great poets of the world, namely Leopardi, Eminescu, Hölderlin, and Rilke (*Filosofia Oggi*, p. 405). In his native country, the former poets are representatives of a generation of innovators, who linked modernity and tradition in Romanian poetry, and managed to synchronize it with European art forms.

Significantly, Uscatescu wrote his poems in Romanian, the language of the place where he was deeply rooted, and thought that poetry actually cannot be translated. Although he expected his poetry to be a part of Romanian culture, his work revealed not only nostalgia for his homeland, but also a kind of nostalgia for a humanist Europe.

In Uscatescu's poetry the traditional topics and symbols of European literature coexist harmoniously with Romanian myths, legends and heroes, projected in a coherent vision onto the modern condition and the 'destiny' of mankind. Each volume is focused on a major theme and is built around a central symbol.

The first volume, *Thanatos*, a title taken from Greek mythology, approaches death as a personification. In the poems, Uscatescu moves from a metaphysical view of death as a supreme experience which opens new horizons to an attitude inspired by a famous Romanian folk ballad, considered by Leo Spitzer as 'one of the great masterpieces of world literature'.[25] Like the anonymous shepherd of the ballad, his lyrical hero accepts death calmly as a comradeship '[t]ogether with stars, fir trees, and wilderness'.[26] Thus, death is not the end, but the continuation of life. The 13 'Poems of silence' included in this volume are wonderful expressions of yearning for homeland which is felt in 'thousands of hypostases'.

The title of the second volume is also inspired by the ancient Greeks.[27] Again, when the author bewails the destroyed Ilium (the Latin name for Troy) he actually expresses his suffering for the lost country. And again, he feels like the Phoenix risen from the ashes of Ilium.

The next volume is built around another metaphor: like a snail, the poet always carries the homeland in his 'shell'.[28] The lyrical treatment of this poetical motif is consistent with his philosophical way of understanding the integration of the individual within universality. The forest is the *leitmotif* of the following volume: the poet answers the calling of the forest' and immerses himself in its 'memory'.[29] This symbolic retreat does not ultimately signify an antihumanist movement, but it is envisioned, on the contrary, as a recapturing of the deeply immersed energies of human soul. Although he enjoys the splendours of each season, the yearning for the homeland which lost its freedom recurs in many poems.

Millenarium evokes the 'dying millennium', but is also a call for celebrating a new beginning.[30] Although his personal hope for a 'meeting' with the year 2000 was uncertain – and, unfortunately, he was right, as he died five years before the millennium – Uscatescu calls for a rediscovering of freedom, considered to be the essential condition of a better future. One of the last volumes is a kind of 'autobiography', which evokes his dearest ones, and compares life in exile with that of a 'vagabond dog'. Significantly, a poem dedicated to Eminescu is included: he is named the poet of 'plenary dreamings', who can 'read' the stars and the signs of the time.[31]

Not accidentally, the corollary of Uscatescu's poetic work is a 'dramatic poem in prose' dedicated to the 100th commemoration of Eminescu's death. The eulogy praises Eminescu as 'the greatest poet of our nation', 'the poet of our completion', 'the Poet and the Prophet of the motherland', 'the founder of our poetic language'. As usual, Uscatescu treats his 'character' from the perspective of eternity. According to the author, the poet declares: 'I lived in many times. I knew how to run away with my entire being from my enemy, time.'[32] He loves only the space, which, as a landscape, comprises the entire country. Not only the Poet but also other characters have a symbolic value; some of them are his contemporaries, the others, transcending the centuries, are his companions in eternity. The presence of the author himself is involved, as 'a poet who has remained without a country, but who has retained the passion for the motherland in his blood' (*Luceafarul*, p. 24). The alternation of poems authored by Eminescu and Uscatescu seems to be a dialogue over time. Among those invited to the commemoration is the Philosopher, a character identified with Constantin Noica. He is presented not only in his capacity as a great Romanian philosopher and as one of the best friends of the author, but also acknowledged for his contribution to the revaluation of some unknown writings of the Poet.

Another central figure, often invoked in the poem, is that of Stefan cel Mare (Stephen the Great), the king of Moldavia, who played an important role in stopping the expansion of the Ottoman Empire in the fifteenth century. He is admired for his courage in facing the danger alone, without the help of his European allies, although – as he wrote to the Pope – his country was 'the gate of Christendom' (*Luceafarul*, p. 74). This courage and dignity are why the Poet would like to 'mirror' his own destiny in the king's image.

But this destiny is located on an 'axis' between Putna, the place where Stefan cel Mare is buried, and Vienna, the European capital where Eminescu discovered the romantic spirit, philosophy, the treasures of antiquity and the fascination of science (*Luceafarul*, p. 65). The Romanian poet belonged, as he stated many times, to European romanticism. His masterpiece, *Luceafarul* (Venus) revives the myth of Hyperion, a theme approached by Hölderlin as well. However, Eminescu's Hyperion is basically inspired by a fairy-tale, called 'Youth without age, and life without death'. So, the author underlines that the fascination with immortality is extracted from the folklore and spirit of his people, and, at the same time, corresponds with the spirit of a great European tradition.

In the last pages of the poem the inheritance bequeathed by Eminescu is described through the voice of a young poet: 'He was the first in our world who, in our language and in its poetry, was able to intercept the existence and the infinite spiral of the universe.' (*Luceafarul*, p. 89) The author evinces the universality of the national Poet not only by evoking his major ideas and themes, but also through some staging directives mentioned within the poem: for example, a scene in which verses written in a Romanian folk rhythm are recited ends in a song by Schumann or Beethoven.

No doubt, Uscatescu was fully aware of the limits of poetry as a means of universal communication. In many interviews and essays he stated that the 'poetical atmosphere' expressed in metaphors – including that created by Eminescu – cannot be properly translated into foreign languages.

In spite of these limits he approached poetry as a field of co-existence between his two identities: European and Romanian. The major themes and symbols, the location and the characters of his poems suggest that, although his homeland's culture belongs to the Eastern tradition, remarkable through its mythic potential, it is fully entitled to be considered a part of European culture.

USCATESCU AND THE HISTORY OF THE IDEA OF EUROPE

A well-known series of books on European identity in its various historical, cultural, social, political and economic aspects, entitled *What is Europe?*, is framed by a set of questions:

> What kind of Europe are we building and why? How does this new Europe relate to the patterns and experiences of European history? Are there distinctive European values? Is there a coherent, recognisable European identity? What do Europe and being European mean?[33]

For a reader who has become familiar with Uscatescu's work it is easy to recognize in these questions those explicitly or implicitly expressed in all of his books, essays, and poems.

As previously emphasized, he understood very well that simple answers cannot be given. There have been and are 'many Europes' in terms of perceptions as well as projects. His vision is not an economic union, nor a political union; it is not a technocratic Europe, but rather the cultural community, the 'European spirit'; his continent is a 'mental' one.

One point in the complex question 'what is Europe' refers to the geographical extent of the continent. At a time when Europe was almost exclusively perceived as referring to the western part only, Uscatescu was a strong voice in calling attention to the drama of the 'absent' Europe, and pleaded for a 'return to Europe'. After the end of the Cold War and the collapse of the communist system he was one of those who tried to find rapid ways of re-connecting his native country to Western Europe.

The relationship between European identity and national identity was a major theme of his work. He did not think in terms of exclusion: a strong sense of 'Europeanness' as expression of cultural unity *or* a multiplicity of national identities. He believed in the likelihood of his motherland integrating 'with its own personality' in an 'authentic' community of European nations.

Uscatescu's approach was not only a scholarly exploration of European or Romanian identity. He supported his options in the name of the 'humanism of liberty and truth'. He thought and felt that his literature was a catharsis, and also a demonstration of his choices and ideas. His view of Europe was not a pragmatic one, but rather inspired by the romantic tradition, focusing on the vision of cultural continuity and the inherent values of humanism.

Thanks to his well-balanced view and pleading, George Uscatescu has a deserved place in the very complex history of the idea of Europe after World War II.

NOTES

1. George Uscatescu, 'Autopresentazione', *Filosofia Oggi* 12.3/4 (1989): pp. 393–405 (All quotations are translated into English by the author of this chapter.)
2. Jorge Uscatescu, *Proceso al humanismo* (Madrid: Guadarrama, 1968).
3. George Uscatescu, 'Heidegger e il suo secolo', *Destin* 21–23 (1971): pp. 10–20, here p. 17.
4. Constantin Noica, 'El continente mental trazado por Jorge Uscatescu', *Cultura y existencia humana: Homenage al profesor Jorge Uscatescu*, ed. Jose Antonio Merino (Madrid: Reus, S.A., 1985), p. 257.
5. George Uscatescu, *La mort de l'Europe?* (Paris: Librairie Française, 1957), p. 109.
6. Jorge Uscatescu, *Europa ausente* (Madrid: Editora Nacional, 1953), p. 114.
7. Jorge Uscatescu, *Maquiavelo y la Pasion del Poder* (Madrid: Guadarrama, 1969).
8. Jorge Uscatescu, *Erasmo* (Madrid: Editora Nacional, 1969).
9. George Uscatescu, 'Machiavelli si pasiunea puterii', *Proces umanismului* (Bucharest: Editura politica, 1987), p. 141.
10. George Uscatescu, *Erasmus* (Bucharest: Editura Univers, 1982), p. 95.
11. Ibid., p. 20.
12. Jorge Uscatescu, *Europa, nuestra utopia* (Madrid: Reus, S.A., 1978).
13. George Uscatescu, 'Europa, utopia noastra', *Proces umanismului* (Bucharest: Editura politica, 1987), p. 291.
14. Ibid., p. 297.

15. 'Cuvant inainte', *Destin* 1 (1951): pp. 3–8.
16. Mircea Eliade, 'Popas la cincisprezece ani', *Destin*, Volum comemorativ, Madrid (1966): pp. 13–4, here p. 13.
17. George Uscatescu, 'Este posibila intoarcerea?' *Destin* 24/25 (1972): pp. 3–8.
18. George Uscatescu, *Nou itinerar* (Madrid: Destin, 1968).
19. Jorge Uscatescu, *Nemesis y libertad* (Madrid: Editora Nacional, 1968).
20. George Uscatescu, 'Caracterele culturii romanesti', *Nou itinerar*, p. 22.
21. George Uscatescu, 'Nou itinerar', *Nou itinerar*, p. 49.
22. George Uscatescu, 'Fenomenul nationalist', *Nou itinerar*, p. 79.
23. George Uscatescu, 'Actualitatea lui Eminescu', *Nou itinerar*, p. 7.
24. George Uscatescu, *Brancusi si arta secolului* (Bucharest: Editura Meridiane, 1985), p. 28.
25. Leo Spitzer, 'L'Archétype de la ballade *Miorita* et sa valeur poétique', *Cahiers Sextil Puscariu* (University of Washington, Seattle) 2.2 (1953): pp. 95–120, here p. 95.
26. George Uscatescu, *Thanatos* (Madrid: Destin, 1970), p. 9.
27. George Uscatescu, *Darimat Ilion* (Madrid: Destin, 1972).
28. George Uscatescu, *Melc sideral* (Madrid: Destin, 1974).
29. George Uscatescu, *Memoria padurii* (Madrid: Destin, 1977).
30. George Uscatescu, *Millenarium* (Madrid: Destin, 1980).
31. George Uscatescu, *Autobiografie* (Madrid: Destin, 1985).
32. George Uscatescu, *Luceafarul: la un centenar (poem dramatic in proza)* (Madrid: Destin, 1989), p. 69.
33. K. Wilson and J. van der Dussen, eds, *What is Europe?: The History of the Idea of Europe* (London and New York: Routledge, 1995), p. 9.

10 Eyvind Johnson and the History of Europe: Many Times in One Place
Rolf Hugoson

As we approach the turn of our century, efforts to create a political community called Europe involve not only law and commerce, but necessarily also culture and history. The institutions that represent the peoples of the European Union have already begun to function, yet a European identity remains to be created. Without such an identity, it is difficult or impossible to act legitimately in common, because it will remain unclear what is meant by the 'we' in sentences such as 'we that act in common'. In this essay, I discuss some of the connections between the creation of a political identity ('us') and the writing of history (what 'we' have done). I focus on the work of the Swedish novelist Eyvind Johnson, whose novels offer us a reading of how identities are formed in time. Notably, he shows how the past is never closed off from the present, but remains with us, or even ahead of us. It appears that the past is not just a sequence of events, but rather a multitude of possible stories that continue to engage the present. This means that any democratic efforts to make us into Europeans will have to negotiate continuously with the past, and thus that European history should be something other than a univocal series of events that necessarily lead to the creation of a European political community.

Eyvind Johnson (1900–1976), who received the Nobel Prize in 1974, was born in Norrbotten, Sweden's northernmost province. His only formal education was the compulsory six years in the village school. Supporting himself by taking odd jobs as a labourer, he succeeded in becoming an author, and lived abroad for several years in France, Germany, England and in southern Switzerland.[1] Johnson wrote in Swedish, but after World War II none of his novels was exclusively set in Sweden. Instead, his characters often became involved in crossing borders. As Warme puts it, 'the "international" protagonists could be seen to personify the author's ideal of European cultural unity through a breaking down of national boundaries'.[2] For Johnson, Europe is, thus, not only an exemplary place of many times, but it is also important as an influence upon the author as a person, and it is a setting for his novels.

To give an introductory example (a kind of *hors d'oeuvre*) of Johnson's argument concerning the importance of the past for our political community, we might quote from one of his late novels, *Hans nådes tid* (The Days of His Grace), which is set in the time of Charlemagne. The novel focuses on the Frankish crushing of the Langobard people. Early on, in the year 775, we encounter an image of history as something through which we will have to pass:

> 'Our people's past piles itself up in front of us', he said *'In front of us*. It's beginning to become too much for us. It's like great mounds of leaves in the fall, like enormous drifts of leaves. Soon we'll be trudging in it as in a compost heap. We have to wade through it again, although it ought to lie behind us.'[3]

This image, or this rhetorical figure, is presented in the form of advice to the Langobard compatriots of Deacon Anselm. In the novel, the image is remembered by Johannes Lupigis, who will later become the secretary of Charlemagne. Deacon Anselm, Johannes' uncle, is a somewhat devious person, almost too clever in his use of words. He wishes to avoid the defeat he foresees will ensue if the Langobards engage in an armed revolt against Charlemagne. To this end, the Deacon sets about collecting old stories, as if to safeguard national identity by means of history instead of by arms. Yet, he is afraid that the past – the Frankish occupation, the loss of independence – will become too heavy to bear, and this is why he advises his audience to beware of the past. There will be reason to return to this particular image of the past, but before doing this, I would like to make a more general investigation into the relationships that exist between on the one hand the construction of political identities (such as Langobards, Serbs, or Europeans), and on the other hand the writing of history. I will show how history can be understood as a narration of past facts that decides who we are, and, one should add, who the others are.[4] I will then discuss Johnson's images of how the past can be written, and then conclude shortly by discussing the relationship between different times.

THE NARRATION OF POLITICAL COMMUNITY

The ruler referred to above, Charlemagne, was crowned Emperor by the Pope in the year AD 800. This was, at least in part, an attempt by the church to revive the idea of the Western Roman Empire.[5] In a similar fashion, exponents of the unification of European states have sometimes looked back upon the Frankish realm as an example of what Europe could be like. Such efforts to revive long-defunct institutions as models for contemporary actions are common, and may almost appear to be a natural procedure. Reference to history is an effective solution when a political community faces the perennial problem of legitimating its own existence. To be able to act, a community must necessarily proclaim its identity. As Walzer puts it, emphasizing the collective aspect of identification: 'Politics is an art of unification; from many, it makes one.'[6] Or Heater, with special reference to Europe: 'No project for voluntary political integration would be at all credible unless the putative member states shared some cultural and political traditions and values.'[7]

A communal identity can thus be defined as an ability to unite a multitude of voices in a more or less singular subject: 'we'. It is easier to make this political and linguistic operation legitimate, if the referent of 'we' appears to be obvious. We and our communal organization will appear obvious if we can appeal to a significant number of similarities that unite and differences that separate 'us' from 'them'. Examples of such distinguishing attributes of a community can be the particular place where we live, our particular religion, our particular looks, our particular ability to conduct war or trade, our particular customs or our particular language. These sources of traditions and legitimacy, and their importance for stable government, are already an important topic of analysis in, for example, Machiavelli's *Discourses*.

However, our particular history will always be of a more overarching interest. It can connect all other attributes into a complex chain of facts that points out that there is an 'us'. It is necessary that our community appears to be something more than the result of a series of accidents, because unless 'we' are the outcome of intentional actions, it is not likely that 'we' will be able to continue and act in the future. The history of a community must be presented as a voluntary movement, which is an ability to move from the past, in principle unalterable by action, to the future, in principle alterable by action. As Hampshire puts it:

Any action, as an intended bringing about of an effect, has a certain trajectory, a relation of before and after within it. This continuity of an intentional action gives the assurance of my own existence as a continuing object of reference. 'I did it', as opposed to 'It just happened' or 'Someone else did it', is the primary, unquestionable indication of my own, utterly distinct existence as a an object of reference.[8]

The constitution of a communitarian identity, such as Europe, must tread a difficult path between the stability of its referents and its ability to adapt to the future. It is true that the distinguishing attributes, the referents that give us our identity, will appear firmer the more they appear to be beyond our control, as when the country or the continent appears to be a clearly demarcated terrain, or the race appears to be a representation of nature.[9] Nevertheless, such a seemingly natural 'us' must also be able to show its ability to project itself into the future, and must, therefore, negotiate with culture. A political 'we' cannot allow itself to just tag along, but it must be able to make promises for times to come.[10] Reference to history can solve this dilemma, because the past can be shown to be both an accomplished fact and a voluntary movement.

Unless we assume the myth that naming has taken place once and for all, European identity will, therefore, appear as an almost kaleidoscopic historical narrative: 'about how the Europeans have conceived themselves and the others, how they have drawn the borders on the map, in the terrain, in the inner worlds where we, with feelings and reason, distinguish between friends and enemies'.[11] This relationship between the plural pronoun of a political community (we) and its referents (what makes us who we are) must, however, point to the ambiguous fact that it is a constitutional or normative relationship, a self-declaration performed in language and in society, a naming as creation.[12]

To understand what Europe is, we have to listen to how the Europeans continuously narrate their own identity, that is, how 'the Europeans' appears both as the subject and the object of the phrase: we are those who make us into ourselves. Identity is, thus, created when somebody chooses to interpret objective or symbolic referents (geography, biology, language, the past) as opportunities to give a name. Our history is not discovered by chance, but it is decided upon, and we can talk about community as a series of agreements and disagreements to act upon texts. The question, as always, will then be 'what texts, as interpreted by whom?' This question opens up for relationships between different kinds of historiography.[13] Different countries and different disciplines take on different traditions of presenting texts as decisions of what the past was like, and how it is connected to the present. Furthermore, it seems that novels could play an increasingly important role in such narratives, inasmuch as reading encourages reflection, which is needed when political action is about making choices, taking on responsibility, and assuming social identities.[14]

When Benedict Anderson made his seminal analysis of the construction of nationality in different cultures, he focused on the establishment of a common time, unknown before the coming of the modern nations or, indeed, the modern novel.[15] A nation (or, I would like to add, a political community in general) needs a sovereign 'we', a subject that makes it possible for many people (or peoples) to act together. This acting together can be accomplished above all by the invention of a common, or simultaneous, time that makes it possible for people who live in different places to act at the same time, without knowing each other. The coordination of simultaneity is in part established with the help of rapid communications of ideas, such as bookprinting and the post.[16] It is also established by acts of imagination, which Anderson explains with reference to the time of a 'traditional' Balzacian novel, where a certain plot allows characters that are unaware of each other to move about and do things at the same time. The temporal order of the novel is therefore an allegory for the timespace of the modern nation: the nation is imagined as a number of people who perform their activities at the same time, even while they remain completely unaware of each other's existence.

Because simultaneity is a temporal order, it cannot be established without appeal to a common past. At this point, there is a choice of possibilities. As a preliminary example, we may look back to 1915, when the acclaimed Swedish explorer and writer Sven Hedin visited Germany. In spite of the war, he found that the spirit in Germany was so good that he could proclaim his belonging to an imperial Western Europe: 'Romanus sum', Hedin exclaimed. In March, when he was approaching the front in East Prussia, he also imagined chosen parts of Swedish history, namely Charles XII's attack upon Russia in the early eighteenth century, now interpreted as a piece of European history:

> I knew, that I could not take one step forward in this country that lay ahead of me without treading in Swedish footsteps. They now gleam of blood that others have shed, but for the same cause. The soldiers of Charles XII, they who rest in the Polish soil, can henceforth sleep in peace. Their revenge is late, but it comes surely. The cause of King Charles XII has rested for two hundred years, but now it is alive again.[17]

Hedin's almost lyrical identification functions as a narrative act of constitution of identity. The path of the forerunners, the soldiers of Charles XII, offers a concrete, albeit invisible, exemplum. It is as if a past effort to accomplish a goal has been lying waiting in the terrain until it can be picked up again, like a standard, and be declared continuously legitimate. The problem with Sven Hedin's discovery of the past is not just his racism and his belligerence but, more importantly, his way of offering the meaning of the past as something univocal. To Hedin, there is no doubt about the direction the past will pursue, as soon as it has been retrieved by memory and by repetition. This lack of doubt shows that the Swedish explorer is trapped by his adherence to an ideology and, somehow, he resembles Defoe's Robinson Crusoe, who discovers a foreign footprint on the island he thought his own. Brantlinger comments upon this event:

> Perhaps there was a real foot corresponding to the footprint Crusoe discovers; perhaps there were real cannibals corresponding to the images and shadows of cannibals he dreads, fights and either kills or drives away. But he knows only the images; he finds in the island and in his experience only that which he wishes or dreads to find.[18]

The possibility of this unfortunate perception of the past hinges on the fact that the past always has to be imagined, because by definition it is no more. Truly, it does not yield itself to be freely imagined, because unlike events that may occur in the future, past events have already happened. But what they mean to us has to be negotiated in the present. As Koselleck says:

> Every event historically established and presented lives on the fiction of actuality; reality itself is past and gone. This does not mean, however, that a historical event can be arbitrarily set up. The sources provide control over what might not be stated. They do not, however, prescribe what may be said.[19]

Bakhtin has coined the concept of chronotope (timespace) to analyse how literature functions, in different ways, by fusing time and space into a concrete whole.[20] But Bakhtin is perhaps more famous for insisting that discourse is also a concrete event, taking place in a dialogue between text and reader. The form of the discourse, especially its chronotope, will then also be dependent upon the chronotope of the world where the text is to be found, that is to say the contextual fusion of time and place that surrounds the writing and the reading of the text. Bakhtin's conclusion is, in short, that: 'although the "event" that is narrated in the world and the "event" of this narration itself need to be recognized as taking place in different temporal and spatial relations, these two events are nevertheless united in the single "event" of the actual text in question.'[21] In Hedin's text, we can first distinguish the chronotope created within the text, where he describes his marching to the front as a temporal and spatial continuation of both the march of the soldiers of Charles XII and the march of the German Army. Secondly, this chronotope must be connected to the 'contextual' chronotope in which Hedin's text is involved as something which is written and read. The latter chronotope involves Hedin's particular address to the reader. By being affirmative about how the past should be interpreted, he tries to shape the reader's perception. His description of moves and memories is an appeal to how the readers should place themselves in time and space, in the history of Europe. It is an old-fashioned appeal, one that fails to make its case in the present.

IMAGES OF WRITING THE PAST

In Eyvind Johnson's novels, we encounter more complex and more appealing ways of constructing chronotopes. If we return to the quote from *The Days of His Grace* above, the past is said to be something upon which we are forced to trudge. In the same novel, in the year 828, more than 50 years after the first occurrence of this image, it is recuperated by the chronicler of Johannes Lupigis' life, Agibertus, a narrator (one among many possible, as so often in Johnson's novels) who is trying to bring back the past through a reading of old documents:

> The past, which belongs to me and to Johannes Lupigis and others, has begun to pile up ahead of me like a future which I must

penetrate. This is how the past piles up before us all. We stand and trudge in this, and we must penetrate it to attain knowledge. We have experienced – or gulped down – parts of it, and now we must penetrate and swallow it again to become free through the knowledge of what it was like. This is probably the law of knowledge, the way to the acquisition of experience, as Deacon Anselm has said.[22]

Ahead of us there are the heaps of leaves or of dung that represent the presence of the past, not as a glorious battlefield, but like something that sticks to our shoes. The Deacon is not trying to conquer the past. Instead he presents the past as something slightly beyond our control, a past we might have to doubt, to resist, or to fear. Although the image of leaves presents the past as something natural, this is balanced (by Johnson) by it also being used in an operation of persuasion, as an effort by the Deacon to conquer the vision of the audience. He wants the audience to understand that they shall have to pay attention to the past, because it has the power to direct the future. The Deacon observes that other stories from the past might entice the Langobards into acts of futile violence, and he resists this. In Johnson's story, the Deacon's storytelling appears to be in vain, because he cannot prevent the failed revolt. Yet, even if the Deacon's storytelling fails in its own time, Johnson's recalling of the Deacon's efforts not only saves them from meaningless oblivion, but also restores something of their apparently conditional power. Johnson's readers are reminded that we can try and avoid being trapped by stories of the past that present what has happened as a univocal sign, as an unambiguous call for action.

If this effort to persuade would fail again, nevertheless the storytelling of a Langobard chronicler has allowed the novelist to improve his plot, because the character of Deacon Anselm is in part a representation of the Deacon Paulus, the ancient author of a history of the Langobard people, whose book Johnson bought in Berlin in the 1920s, and used as one of the sources for his own return to the Langobard resistance.[23] Deacon Anselm is thus a fictive representation of a real source that has allowed Johnson to incorporate reality into his novel. On this course, we can note that in a sense Johnson himself is also portrayed in the novel, in the person of the chronicler Agibertus. Agibertus, as we saw, recalls the Deacon's image of the past as a heap of leaves, in part as an interpretation of his own writing about the past. This is also how Johnson uses the image and, perhaps, it might be used accordingly by the reader. Over and over again we see that the past is not allowed to remain with the Deacon as a single, closed-off event, as if it were a figure of speech that hardly made sense in its own time. And neither is the past just a cause of the present, as if history could push the story forward without being continuously interpreted.

The complex chronotope at work here is common enough in Johnson's novels to be called a trade-mark for his writing: the *mis-en-abîme*, the presentation of a thought or a story as reflected through a series of readers and writers, as stories placed as boxes-within-boxes.[24] This is a way of showing how texts are not just constructed in a singular and closed relationship with the reality depicted, as Hedin and others would have us believe. Johnson demonstrates that the novel may move beyond such constructions, reflecting upon them as constructions that, for whatever purposes, have to be recalled by somebody willing to entertain a dialogue between the past and the present, the act of writing and the act of reading. The frame is brought into the picture. The freedom of our world between past and present is compromised by the roles that are given to beginnings and to endings. As Peled Ginsburg says in a different literary context, such a particular

> [...] historical consciousness [...] undercuts not only the nostalgic idealization of the past (as totally different from the present), but also the view of the present as in some sense 'beyond' the past – a vantage point from which one can apprehend the past, turn the 'pastness' of the past (its being irrevocably lost) into its knowledge.[25]

It has also been noted that Johnson often preferred to write hesitantly, somehow unwilling to allow a single word to finish off the descriptions. In particular, words that may appear to be marginal, or subordinated, can give the text important shifts in nuance, or sometimes place arguments in positions of ironic contradiction.[26] Because of this, some early critics suggested that parts of his long novels could have been more concentrated: reduced to their essential messages.[27] Johnson did not agree. With particular reference to James Joyce and Thomas Mann, he says: 'The dependent clauses, that in the method of "concentration" appear unnecessary, or heavy, are the life of these novels. The disappeared, the in-between tone, the hunch.'[28] Setterwall supports this stance in seeing modernist prose as intent on creating places for reflection, rather than just allowing for a linear reading: 'the narrator as a reconstructor of past experience through present time reflection requires the reader's reflexive rather than linear participation'.[29]

The readers are required to reflect on the ability of words and figures to carry an overload of meaning, otherwise they will lose their way in Johnson's long chains of metaphors that continuously displace meaning. Such a metaphorical displacement occurs, for example, in Bordeaux in the 1920s, when a narrator of *Livsdagen lång* (Life's Long Day) imagines what would happen if a winecask he sees were to fall from a wagon and burst, in turn allowing him to imagine blood pouring out of open wounds, if it were red wine, or traces of horses, if the wine were white. The narrator says that it probably was red wine: he then imagines that he hears the cask landing with 'a thud on the pavement, a heavy drum-beat on the drum-skin of the street, terrified, surprised, angry shouts – or happy ones? Signs of rebellion, revolution, important changes in the world for the better or for the worse.'[30]

Johnson is especially keen on playing with words and figures in places where identity is guarded, a subject of controlling institutions. In *Favel ensam* (Favel Alone), the names of the main characters are Favel-Hyth, a journalist of German origin, with a British passport, living in Rome, and Charlon-Loday, a painter and a doctor, who appears to have a long record of being arrested and interrogated by the police of different regimes. Playfully, the names are in part derived from the protagonist traveller in Thomas More's *Utopia*, Charlonhyth.[31] Both characters share characteristics with Johnson, and Charlon-Loday also resembles both Thomas More and Rudolf Rocker, the anarchist Krapotkin's secretary, whom Johnson had met in Berlin in the 1920s. In the novel, Favel-Hyth has come to England to tell the truth about certain events that occurred in Berlin in 1934. He soon begins to doubt the necessity of revealing what happened, and he starts to question his motives for telling the truth. He understands that there are strategies and passion involved in truth-telling. The truth is not only a passive reflection of what has happened, but rather, to tell the truth is an act that has an effect upon the world, an act that will take place on a field where different strategies compete. This means, that even if there is reason to tell the truth about history, about identity, we are still not allowed to separate truth-telling from ideology. As the character Crofter Brace says in another novel:

What makes me a European – if I am one? A certain amount of reason, which isn't ice-cold. Ice-cold reason is a mere phrase. There's no reason without some measure of passion. But what is the passion for power? Is it cold or hot? A desire to commit violence to the goddess of history? Also a phrase, but with truth to it: the passion for power is a desire to rape. But cold reason, does that exist? Why, even the desire to analyze is passion.[32]

Favel-Hyth comes to understand that false dreams may be better than ravaged utopias, but Johnson seems to say that it is only in borderlands that utopian or other stories of pleasure can play a soothing role, while there is a perpetual risk that they turn into monsters if they are moved to the centres of national narratives. In *Favel ensam*, an example of this is a particular story, set on the border, for the moment retold by Charlon-Loday, who was once questioned at British Customs by Scotland Yard.[33] The Yard ask the 'usual' questions: Who is Charlon? He answers: 'I presumed every thinking human being – except of course the Scotland Yard-people – to be uncertain of their identity.' He says he has been 'investigating the mysteries and the possibilities of prisons as motives in relation to words and pictures, primarily oil-paintings'. Such research was made 'to increase one's prison-knowledge, for example, by comparing certain prisons to the Tower and to other important monuments of culture and human nature', and this turns out to have been a part of his inquiry about 'the possibility of happiness for mankind'. The officers from Scotland Yard finally ask Charlon to describe the place where he lived – England – allowing Charlon-Loday to indulge in a realistic description of the extensive amount of history that may be found where people live, thereby resisting any simple definition of the identity of a place:

> I continued for such a long time that all possible plausible spies surely had the opportunity to sneak into the country, due to the one-sided or lack of attention on the part of the police; and afterwards I guess I was sorry about that perhaps happening. You see, I started with the Danish Founder and the founding, almost at the bottom.[34]

We may compare this lack of trust in the possibility of giving a conclusive explanation of truth, identity and history, with Johnson's complex understanding of the pleasure of reading about history, the curiosity that gives people a lust for the past. In a speech, the novelist says that to explain this kind of curiosity would require

[...] a lot more time than I now have at my disposal this week or this month. A roundtable question to be answered in detail during the decades to come by all the world's historians, cultural historians, archaeologists, linguists – yes, only those who think that a new culture starts with every new minister of culture in every country, do not need to bother about this.[35]

There are, then, plenty of reasons to be wary of the possibility of taking for granted the immediate content of the pictures that Johnson purveys, as if every image was an unambiguous concentration of meaning. Nevertheless an interesting image is given by Crofter Brace, a writer of drama escaping from a revolution, in the novel *Lägg undan solen* (Put Away the Sun). Crofter Brace is envious of the ability of painters to represent simultaneity in their paintings, while narrators remain trapped in the order of events that follow each other in time. This argument rests on Gotthold Ephraim Lessing's thesis that signs arranged side by side, such as in painting, can express only subjects arranged side by side, like a landscape, whereas signs which succeed each other, as in poetry, can express only subjects which succeed each other, like actions.[36] Bäckman takes this figure to be a key to what Johnson's writing is all about: a more or less vain effort to present simultaneity, or, as Bäckman says, a search for the 'timeless history'.[37] But this would make Johnson's approach to time univocally utopian, and one would be tempted to quote Patrick Wright: 'history becomes "timeless" when it has been frozen solid, closed down and limited to what can be exhibited as a fully accomplished "historical past" which demands only appreciation and protection.'[38] If this was true, one would be able to make a systematic model of how things can remain timeless, for example how institutions can be preserved, or identities remain essential. Such timelessness is, however, contested not only by Johnson's irony, but also by alternative images of time that he has presented.

In Johnson's novels there occurs only a precarious simultaneity of actions among people who are unaware of each other.[39] As I have pointed out, he has an understanding for the soothing function of utopian narrative when straddling the borders of nations. But more often his writing tends to complicate even such pictures of place and time, rather than to make them appear obvious. We need to write stories about the past to account for our present identities, but he argues that such writing can rarely be an effortless recuperation of a single history. The all-pervasive chronotope of Johnson's work is his demonstration that every place and every identity, especially in Europe, can be read as the outcome of a plethora of stories. A word Johnson uses to describe such a reading is 'penetration'. As again one can read in *Hans nådes tid*:

> In Johannes Lupigis' memoirs, one can read:
> 'I write these words now:
> Penetrate. To penetrate the world as it is, in order to find out how it is and as I still am able to see it [...] – to penetrate the memory of pain to dissolve it in contemplation. Penetrate the past so that one is there – and behold, I am part of it now, and I say: remembrance is there and it belongs to what is alive, it belongs to life in the present.'[40]

The word 'penetrate' indicates a connection to the philosopher Henri Bergson, whose theories of history were particularly influential in the early twentieth century.[41] Bergson proposed to understand time as an almost phenomenological experience of duration, instead of the more familiar geometrical conception of time as events that follow each other like points on a line. In a letter written in 1929, Johnson refers to his reading of Bergson:

> History will according to Bergson (am I right?) not offer us any *conclusion*, but it will continue to tie together small trifles, continue to bump and scrape against each other the small causes of the generations' life and death, just like the sea at the shore scrapes and bumps gravel into a certain form.[42]

This vision of time as duration makes decisive, revolutionary changes almost impossible, not because everything is set, but on the contrary because it cannot ever settle, and thus there is no sense in voting for the revolutionary alternative of turning things upside down. In another letter from 1929, Johnson, once a follower of Krapotkin, confesses that he appreciates the moral integrity of the communists, although he criticizes their ideology. Yet, he continues: 'although if a revolution were to break out now, like the others I would grab a gun and mount the barricades'.[43]

THE STORIES AMONG US

In a novel from 1964, Johnson remembers the 1920s, where a young narrator tells how place can be imagined, on a square in Bordeaux where once a seventeenth-century rebellion had ended in the execution of the revolutionaries:

> One time changes place with another, times shift, change place on the chessboard, but they do not disappear: they remain. One time watches another time. None of them is effaced for ever. Times remain in the stones of the street, in the houses, in inherited movement. Time is preserved, there are time-preservers.[44]

On this square in Bordeaux we seem to have encountered another time, a time which is not our time, because it 'watches' our time, and it is therefore clearly another – its presence in our time is not a simultaneity, an absence or a total presence of time, but it is a meeting, a coming together. Of course, this is not an entirely unique argument, and Johnson shares his awareness of the discontinuity of history with many other novelists. For example, the Bordeaux writer Phillippe Sollers has argued that the layered presence of many times does not necessarily involve any recognition between the different times. Without the intervention of the novelist, times might therefore remain unaware of each other:

> So the History that marches and moves around, tumult and rage, does then leave intact the flowers that grow indefinitely in the same ground, on the surface, where conquests and bloody battles have taken place, anguish and massacres. There they are again, 'fresh and cheerful as in the days of battle'.[45]

Johnson, however, allows the times to watch each other, and to enter into dialogue. The chronotopes of stories and histories are not efforts to find a unique and unambiguous relationship between place and time, identity and history, but rather a way of opening up places by means of a discussion between different times. They are a way of retelling Europe as a discussion between different stories. Other times and other stories may be framed by narrators, arranged so that they can be seen, or perhaps even so that the other times can see us. In *Några steg mot tystnaden* (A Few Steps towards Silence), the picture-framer Peidar, while framing some old paintings, is thinking about the words of his cousin Giachim, owner of an hotel filled with portraits, on the Swiss–Italian border:

> Giachim wants the framed faces to be at their advantage, yes, that is self-evident. To turn to the observer, as he said, to 'attract, allow their appearance to please'. Or the better to be able

to watch the observer, to notice the life that passes before the eyes of the portrait, to look closely at the visitor and his or her present. One can't make Giachim out, he sometimes says such unexpected things.[46]

Now, perhaps one should not take Peidar so seriously, when he claims that Giachim says unexpected things. We already know that governments wish that the past speak to us in a pleasant way. At the limit, the past is brought in just to state its finitude, its inability to be of interest to our present, 'the hopeful promise of our common future'. Every representation of a political community will allow the past to speak, and we expect that official narrators, whether hotel managers or European commissioners, will try to frame history so as to legitimate governance.

What may be unexpected in Johnson's novels is, instead, his rich, yet hesitant, figuration of the kind of writing we can use to make the past speak. Apparently we may play around with the past, even when we tell the truth, which we may do for one reason or another. It is interesting to note that such a playing around need not mean that serious subjects are forgotten (unless, of course, serious is taken to be the equivalent of what is useful for a certain regime). Literature can be a distinctive source of knowledge mainly because of its ability to establish identity in an alternative, overtly fictitious way. It allows the reader time to play; time to gain a new perspective upon the world. Such playing around can be uncomfortable and unsettling for ideologies that become legitimate only by hiding the ambiguities of governance and identity-making.

In contrast to many other authors, Johnson does not offer us anything drastically new, and he doesn't promise that the future will be full of changes. His novels do not offer us an image of a singular place or a singular time, and it is not possible to extract any univocal definition of what a European history or a European identity would be like. Indeed, the objective of this chapter has not been to extract any such message from Johnson's novels, but rather to show how they may be read as a comment upon the way Europe will have to negotiate its past more carefully than might seem to be the case in texts that urge us to hurry on if we wish to catch the promises of the future.

The novelist argues that history can answer back, even while it is addressed only to legitimize the present. If Europe is becoming a new place, with an increasingly common history, it might be a good thing. However, following Johnson, we should know that stories about the past and the present will remain, that they already are lying around for us to trudge through or to pick up: times remain in the stones of the streets. Johnson reminds us that the modern chronotope of simultaneous time is too strong an allegory for Europe. This particular community should rather be read as a place with many times.

An early version of this article was presented at the ECPR conference of political scientists in Bordeaux in 1995, and I would like to thank the participants in the 'Politics and the Arts' workshop for their comments.

NOTES

1. Johnson's life before his decision to be an author is the subject of his novel *Romanen om Olof* (Stockholm: Bonnier, 1935). The standard biography is in two volumes: Örjan Lindberger, *Norrbottningen som blev Europé* (Stockholm, 1986), and *Människan i tiden* (Stockholm, 1990). See also Gavin Orton, *Eyvind Johnson* (New York, 1972).
2. Lars G. Warme, 'Eyvind Johnson's *Några steg mot tystnaden*: an Apologia,' *Scandinavian Studies* 49 (1977): pp. 452–63, here p. 452.
3. *Hans nådes tid* (Stockholm, 1960) p. 72. All quotations from Johnson's novels are my translations.
4. For an interesting study of the times of the others, see Michael Taussig, *Mimesis and Alterity: a Particular History of the Senses* (New York, 1993).
5. Derek Heater, *The Idea of European Unity* (Leicester, 1992), p. 2.
6. Michael Walzer, 'On the Role of Symbolism in Political Thought', *Political Science Quarterly* 82 (June 1967): pp. 191–204, here p. 194.
7. Heater, p. 180.
8. Stuart Hampshire, *Thought and Action* (London, 1960), p. 71. Or, as Frank Kermode says, 'sequence goes nowhere without his doppelgänger, or shadow, causality.' 'Secrets and Narrative Sequence', *Critical Inquiry* 7.1 (1980): pp. 83–101, here p. 84. Cf. Helga Nowotny, 'Time and Social Theory: Towards a Social Theory of Time', *Time & Society* 1.3 (1992): pp. 421–54.
9. For a critique, see George C. Bond and Angela Gilliam, eds, *Social Construction of the Past: Representation as Power* (London, 1994); or John G. Ruggie, 'Territoriality and Beyond: Problematizing Modernity in International Relations', *International Organization* 47.1 (1993): pp. 137–74.
10. Cf. Ole Waever, 'Europe since 1945: Crisis to Renewal', *The History of the Idea of Europe*, eds K. Dussen and J. van der Dussen (London,

1995), pp. 151–210, here p. 152: 'the *promise* of Europe – which might mean the possibility of freeing oneself from the old Europe'.
11. Janerik Gidlund and Sverker Sörlin, *Det europeiska kalejdoskopet* (Stockholm: SNS, 1993), p. 22.
12. Cf. the Yugoslavian state, which 'was born in 1918, upon the collapse of the Ottoman and Habsburg Empires, *in the name* of the principle of self-determination of nations. It died in 1991 *in the name* [my emphasis] of the same principle'. *Unfinished Peace: Report of the International Commission on the Balkans* (Washington: Carnegie Endowment for International Peace, 1996), p. 28. For a philosophical analysis, see Slavoj Zizek, *The Sublime Object of Ideology* (London, 1989), pp. 87–99. See also Alain Boureau, 'L'adage vox populi, vox dei et l'invention de la nation anglaise (VIIIe-XIIe siècle)', *Annales: Economies, Sociétés, Cultures* 4/5 (1992): pp. 1071–89. On the uses of history as a way of proving theory right, see the debate between Markus Fischer and Bruce Hall & Friedrich Kratochwil, *International Organization* 43 (1993), pp. 479–500.
13. See, for example, Dominick LaCapra, 'History, Language and Reading: Waiting for Crillon', *American Historical Review* 100.3 (1995): pp. 799–828.
14. Maureen Whitebrook, 'Taking the Narrative Turn: What the Novel has to Offer Political Theory', *Literature and the Political Imagination*, eds. J. Horton and A. Baumeister (London, 1996), pp. 32–52. Cf. Michael Shapiro, 'Literary Production as a Politicizing Practice', *Political Theory* 12.3 (1984): pp. 387–422.
15. *Imagined Communities: Reflections on the Origin and Spread of Nationalism* (London, 1983), pp. 28–40.
16. Geoffrey Bennington, 'Postal Politics and the Institution of the Nation', *Legislations: the Politics of Deconstruction* (London, 1994); Andrew Hadfield, *Literature, Politics and National Identity: Reformation to Renaissance* (Cambridge, 1994).
17. Sven Hedin, *Kriget mot Ryssland: Minnen från fronten i öster, mars – augusti 1915* (Stockholm: Bonnier, 1915), p. 38. Hedin, just like today's Swedish skinheads, seems to ignore Voltaire's comment: 'Certainement, il n'y a point de Souverain, qui en lisant la vie de Charles XII. ne doive être guéri de la folie des conquêtes.' *Charles XII: Roi de Suède*, p. 31, from *Collection complette des ouvres* (Geneve, 1757).
18. Patrick Brantlinger, *Crusoe's Footprints: Cultural Studies in Britain and America* (London: Routledge, 1990) p. 2.
19. Reinhart Koselleck, *Futures Past: On the Semantics of Historical Time* (Cambridge, Mass.: MIT Press, 1985), p. 112, English trans. of *Vergangene Zukunft: Zur Semantik Geschichtlicher Zeiten* (Frankfurt am Main, 1979).
20. Mikhail Bakhtin, 'Forms of Time and of the Chronotope in the Novel', *The Dialogic Imagination: Four Essays* (Austin, 1981) pp. 84–258, here p. 84, English trans. of *Voprosy literatury i estetiki* (Moskva, 1975). Without using this concept, Niklas Luhman also writes about the importance of a fusion of time and space for the maintenance of 'social systems', for example, 'Complexity, Structural Contingencies and Value Conflicts', *Detraditionalization: Critical Reflections on Authority and*

Identity, eds. Heelas, Lash, Morris (Cambridge, Mass., 1996); see also Ulrich Beck, Anthony Giddens, Scott Lash, eds, *Reflexive Modernization* (Cambridge, 1994). All these authors want to avoid defining structures too rigidly. For a more closed model of European integration, see Staffan Zetterholm, 'Why is Cultural Diversity a Political Problem?: a Discussion of Cultural Barriers to Political Integration', *National Cultures and European Integration*, ed. Zetterholm (Oxford, 1994), pp. 65–82. For a discussion of the limits of openings, see Umberto Eco, *Lector in fabula: La cooperazione interpretativa nei testi narrativi* (Milano, 1979).
21. Stuart Allen, '"When discourse is torn from reality": Bakhtin and the Principle of Chronotopicity', *Time & Society* 3.2 (1994): pp. 193–218, here p. 210; Bakhtin, p. 255.
22. *Hans nådees tid*, p. 186
23. Bo G. Jansson, 'Självironi, självbespegling och självreflexion: den metafiktiva tendensen i Eyvind Johnsons diktning', diss: Uppsala University, 1990, p. 125.
24. Jansson, passim. Cf. Hayden White, 'The Question of Narrative in Contemporary Historical Theory', *History and Theory* 23.1 (1984): pp. 1–33.
25. Michal Peled Ginsburg, *Economies of Change: Form and Transformation in the Nineteenth-Century Novel* (Stanford: Stanford University Press, 1996), p. 81.
26. Ingrid Öberg, 'Upprepning och variation i Eyvind Johnsons roman Hans nådes tid', *Svensklärarföreningens årsskrift* (1972): pp. 122–43.
27. For example, Hallberg regards Johnson's playfulness as a limbering-up movement, a preparation for the deed of poetry: Peter Hallberg, 'Eyvind Johnson, ordet och verkligheten', *Bonniers Litterära Magasin* 27.7 (1958): pp. 538–48, here p. 539.
28. 'Anteckningar om romanförfatteri' (1949) in *Personligt, politiskt, estetiskt* (Stockholm, 1992), pp. 176–82, here p. 181.
29. Monica Setterwall, 'The Unwritten Story', diss., University of Wisconsin-Madison, 1979 (Ann Arbour, 1981), p. 67.
30. *Livsdagen lång* (Stockholm, 1964), p. 12. In Dickens's *A Tale of Two Cities* a winecask really breaks, and announces the coming of the French revolution. See Jansson, 109f.
31. *Favel ensam* (Stockholm, 1968). Cf. Paul Turner's remark on Thomas More's characters, quoted in Jansson, p. 88: 'It is clear from an ironical passage in a letter [...] that More expected the educated reader to understand these names.' On the utopian in *Favel ensam*, see also Thure Stenström, *Romantikern Eyvind Johnson* (Uppsala, 1978), pp. 73–196.
32. *Lägg undan solen* (Stockholm, 1951), p. 96.
33. *Favel ensam*, pp. 125–30.
34. ibid., p. 128.
35. 'Att dröja vid det förflutna' (1967) in *Personligt, politiskt, estetiskt*, pp. 209–220, here p. 217.
36. With particular reference to Lessing and his allegories, Carol Jacobs warns against the too-abrupt interpretation, 'Fictional Histories: Lessing's

Laocoön', *Telling Time* (Baltimore, 1993) p. 118.
37. Stig Bäckman, 'Den tidlösa historien: En studie i tre romaner av Eyvind Johnson', diss., University of Lund, 1975.
38. Quoted in Tony Bennett, *The Birth of the Museum: History, Theory, Politics* (London: Routledge, 1995), p. 134. Johnson often defines his writing in terms of a construction of pictures. See Ulf Linde, 'A Trip to Gotland', *Artes: an International Reader of Literature Art and Music* 3 (1996): pp. 27–34, here p. 31.
39. Staffan Björck, *Romanens formvärld* (Stockholm, 1953), pp. 186–226; Göran Rossholm, 'Sub Specie durationis: En studie i Eyvind Johnsons roman Hans nådes tid i ljuset av Henri Bergsons tidsmetafysik', *Horisont*, 21.6 (1974): pp. 119–33; Hallberg.
40. *Hans nådes tid*, p. 440.
41. Cf. Jean-Francois Battail, *Le mouvement des idées en Suède à l'âge du bergsonisme* (Paris, 1979); Bäckman; Ann Game, 'Time, Space, Memory, with reference to Bachelard', *Global Modernities*, eds Featherstone, Lash, Robertson (London: Sage, 1995) pp. 192–208; Rossholm.
42. Quoted in Lindberger (1986), p. 246f.
43. Ibid., p. 247f.
44. *Livsdagen lång*, p. 11.
45. *Portrait du Jouyeur* (Paris, 1984: Gallimard Coll. Folio, 1986), p. 241, my trans.
46. *Några steg mot tystnaden* (Stockholm, 1973), p. 206.

11 Englishness from the Outside
Ruth Wittlinger

In a study on *The Novel and England since 1945*, D.J. Taylor has recently claimed that the adjective '"English" [...] is capable of describing anything from a limp handshake to class hatred.'[1] The aim of this essay is to examine the concept of Englishness from different perspectives. One, a view 'from the inside' provided largely by people who have a particular interest in preserving this 'national fiction' for identificatory purposes – that is, politicians – and the other, a view 'from the outside',[2] provided by Naipaul, a post-colonial writer who describes his experience and encounter with England in his autobiographical novel *The Enigma of Arrival*.[3] First of all, however, it is necessary to look briefly at the recent discussion on the concept of the nation which forms the basis for related constructs such as national identity, in general, and Englishness, in particular.

EUROPEAN INTEGRATION AND THE NATION-STATE

As other essays in this collection illustrate, discussing the *idea of Europe*, a *European identity* or, in a more practical sense, *European integration* requires in most cases an examination of the concept of the nation, since, as Benedict Anderson puts it, 'nation-ness is the most universally legitimate value in the political life of our time'.[4] This is particularly important to bear in mind in the context of an integration process in which the main building-blocks are nation-states.

Along with many fellow-academics discussing the alleged crisis of the nation-state, and, in contrast, its continued resilience, John Dunn reminds us of the deeply flawed notion of a 'nation-state' when he points out that

> [a] true nation state, therefore, would consist only of those who belonged to it by birth and of those who were fully subject to its

sovereign legal authority. By this (for practical purposes, no doubt absurdly stipulative) criterion it is unlikely that there is a single nation state in the world at present, and moderately unlikely that any such state has ever existed. But, as with most political ideas, the force of the idea of the nation state has never come principally from its descriptive precision. What it offers is a precarious fusion of two very different modes of thinking: one explicitly subjective, urgent and identificatory, and the other presumptively objective, detached and independent of the vagaries of popular consciousness.[5]

Eric Hobsbawm, criticizing the criteria commonly used to define nationhood such as 'language, ethnicity or whatever' finds them 'fuzzy, shifting and ambiguous' which 'of course, makes them unusually convenient for propagandist and programmatic, as distinct from descriptive purposes'.[6] Along similar lines, Anderson has a strong case arguing that nations are 'imagined communities' or even 'cultural artefacts of a particular kind'.[7] On the other hand, however, the importance and popular appeal of related constructs such as 'national identity' are not to be underestimated. Regardless of the assessment of the concept of the nation by the academic community, appealing to the nation and a national identity with the help of national symbols or, in a wider sense, texts, still provides a populist and powerful instrument used not only by politicians during election campaigns.

At the same time, however, the postmodern trajectory suggests that subjectivity is largely characterized by diversity, fragmentation and multiple identities, and that the nation-state increasingly loses its importance in a globalized world in which consumer fetishism not only unites classes, as Marcuse claimed, but also renders national affiliations less and less important. In other words, 'the nationally imagined identity is diminishing in importance, as compared with imagined "life-style" groups of consumers.'[8] Michael Billig, however, claims that the postmodern thesis of the disappearing nation-state and the notion of a 'global village' tend to ignore what he termed 'banal nationalism'[9] which, he stresses, certainly does not mean that it is benign in nature. In his view,

> [n]ationalism is not confined to the florid language of blood-myths. Banal nationalism operates with prosaic, routine words, which takes nations for granted, and which, in so doing, enhabit them. Small words, rather than grand memorable phrases, offer constant,

but barely conscious, reminders of the homeland, making 'our' national identity unforgettable.[10]

Whether we like it or not, nationhood provides a continual background for political discourses as well as cultural products and we are daily reminded of 'our' national place in a world of nations.[11] After these general considerations on the role of nations, I would now like to turn my attention to national identity and examine in more detail the British variant, which is, ironically, usually referred to as 'Englishness'.

ENGLISHNESS

National identity is a very elusive and constructed concept in any case, but Englishness appears to be particularly adaptable and persuasive at the same time as being difficult to grasp and analyse. In their introduction to a sourcebook entitled *Writing Englishness* Judy Giles and Tim Middleton explain the meaning and function of Englishness as follows:

> Englishness is not simply about something called 'the national character' but has to be seen as a nexus of values, beliefs and attitudes which are offered as unique to England and to those who identify as, or wish to identify as, English. In other words Englishness is a state of mind: a belief in a national identity which is part and parcel of one's sense of self.[12]

Englishness has been a popular theme in many cultural texts – painting, music, literature[13] – as well as in academic research in many disciplines and sub-disciplines, from political thought to literary and cultural studies.[14] As the quote from Taylor at the beginning of the chapter indicates, in some respects it appears as if Englishness merely provides the empty shell which can be filled according to taste, the taste being determined by the dominant discourse of a particular time and place. It is therefore hardly surprising that Englishness through the course of its history has been renegotiated and adapted to different circumstances. In the context of European integration Stephen Haseler even argues that Englishness is the culprit responsible for Britain's difficult relationship with Europe and the EU.[15] At the same time, however, he suggests that the 'twin pressures of global capitalism and European union' might even mean a 'potentially terminal crisis' for Englishness.[16] As I will show with some examples from recent political rhetoric, however, it appears as if these 'twin pressures', rather than threatening the existence of Englishness, seem to support its continued existence and even offer a chance for Englishness to reassert itself, possibly exactly because it is portrayed and perceived to be under threat.

I would therefore argue that it is no surprise that there are plenty of examples in recent British political history which illustrate how Englishness has been evoked, for example, by using the past in order to provide identification for the present as well as a vision for the future. This point can be particularly well illustrated by Thatcher-style Englishness[17] which provides prime examples in this context. Although Margaret Thatcher was on the one hand rightly accused of breaking with 'One-Nation Toryism', that is, her policies are said to have widened the gap between the rich and the poor, the haves and the have-nots,[18] on the other hand, she never got tired of using strong rhetoric, appealing to the idea of the nation as a unifying force to (re)construct some common identity. This was particularly obvious at the time of the Falklands War when she referred to the Falklanders as 'British in stock and tradition'[19] but even in less 'extreme' circumstances she managed to provide a vision in claiming that '[s]omewhere ahead lies greatness for our country again. This I know in my heart.'[20] In the European context, the strong nationalist rhetoric she used is best illustrated in the Bruges speech in which she identifies in no uncertain terms the enemy that threatens the 'achievements' of Britain: 'We have not successfully rolled back the frontiers of the state in Britain only to see them reimposed at a European level, with a European super-state exercising a new dominance from Brussels.'[21] 'Rolling back the frontiers of the state' in the economy was an 'achievement' of Thatcherite Britain in terms of deregulation which was part of her 'elimination of socialism' project. Destroying socialism, 'the enemy within', was her declared aim. It was, however, a much more useful technique to identify, locate and demonize the main enemy of Thatcherism in Europe (which, significantly, in popular speech is usually taken to exclude Britain) instead of in domestic politics.

Possibly a softer but perhaps not necessarily less powerful and effective image was favoured by her successor with '[h]is central vision of contemporary Britain [which] was inspired by people watching the sun set over the village cricket ground, before retiring to the pub for warm beer and amicable conversation between teams and locals.'[22] A recent example shows that this technique is, however, certainly not the prerogative of Conservative prime ministers. In the British General Election campaign of 1997, a party political broadcast by New Labour featured a bulldog which 'is often used, even for political purposes, as a symbol of Englishness *per se* and as a personification of slowness and determination'.[23] Without naming the beast, Margaret Thatcher had used the same image in a speech towards the end of her General Election campaign in 1979: 'It is a Britain of thoughtful people, tantalisingly slow to act, yet marvellously determined when they do.'[24]

Apart from politics, it is probably in the area of imaginative literature that Englishness has received most attention. The literary canon as it has been known and established[25] contributed considerably to the construction and persistence of the concept by repeating and thereby reinforcing familiar motifs of Englishness such as the 'Gentleman Ideal',[26] the 'English Landscape' and so on. It is interesting to note here that the most persistent motifs are very often exclusive rather than inclusive through their portrayal of certain sections of society only, for example, cricket fans.

Before turning to Naipaul's narrative, it is necessary to briefly explore the relationship between 'nation' and 'narration', concept, which, to a large extent, are both products of the imagination.

NATION AND NARRATION

There are several potential connections between 'nation' and 'narration'. From a historical perspective, for example, the nation developed almost simultaneously with the novel. Aldous Huxley even attributed some responsibility for the creation of nations to novelists by claiming that '"nations are to a very large extent invented by their poets and novelists"'.[27] Homi Bhabha has pointed out another link between 'nation and narration' by claiming that '[n]ations, like narratives, lose their origins in the myths of time and only fully realize their horizons in the mind's eye'.[28]

It is particularly since the emergence of 'post-colonial literature and criticism', a category which has recently received increasing attention, that literature in English has been actively engaged in a critical discussion and questioning of Englishness. Post-colonial narratives, imaginative ones as well as those produced by literary criticism and cultural studies, have facilitated a discussion which has redirected and renegotiated the focus from a perceived centre to what has long been seen to be the periphery. Along with that, an interest developed in the perception of 'Englishness from the outside', or, as Homi Bhabha put it, 'the peoples of the periphery return to rewrite the history and fiction of the metropolis. [...] The bastion of Englishness crumbles at the sight of immigrants and factory workers.'[29]

In the following section, I will focus mainly on the question of national identity in the context of displacement, as presented and discussed in *The Enigma of Arrival*.

NAIPAUL'S *ENIGMA OF ARRIVAL*

Similar to the 'narrative of the nation' which combines historical and geographical 'realities' with myths, Naipaul's narrative is called an 'autobiographical novel'. This allowed Naipaul to merge fact and fiction, by the same token assigning it more general relevance than a 'mere autobiography' *and* acknowledging the inherently fictitious character of any autobiographical account. It can therefore be seen as an example of 'post-colonial counter-discourse' to the

> European constitution of the colonial subject, [in which] texts and textuality play a major part. European texts constructed colonial worlds, judging the colonized 'other' assimilatively through European cognitive codes, while reading that alterity as absence or negation against those codes.[30]

The autobiographical nature of the novel is of particular relevance, since, as Tiffin points out, 'English and European autobiographies [...] were part of the process of the 'othering' of the Caribbean by Europe.'[31] Thus, it is also through the choice of genre that Naipaul's account provides a contribution towards this counter-discourse or, in other words, an example in which *The Empire Writes Back*[32] and reflects on the encounter of the periphery with the centre.

From a non-European perspective, but certainly not without some perceptions of Europe and Britain, *The Enigma of Arrival* discusses, amongst other themes, questions of identity, particularly with regard to displacement. In this respect, the novel falls easily into the category of post-colonial literature since, as Ashcroft pointed out '[a] major feature of post-colonial literatures is the concern with place and displacement. It is here that the special post-colonial crisis of identity comes into being; the concern with the development or recovery of an effective identifying relationship between self and place.'[33]

The Enigma of Arrival tells the story of an unnamed Caribbean writer with Indian ancestry who left his home in Trinidad for England, the homeland of the former colonizers, at the age of 18 to take up a scholarship at Oxford. It is not just a journey removing him physically from his homeland. Metaphorically, it is a journey during which there are many *arrivals* in the context of his new, for a long time only, 'place of residence' rather than 'home'. During his journey, or, what Srinivasau calls 'Naipaul's odyssey',[34] the author-narrator has to revise and renegotiate his own version of Englishness which he received and formed in Trinidad. The following passage illustrates the author-narrator's, at times by his own account, very romantic notion of England and Englishness constructed by his former cultural environment:

> I had seen the cows on the hillsides against the sky, heads down, grazing, or looking with timorous interest at the passing man. And they had seemed like the cows in the drawing on the label of the condensed-milk tins I knew in Trinidad as a child: something to me as a result at the very heart of romance, a child's fantasy of the beautiful, other place, something which, when I saw it on the downs, was like something I had always known. (*EA*, p. 80)

During his time in the countryside, however, he is forced to accept the inevitability of change which also makes him reconsider previously held ideas, adding different and less romantic dimensions:

> The cows themselves eventually disappeared. Some would have been sold; but whether sold or not, what would have happened to them would have been what always happened to cows when their time was judged to have come: batches of them were regularly taken off in covered vans to the slaughterhouse. (*EA*, pp. 79–80)

In spite of Naipaul's reputation of being the personification of 'global homelessness', it is interesting to note here that the author-narrator, in his search for identity, regularly recalls images from his former homeland in order to make sense of his new surroundings. In the passage following the above quote, for example, he ponders at length over the role and status of cows in the society to which he previously belonged. In this respect, it can be argued, that no matter how homeless the subject might be, the previous cultural environment co-determines the parameters against which the new context is measured, thereby exerting considerable influence on the formation of a renegotiated identity.

Bruce King describes the author-narrator's dilemma of having to come to terms with the provisional nature of all perceptions as follows:

> As he begins to understand where he is, he also realizes that his notions of and associations with his new home have been wrongly influenced by his colonial education and readings in English literature. He must learn to see anew, to understand what he is actually seeing rather than what he expects to see. Again and again his perceptions are found to be wrong. No sooner has he corrected one mistake than the correction needs to be corrected by further information or someone else's point of view. People and places need to be seen in context and studied to get at the truth; but the people, places and contexts keep changing.[35]

For ten years he lives in a rented cottage near Stonehenge on Salisbury plain, a well-chosen location for an encounter with the historical dimension of Englishness. In the reclusion of this cottage and the surrounding manor grounds, he experiences what he calls a second childhood and reflects on his development from an 18-year-old scholarship student who left Trinidad to become a writer, to the mature writer he has become after several arrivals. This second childhood is characterized by an acceptance of the transitory and negotiable nature of alleged 'realities' and their perception.

The title of the novel 'serves more as metaphor than event'[36] and suggests that there is no clearly defined place of arrival; it is an enigma. Every arrival is provisional, possibly offering a new point of departure in the search for identity but never reaching a final point. Throughout the novel this metaphor for the author-narrator's personal development, or journey, is being reinterpreted and renegotiated according to his ever-changing perspectives created by different contexts and influences.

The main character comments on a painting which he has found by accident in a booklet which was left behind by the former tenants of his cottage: 'What was interesting about the painting itself, "The Enigma of Arrival", was that – again perhaps because of the title – it changed in my memory. The original (or the reproduction in the

"Little Library of Art" booklet) was always a surprise.' (*EA*, p. 91)

The painting itself depicts a Mediterranean quayside scene. In the background, the top of the mast of a vessel can be seen and in the foreground there are two figures: 'one perhaps the person who has arrived, the other perhaps a native of the port' (*EA*, p. 91). The author-narrator comments on the atmosphere of the scene: 'The scene is of desolation and mystery: it speaks of the mystery of arrival.' (*EA*, pp. 91–2)

In the following passage, he tells us of the story he might write one day about this scene. Metaphorically, it is really 'his story', in terms of identity-formation in the context of displacement:

> My story was to be set in classical times, in the Mediterranean. My narrator would write plainly, without any attempt at period style or historical explanation of his period. He would arrive – for a reason I had yet to work out – at that classical port with the walls and gateways like cut-outs. He would walk past that muffled figure on the quayside. He would move from that silence and desolation, that blankness, to a gateway or door. He would enter there and be swallowed by the life and noise of the crowded city (I imagined something like an Indian bazaar scene). The mission he had come on – family business, study, religious initiation – would give him encounters and adventures. He would enter interiors, of houses and temples. Gradually there would come to him a feeling that he was getting nowhere; he would lose his sense of mission; he would begin to know only that he was lost. His feeling of adventure would give way to panic. He would want to escape, to get back to the quayside and his ship. But he wouldn't know how. I imagined some religious ritual in which, led on by kindly people, he would unwittingly take part and find himself the intended victim. At the moment of crisis he would come upon a door, open it, and find himself back on the quayside of arrival. He has been saved; the world is as he remembered it. Only one thing is missing now. Above the cut-out walls and buildings there is no mast, no sail. The antique ship has gone. The traveller has lived out his life. (*EA*, p. 92)

This quote also illustrates the uprootedness of the traveller. Although he gains entry into houses after his arrival, he has the feeling 'that he was getting nowhere'. At the same time, however, he cannot 'reverse the arrival' and go back. The fact that the walls and gateways at the port where the traveller arrives are like 'cut-outs', points to the notion that it is the traveller who has to make them 'real' by supplying his own perspective.

And it is not until later that the author-narrator acknowledges the relevance of the story to his own life: '[...] it did not occur to me that that Mediterranean story was really no more than a version of the story I was already writing'. (*EA*, p. 93)

Parallels to the postmodern perception, as expressed by Bauman, that 'the postmodern citizen is a nomad wandering between unconnected places'[37] are striking in this key image of the novel.

At one point, the narrator spells out clearly the relevance of the painting to his own story:

> And it was out of that burden of emotion that there had come to the writer, as release, as an idyll, the ship story, the antique-quayside story, suggested by the 'Enigma of Arrival'; an idea that came innocently, without the writer suspecting how much of his life, how many aspects of his life, that remote story [...] carried. (*EA*, p. 96)

Although there are several other characters in the book, mainly people working in the manor grounds of which the cottage is part, apart from Jack the gardener and his landlord, Naipaul does not portray them in great depth. The narrator's main concern during his time at the cottage appears to be the countryside which takes on near-character-like status. As Nixon points out '[t]ere is decidedly no other British writer of Caribbean or South Asian ancestry who would have chosen a tucked-away Wiltshire perspective from which to reflect on the themes of immigration and post-colonial decay.'[38] This is particularly relevant since the English countryside is one of the prime motifs of Englishness and the relationship between the place and the self is said to be one of the main concerns of identity formation. According to Homi Bhabha, the role of the landscape is a 'recurrent metaphor [...] as the inscape of national identity'.[39]

The ever-changing perspectives which Naipaul uses, for example those in the countryside caused by the seasons, have resulted in the novel being labelled 'postmodern'. Naipaul uses these different perspectives in order to illustrate the lack of certainty and the negotiable position of the 'self' as well as the 'other'. This becomes particularly obvious in the case of the 'Negro' whose changed status, caused by a different location and cultural environment, the narrator describes as follows:

> There had been a Negro in the hangar or airport shed in Puerto Rico where, after many hours, and in the late afternoon, our little aeroplane had made its first halt. Already the light had changed; the world had changed. The world had ceased to be colonial, for me; people had already altered their value, even this Negro. He was bound for Harlem. At home, among his fellows, just a few hours before, he was a man to be envied, his journey indescribably glamorous; now he was a Negro, in a straw-coloured jacket obviously not his own, too tight across his weightlifter's shoulders (weight-lifting was a craze among us). Now, in that jacket (at home, the badge of the traveller to the temperate North), he was bluffing it out, insisting on his respectability, on not being an American Negro, on not being fazed by the aeroplane and by the white people. (*EA*, p. 101)

Naipaul illustrates here that a different place does not only make a difference to the identity of the self, but also to the way the self is assessed and judged by the others. From having been in a position of being envied, a change of location causes the 'Negro' to have to 'bluff it out and insist on his respectability'.

And although the narrator 'had sought him out and even claimed kinship with him', he was glad that the man did not respond in a friendly way since he (the narrator) 'felt the gestures of friendship to be false'. (*EA*, p. 101) In spite of that, however, the 'kinship' is acknowledged in a way that makes it hardly noticeable: 'weight-lifting was a craze among *us* [my emphasis]'. This seems to give weight to Billig's argument, presented earlier in this essay, claiming the omnipresence of 'banal nationalism' which is expressed in 'small words' rather than 'blood-myths'.

Changing locations and the resulting feeling of displacement is a constant feature of the narrator's character. As the following quote shows, even after many years in England, he still feels displaced, constantly arriving somewhere physically without ever getting the feeling of belonging:

> The idea of ruin and dereliction, of out-of-placeness, was something I felt about myself, attached to myself: a man from another hemisphere, another background, coming to rest in middle life in the cottage of a half-neglected estate, an estate full of reminders of its Edwardian past, with few connections with the present. (*EA*, p. 19)

In contrast to the narrator's displacement stands Jack the gardener's life which the narrator sees as 'genuine, rooted, fitting: man fitting the landscape' (*EA*, p. 19).

Although the narrator feels that '[f]ifty years ago there would have been no room for me on the estate; even now my presence was a little unlikely' (*EA*, p. 52), he feels great sympathy for his landlord, a character closely linked to representations of Englishness like the 'Gentleman Ideal' living in an 'English Manor House'. In spite of their opposing places in terms of colonizer and colonized, the narrator conveys more commonality with the landlord – 'the wild garden his taste [...] and also mine' (*EA*, p. 53) – than with the 'Negro' with whom he shared his geographical origins.

The reception of Naipaul as a post-colonial writer has been diverse. The dominant Anglo-American perception of him is one of 'a permanent exile, a refugee, a homeless citizen of the world, and an extranational writer' who is 'haunted by a global homelessness that is inseparably geographical, existential, and literary',[40] in other words a 'cultural hybrid' par excellence.[41] However, his fellow postcolonial critics have also accused him of being prone to Eurocentrism: – '"[h]e travels to confirm his Eurocentric prejudices"'.[42] In other words, he could be seen to confirm his own 'fictions' of reality. It is reassuring to see that Naipaul's central message, the changing perspectives depending on time, place and context, have also inspired literary criticism and have thus produced different readings of his works.

CONCLUSION

The narratives presented by historians, political scientists and an imaginative writer and discussed in this essay, indicate that nations and their related concepts such as national identity can be demystified. In the context of European integration, this appears, at first sight, to be good news. Transcending national boundaries opens up the possibilities of further integration. Just as a British identity is arguably produced mainly by myth-making, we (!) could attempt to construct a 'European Identity' built on myths with an emphasis on a common European culture, in other words, open ourselves up to Eurocentrism, something which has been a major criticism made by poststructuralists. The question, however, is whether the creation/construction of a common European identity that transcends the nation-state is so desirable, since, as mentioned above, it would first require the establishment or construction of difference which is so important in terms of identity formation. This is no doubt a dubious aim to pursue because it would merely shift the border of exclusion to a different level, with a still very artificial and restricted division of the world into 'us' and 'them', the binary opposition still being intact. In an economic sense, this politically constructed border already exists.

Jacques Delors made the exclusive nature of his vision of Europe quite clear when he suggested that 'Europeans unite behind the label of "Christian European Civilization"'.[43] As Billig observantly notes, this 'label indicates an amorphous otherness: a non-Christian, non-European lack of civilization massing beyond the boundaries.'[44] This should not be forgotten in the euphoria of a common European identity.

NOTES

1. D.J. Taylor, *After the War: the Novel and England since 1945* (London: Chatto & Windus, 1993), p. xxiii.
2. It is worth pointing out, however, that there is only very limited merit in using the terms 'centre' and 'periphery' or 'insider' and 'outsider' since their logic is based on a construction of binary opposition which is, on closer examination, not very convincing. On different societal levels (the national, group as well as the individual level) the 'insider' requires the 'outsider' in order to define itself. In other words, in order to create identity, difference must first be established. In addition to that, there is no 'pure' and 'uncontaminated' view from the inside nor the outside because both perspectives carry some ideological baggage in terms of preconceptions. This is particularly the case in the postcolonial context.
3. I use the edition by Penguin, Harmondsworth 1987. After quotations the novel is referred to as *EA*, followed by the page number.
4. Benedict Anderson, *Imagined Communities: Reflections on the Origin and Spread of Nationalism* (London: Verso, 1991), p. 3.
5. John Dunn, 'Introduction: Crisis of the Nation State?' *Political Studies* 42, *Special Issue* (1994): pp. 3–15, here p. 3.
6. Eric J. Hobsbawm, *Nations and Nationalism since 1780: Programme, Myth, Reality* (Cambridge: Cambridge University Press, 1992), p. 6.
7. Anderson, p. 4.
8. Michael Billig, *Banal Nationalism* (London: Sage, 1995), p. 132.
9. Billig, p. 128.

10. Billig, p. 93.
11. Billig, p. 8.
12. Judy Giles and Tim Middleton, eds, *Writing Englishness 1900–1950: an Introductory Sourcebook on National Identity* (London: Routledge, 1995), p. 5.
13. A good discussion of these national myths in paintings, music, literature etc. can be found in Raphael Samuel, ed., *Patriotism: the Making and Unmaking of British National Identity*, Vol. III: *National Fictions* (London: Routledge 1989).
14. For example: Robert Colls and Philip Dodd, eds, *Englishness: Politics and Culture: 1880–1920* (London: Croom Helm, 1986); Brian Doyle, *English and Englishness* (London: Routledge, 1989); Stephen Haseler, *The English Tribe: Identity, Nation and Europe* (London: Macmillan, 1996).
15. Haseler, p. 65.
16. Haseler, p. vii.
17. See also Thomas Noetzel, 'Political Decadence? Aspects of Thatcherite Englishness', *Journal for the Study of British Cultures* 1.2 (1994): pp. 133–47.
18. Rather than abolishing class distinctions and uniting the country in socio-economic terms, it has been argued that her policies were responsible for the emergence of a new class, the so-called underclass.
19. Billig, p. 3.
20. Peter Riddell, *The Thatcher Government* (Oxford: Blackwell, 1985), p. 8.
21. Margaret Thatcher, *The Downing Street Years* (London: HarperCollins, 1995), pp. 744–5.
22. Roger Eatwell, ed., *European Political Cultures: Conflict or Convergence?* (London: Routledge 1997), p. 50.
23. Noetzel, p. 144.
24. Noetzel, p. 133.
25. For some comments on the literary canon of English, see Marion Frank-Wilson's contribution in this volume.
26. See also Susanne Fendler's contribution in this volume.
27. Quoted in Sarah M. Corse, *Nationalism and Literature: the Politics and Culture in Canada and the United States* (Cambridge: Cambridge UP, 1997) p. 7.
28. Homi K. Bhabha, 'Introduction: Narrating the Nation', Homi K. Bhabha, ed., *Nation and Narration* (London: Routledge, 1990), pp. 1–7, here p. 1.
29. Bhabha, p. 6.
30. Helen M. Tiffin, 'Rites of Resistance: Counter-discourse and West Indian Biography', *Journal of West Indian Literature* 3.1 (January 1989): pp. 28–46, here p. 29.
31. Tiffin, p. 30.
32. Title of a study on the theory and practice of post-colonial literatures by Bill Ashcroft, Gareth Griffiths and Helen Tiffin (London: Routledge, 1989).
33. Ashcroft, pp. 8–9.
34. A. Srinivasau, 'The Enigma of Arrival – Naipaul, V.S.', *Indian Horizons* 37.3/4 (1988): pp. 87–89, here p. 88.

35. Bruce King, *V.S. Naipaul* (London: Macmillan, 1993), p. 138.
36. Rob Nixon, 'V.S. Naipaul, Postcolonial Mandarin', *Transition* 52 (1991): pp. 100–13, here p. 102.
37. Billig, p. 136.
38. Nixon (1991), p. 102.
39. Homi K. Bhabha, 'DissemiNation: Time, Narrative, and the Margins of the Modern Nation', *Nation and Narration*, ed. Homi K. Bhabha (London: Routledge, 1990), pp. 291–322, here p. 295.
40. Rob Nixon, *London Calling* (Oxford: Oxford Universtiy Press, 1992), p. 17.
41. A discussion of cultural hybridity can be found in Pnina Werbner and Tariq Modood, eds, *Debating Cultural Hybridity: Multi-Cultural Identities and the Politics of Anti-Racism* (London: Zed, 1997).
42. Nixon (1992), p. 4.
43. Billig, p. 141.
44. Ibid.

12 Memories of Hell: Kieslowski's Vision of European Subjectivity
Roy Boyne

INTRODUCTION: EUROPEAN FILM AND THE ETHOS OF LITERATURE

In his discussion of Western reactions to the breakdown of Communism in Greater Europe, Stjepan Mestrovic asks us to consider 'Balkanization as the breaking up of a unit into increasingly smaller units that are hostile to each other.'[1] If something like that definition was what Bloom had in mind when he wrote, in the closing chapter of *The Western Canon*, that 'the Balkanization of literary studies is irreversible',[2] then there are at least two possible interpretations of his statement. Bloom points us to both of them. Either literary studies is breaking up into mutually antagonistic schools, or the aesthetic whole, of which literature has traditionally been a part, is decomposing.

Because language is the common medium between canonical literature and critical response, the literary field has been peculiarly vulnerable. It has become an ideological slaughterhouse. Many analysts and critics have not been driven by aesthetic experience but, argues Bloom, by *ressentiment* and the ideologies of race, class, and gender:

> Precisely why students of literature have become amateur political scientists, uninformed sociologists, incompetent anthropologists, mediocre philosophers, and overdetermined cultural historians, while a puzzling matter, is not beyond all conjecture. They resent literature, or are ashamed of it [. . .].[3]

Bloom specifies seven types of literary critic, although he only lists six of them: 'Feminists, Marxists, Lacanians, New Historicists, Deconstructionists, Semioticians'.[4] The seventh is typified by his entire approach:

I think that the self, in its quest to be free and solitary, ultimately reads with one aim only: to confront greatness. That confrontation scarcely masks the desire to join greatness, which is the basis of the aesthetic experience once called the Sublime: the quest for a transcendence of limits.[5]

Bloom thinks that great literature is often difficult, but that the experience can be massively rewarding. The locus of that experience is the solitary reader, an existential figure who can draw hope and consolation from the experience of great literature. He thinks that the same is true for art and music, for Matisse and Stravinsky, for example. A recent illustration of the way that the study of literature may be breaking up into antagonistic schools is the recent work on Flaubert by the eminent French sociologist, Pierre Bourdieu. The basic field-analytic position from which Bourdieu sets out his account of Flaubert in *The Rules of Art* is functionalist. He criticizes the aesthetic tradition for what he regards as its continuous reference to the art work's absence of function, to the primacy of its form, and to the disengaged nature of art as art. What Bourdieu does is assemble an ideal type of the attempted universalization of art's essence, and he argues that this ideal type, general though it might once have been, ignores the socio-historical location of the work and its reception. He holds that aestheticism privileges the reader's decontextualized subjective experience of the work of art, and that therefore aestheticism universalizes the particular, translating particularity into transhistoric normativity. He concludes that ignoring the historicity of both the work and its reception precludes the development of anything approaching an adequate view of aesthetic experience.[6]

If Bourdieu's demotion and derogation of aesthetic values is symptomatic, then there is indeed sense to that first interpretation of Bloom's balkanization thesis. In opposition to other forms of literary science, and against aestheticism, Bourdieu's approach will draw attention to the historical context and contemporary function of the literary work, allowing, for example, attention to be drawn to the potential role of literature in advancing trans-national European values. It will also, however, provide some legitimacy for the struggle between ideologies: of race, gender, class and nation. The replacement of aesthetic formalism with ideological functionalism does not, then, provide a template for a civilizing process – unless, of course, one is arguing from one of the competing standpoints. Indeed it may well be, as Bloom hints, quite the reverse. In certain respects, the second interpretation of Bloom's balkanization thesis, that the domain of the aesthetic *tout court* is breaking up, is even more worrying. Bloom suspects that reading is a dying art, that 'the reborn theocratic era will be almost wholly an oral and visual culture.'[7] Geoffrey Hartman, reflecting on contemporary culture, had this to say:

> The substantial effects of film and telecommunications are having their impact. An 'information sickness' caused by the speed and quantity of what impinges on us, and abetted by machines that we have invented that generate endless arrays, threatens to overwhelm personal memory. The individual, we complain, cannot 'process' all this information, this flak: public and personal experience are being moved not closer together but further apart. The arts, it used to be said, aspire to the condition of music; now the 'total flow' of video seems to dominate. Can public memory still be called memory when it is increasingly alienated from personal and active recall?[8]

One aspect of this information sickness is the demand for accessibility, for easy experience, for anaesthesia. It is routinely observed that the contemporary television viewer is inured to tragedy. Our cinematic society means that 'Actuality is distanced by larger-than-life violence and retreats behind special effects'.[9] How, Hartman asks, within the anaesthetized culture of the facile, also characterized by suspicion of official pronouncements, can we promote awareness of the historical legacy (and the same question needs to be asked in regard to the fulfilment of future potential). He cites Spielberg's *Schindler's List* as a successful reconnection to the past, and goes on to suggest that 'Art as a performance medium – art not reduced to official meaning or information – has a chance to transmit this inheritance most fully. When art remains accessible, it provides a counterforce to manufactured and monolithic memory.'[10]

The balkanization of the aesthetic was, in fact, announced by Walter Benjamin, in his famous essay, 'The Work of Art in the Age of Mechanical Reproduction'. He saw that Abel Gance's enthusiasm for the way that film might revivify 'Shakespeare, Rembrandt, Beethoven' promised liquidation rather than resurrection.[11] A part of its destructiveness was the way that cinema imposed itself on the spectator, impacting upon the viewer like a bullet, subjecting the audience to a fusillade of moving images. The mind of the viewer is taken over, not allowed to reflect but forced on to the next image. The cinema inaugurates the era of the spectacle, and so it is that a film like *Schindler's List* can work to reconstitute memory; Hartman says that this film works 'albeit by spectacular means', but Benjamin's point would be that it would work *precisely* by spectacular means. This is, however, only one part of the contemporary effectivity of cinema. A second aspect concerns the distrust of official discourses in the electronic age of democracy,[12] and raises the question of the popular distrust of literature arising out of its formal educational function.

Whichever interpretation we take of Bloom's notion of the balkanization of literary studies, its consequence is a certain suspicion, whether of the indoctrination potential of ideological functionalism or because of the mass rejection of a difficult art that is, in any event, tainted by official approval. Neither of these lines of thought is in any way sufficient for us to celebrate the end of literature, but both may lead us to consider seriously giving the kind of attention to film that has formerly been reserved for the high terrain of literature, music and art. We are then, however, immediately faced with the issue of the kind of approach to be adopted, and perhaps a certain anti-balkanism would be in order, treating film as both aesthetic object and as socio-historically located. So far as the formal properties of the medium are concerned, we may take our lead from Noel Burch's comparison of Renoir's *La Regle du jeu* and serial music:

> Even taking the term in its simplest sense, the subject is contained in microcosm not only in each sequence but in almost every shot, on a certain level of analysis at least [...]. Serial composers appear to us to have a very similar conception of the relationships between the basic choice of a tone row or tone rows (which provides a musical work with its 'subject', what classical musicians call the 'theme' of a work, although tone rows function quite differently) and the form of the finished work. Serial composers believe that the entire development of a musical work must be derived from the basic cell or at least be located relative to it, even if the actual cellular unit is never recognizable as such.[13]

In what follows, we will allow the work of Kieslowski, in its socially located aesthetic sense, to communicate, frame by frame, something of the vulnerability and (*mirabile dictu*) persistence of historically specific European subjectivities.

THE LIMITS OF PERSONAL HELL

Krzysztof Kieslowski died from his second heart attack on 13 March 1996. His 1993 film, *Trois Couleurs Bleu*, was the first of a trilogy. The film was co-scripted by Kieslowski and his long-standing co-writer, Krzysztof Piesiewicz. They had worked together since the 1984 film, *No End*, and had collaborated as joint script-writers on *The Decalogue*, Kieslowski's series of ten films for Polish television, from 1988, which reflect, one by one, on the Ten Commandments, and therefore, it may be argued, on the European subjective condition.

The trilogy, of which *Three Colours Blue* is the first, was conceptualized by Kieslowski as follows:

> Blue, white, red: liberty, equality, fraternity. Piesiewicz had the idea that having tried *Dekalog*, why shouldn't we try liberty, equality and fraternity? [...] The West has implemented these three concepts on a political or social plane, but it's an entirely different matter on the personal plane. And that's why we thought of these films.[14]

Three Colours Blue, then, deals with liberty on the personal plane. As Nigel Andrews, film critic of *The Financial Times*, put it: '*Blue* is about [...] Liberty from memory, from grief. Liberty from the panaceas of the well-meaning.'[15] What Kieslowski found was that freedom of the will and subjective self-determination are socially constrained; and he discovered the social prohibition and sociological impossibility of willed amnesia, pointing therefore to the underlying sense of 'coming to terms with' and 'learning to live with' as the foundation of all effective post-traumatic therapies.

Julie de Courcy, Patrice her composer-husband and Anna their child are on a car journey. The car has a leaking brake pipe. There is an accident.[16] The car goes off the road at a bend and hits a tree. Julie is alive, but the others are dead. A young man named Antoine is close by and runs to the scene. He can do little, but we will hear from him again. Julie regains consciousness in hospital. Kieslowski tells us he used that moment of regained consciousness to indicate how much inside Julie's experience he wanted to take us:

> We wanted to convey Julie's state of mind. When you wake up on an operating table what you see first is the lamp, the lamp becomes a great white haze and then it becomes clearer and

clearer. After the accident, Julie can't see the man who brings her the television set clearly. She opens her eyes and, for a while, she sees a blur. It's typical of her mental state of absolute introversion, of focusing in on herself.[17]

The reference to the television set probably referred to an earlier cut, since in the film as released it is the doctor who tells her of the death of her family who is seen first in a haze, and then reflected in Julie's eye, and so, strictly speaking, her blurred vision is a pre-figuration of rather than a symptom of her inward-focusing. Additionally, 'the man' who brings her the television set is Olivier, as we will see hardly just 'the man' in the sense of 'the man who brought the TV set'. In any event, her first activities are deliberate but beyond her capacities. She breaks a window in the hospital corridor in order to distract the nurse while she takes tablets from a locked cabinet and then attempts to swallow them. Her own body proves much more obdurate than the plate glass window she broke, and it rejects the tablets she tries to swallow, despite her obvious determination.

The distantiation and self-isolation which the film explores has its second major moment (the accident, of course, being the first) with Julie's viewing on television of the funeral of her husband and child. The process of alienation is further developed with her matter-of-fact instruction to her lawyer that all her property should be sold. Julie insists that no one must know any details, that the money will go into a numbered account, although she is concerned to ensure that her mother will be provided for in her nursing home for as long as she lives. Perhaps the strongest sign of her resolve to erase the past comes with the settling of accounts with her husband's music. He was a world-renowned composer. He had been commissioned to write a *Concerto for Europe*, which was to be performed simultaneously by twelve orchestras in twelve European cities. It was part-written, and there had been some indication that Julie had been actively involved in the writing of her husband's work – perhaps as an editor, perhaps even more. There is a moral question here: does Julie have the right to destroy this music? Her answer is unequivocal. She visits the agency where the music has been deposited, collects what we take to be the only copy, and hurls it into the jaws of a refuse van which minces the concerto along with the black and purple plastic bags. The film critic of *Variety* suggested that the music in this film is a character in its own right[18] and Julie's act of destruction has all the symbolic and emotional force of a murder.[19]

The locking away of the past, both as memory and as potentiality, continues with Julie's ritualized consumption of her daughter's second lollipop – Anna had eaten the first on the car journey – and then goes further with her attempt to persuade the key friend of the family, Olivier, who loves her, that she is just unremarkable flesh and will be easily and painlessly forgotten. As she walks away from the house in the morning, with just a bag and a cardboard box tied up with string, she scrapes her knuckles along the rough wall at the side of the road: 30 metres of pain to shift her focus from the past to the present.

She intends to live alone and (with the single exception of her mother who is becoming senile) out of contact completely with everyone from her former life. When she is searching for somewhere to live, the estate agent asks her what she does. He has the thought that this will help him judge what kind of property will be most suitable. Her reply is that she does nothing, *'absolument rien'*: a further mark of the emptying out of identity which is taking place, as she plainly rejects any notion of self-fulfilment other than perhaps through the simple fact of her continuing existence.

There are weak points in the carapace Julie is forming about herself. The first of these relates to an exception to her excision of the past. This exception is her mother. She is in a nursing home, and Julie visits her. This may be an act of duty. It may also be safe because her mother will make neither demands nor connections as long as she has her television. However, whether done out of love or duty or magnanimity or irrelevance, there is no need of psychoanalytic theory to establish that this active link to her mother is also a thread back to the past Julie is seeking to escape. A second weakness is demonstrated by her requirement that whatever building she lives in must not have any children living in it: this is her (and Kieslowski's) acknowledgement that the will is not strong enough to resist the normal triggering processes of memory, that the insistent presence of children will be intolerable. The third element she cannot choose to disregard is her husband's music. Kieslowski thought that the music was the one thing she could not get away from. He wrote this about it:

> Music is important in *Blue*. Musical notes often appear on the screen, so in this sense the film's about music, about the writing

of music, about working on music. For some people Julie is the author of the music we hear. At one stage the journalist asks Julie: 'Did you write your husband's music?' And Julie slams the door on her. So this possibility does exist. Then the copyist says: 'There are a lot of corrections'. There had always been a lot of corrections. Did Julie only do the corrections? Maybe she's one of those people who aren't able to write a single sheet of music but is wonderful in correcting a sheet which has already been written. She sees everything, has an excellent analytical mind and has a great talent for improving things. The written sheet of music isn't bad but when she's improved it, it is excellent. But it's not all that important whether she's the author or co-author, whether she corrects or creates. Even if she only does do the corrections she's still the author or co-author because what has been corrected is better than it was before. The music is cited all through the film and then at the end we hear it in its entirety, solemn and grand. So we're led to think that she's played a part in its creation. In this sense the film's about music.[20]

The massive presence of the music is inescapable, and is synecdochically linked to the presence of Patrice and Anna in Julie's life.

Her mother, her aversion to children now, and the music are not the only things that tie Julie to the past. Her first act when she steps into her new flat is to open her cardboard box and take out the blue light-fitment, the only thing that remained in the 'Blue Room' of her former house, which she had ordered to be cleared. As she puts up the blue hanging stone chandelier, she is crying inside. It would, at this point, be an error to think that this partial preservation of the past is a sign of choice on Julie's part. The clearing away of all detritus to leave a pure subject, a *tabula rasa* recreated and ready to be written on again but as if for the first time, was surely exposed as an impossible dream, most definitively by Jacques Derrida, writing of the inseparability of repetition and erasure, and of the non-existence of the subject, 'if we mean by that some sovereign solitude of the author'.[21] As Derrida put it in his *Grammatology* essay:

> The outside [...] which we believe we know as the most familiar thing in the world, as familiarity itself, would not appear [...] without *différance* as temporalization, without the nonpresence of the other inscribed within the sense of the present, without the relationship to death as the concrete structure of the living present.[22]

For Derrida, the idea of a subject with memory control would be untenable. For Julie, perhaps the choice to take the light-fitment forward into her new life was something over which she had some control; one can say the same thing about the scrap of music in her bag, but she had no control over the fact that things would go with her. It is this link between the inside and the outside, between the subject and its social context, that the film shows to be outside of the will to power.

Kieslowski will not only find that memory is outside of the will, so too is social existence. The insistently threatening invasions of everyday life are announced with a fight outside Julie's flat. She contrives to lock herself out when she goes to see what is happening, spending the night on the landing and thereby beginning a process of connection with her neighbours. She rebuffs their first approach, from a neighbour who asks Julie to sign the petition to eject one of the tenants because she is sex-worker. The pressure upon her is considerable: 'everyone else has signed!'. Nevertheless, Julie resists, saying it is nothing to do with her. The fortuitous and contingent visit her again with a call from the young man who was first on the scene of the accident. He bears the twin gifts of her husband's last words, and the neck-chain which had been lying at the scene, and which we later learn was a definitive sign of Patrice's love. Julie deals with both in a detached way, explaining the words and telling Antoine that he can keep the neck-chain. The third intrusion opens what will be a new path: Lucille calls with a bunch of flowers, to thank Julie for not signing the petition; and soon after that, with a certain inevitability, Olivier, who has been searching for her for months, finds Julie in her local café.

Both the past and the future seem as if they are converging on her, denying any prospect of success to her fight to remain in the present, without links to the past and without debt to the future. Her childhood phobia about mice is revived as she finds a nest in the larder. Her mother thinks she is dead, which is the condition she aspires to, at least in the eyes of the *other*, but Julie cannot resist correcting her. Kieslowski's construction of the mother presents an image of disconnectedness. If this is an example of what willed amnesia might do, it carries the stigmata of social dysfunctionality, dependence, disease and the pathos of repeated misrecognitions. Even though Julie could surely not want this, she has not yet acknowledged the lesson, and says to herself as much as to her mother, 'I want no belongings, no memories, no friends, no love: they are all traps.' If the condition of isolated subjectivity were an existential possibility, then the increasing pressure from past and future might be resisted, but the successful strategies which Kieslowski gives us are suicide and senility. Julie cannot kill herself (although she goes to the edge of this again – in the swimming pool) nor will herself into oblivion. So she begins to face what has happened and will happen. She borrows (creating a debt) a cat to deal with the mice, and then her submission to Lucille's offer to clean up the mess is more a sign of the strength to enter into reciprocities, than it is of weakness in dealing with a phobia. She is called upon to repay this second debt very soon, as Lucille asks her to come to the club on Place Pigalle where she works. It is 11.30 at night and Lucille needs help. Julie goes. It is for Kieslowski the sign that she is ready to be sutured back into the rest of her life.

At the sex club where Lucille works, Julie sees herself on television. Olivier has obtained a copy of Patrice's unfinished manuscript. He says he is going to try and finish the work. Julie had not destroyed the only copy after all. The media are very interested, and they show a range of still pictures of Patrice as accompaniment to the story. There are some of Patrice and a woman that Julie does not know. This double jolt sends Julie to Olivier. There is an exchange at the heart of their meeting: she gives him the words that are meant to go with the *Concerto* (St Paul's Epistle to the Corinthians 1, Ch. 13),[23] he gives her the story of Sandrine, Patrice's girlfriend for several years. Julie meets Sandrine, who is pregnant with Patrice's child. Sandrine says, at the end of their first encounter, 'You want to know if he loved me?' 'Yes,' replies Julie, 'That's the question I wanted to ask, but I know the answer now.' Sandrine is wearing Patrice's neck-chain.

Kieslowski forces Julie to a final decision: suicide or senility. She can neither stay under the water, nor countenance her mother's existence. Thus she turns to Olivier, and considers what fate has done. Had Olivier not removed a dossier from Patrice's desk, Julie would have destroyed it unexamined and the pictures of Sandrine it contained would have been no more. 'Maybe it's better this way,' says Julie, as she turns to the manuscript from Patrice that Olivier is working on to see what he has done so far. They work on it together, but the finale is missing. Then Julie remembers the scrap of sheet music in her bag.

Four moments complete the film. The house will not be sold, and Sandrine and her son, to be called Patrice, will live in it. Olivier refuses to acknowledge the music that Julie has completed unless its writers are named. Julie takes the completed manuscript to Olivier, and they make love on the mattress that he had bought when the possessions from Julie's house were sold. The concerto's main themes are played to their textual accompaniment, with a foreground collage of Julie, Olivier, Antoine, Julie's mother, Lucille and her husband's unborn child.

THE HISTORY OF EUROPEAN SUBJECTIVITY

If we imagine that Kieslowski's film was an attempt to present a credible version of a self isolated from its past, if we understand the film as a failed experiment to construct a subject insulated from its social context, and if we thematize the priority established by the end of the film of love and sociality over self and autonomy, a certain picture of the self emerges. This self is characterized as an essentially social subject with a relatively inflexible identity possessed of a will with quite definite internally determined limitations (such as the inability to control memory). How does this picture of the self compare with our conventional understanding?

The history of the subject as written from Plato forward moves from being God's creation in His image, through a constrained and physical view of voluntary control over our physical actions in Aristotle, to an Augustinian conception of a unified subject able to choose good over evil, to a Cartesian conception[24] of mental agency as domination over the physical world, to a Kantian view that the agent is inscribed within a world with, broadly, an *a priori* moral structure, to a Freudian view of a composite and imperfectly revealed self, to a postmodern view of fragmented subjectivity. Until the last, Freudian and postmodern, stages, this historical narrative of the self has taken the form of a dialectic of strength and weakness explicating the nature of the unified subject. This will require some further elaboration.

It is generally thought that the notion of free will is specific to Western culture from approximately the fourth century AD.[25] While there are clear pre-echoes of the notion in Plato[26] and a developed account of voluntary action in Aristotle,[27] it was Christian thought that gave clear shape to the idea with its elaboration of inner-directed behaviour. Within Christian thought, the significance of free will may be understood as the emergence of inner compliance to the

Ten Commandments. It represents a change from external obedience to inner harmony with a moral code. The emerging sense from St Augustine onwards was very powerfully of a unified subject, a clear conception of the human individual as having causal powers and moral responsibility, and as operating as a whole force. The inward turn offered by Christianity provided the foundation for the emergence of this conception, which may still be taken entirely for granted, and which both Freudianism and postmodernism have been questioning.

The Augustinian problematic was built upon the human capacity to dwell within the City of God, and in the final analysis the primary reference points of his thought and teaching were otherworldly. A decisive break, however, is marked by Descartes. In his thought a shift is made from human existence as leading to Heaven or Hell, to what Charles Taylor calls the disengaged subject, whose relationship to the world will now be one of instrumental control, and whose relationship to the self will be one where reason controls the passions. Partly in reaction to Cartesian dualism, Immanuel Kant argued that here is an *a priori* moral law. That is to say he thought that the idea of morality cannot be deduced from experience, but is somehow independent of experience and prior to it, that if there were no *a priori* morality then the way that we live in the world would be unthinkably different.

The history of thinking about the self, from Plato to Kant, is a history of religion and morality (or, otherwise put, of politics and duty). Nietzsche's critique of morality was therefore not surprisingly also a critique of the unified moral self. He wrote as follows in 1885:

> Granted that nothing is 'given' as real except our world of desires and passions, that we can rise or sink to no other 'reality' than the reality of our drives – for thinking is only the relationship of these drives to one another [. . .].[28]

This formulation of Nietzsche's is more extreme than Freud's view, but the Nietzschean dismissal of God in the human form of conscience is widely regarded as a prime antecedent for the deconstructionist critique of unified subjectivity.[29] But it is surely Freud's work that underpins the postmodern thesis that fragmentation is the condition of contemporary subjectivity. At the same time that Nietzsche was writing *Beyond Good and Evil*, Dr Freud was becoming an authority on childhood cerebral palsy and working under Jean-Martin Charcot, whose lectures on hysteria were gaining wide attention. In 1895 Freud and Josef Breuer published the case study of Anna O. She had a right-side paralysis for two years, together with defective vision, intermittent anorexia, a nervous cough, and frequent bouts of delirium. Breuer had noticed that during her hysterical attacks Anna would mutter things, and he decided to explore the connotations of these mutterings by putting Anna under hypnosis and questioning her. Her condition improved, and it was Anna herself that referred to this early version of psychoanalytic therapy as the 'talking cure'. Through further work, Freud developed the theory of repression, probably the foundational concept of the whole psychoanalytic edifice.[30] To get a picture of the subject according to Freud, however, it is not enough to understand the mechanisms of id, ego and superego – one must add in his theory of development, which has five critical moments: first, the shift from auto-eroticism to sanctioned object-choice; second, the movement from polymorphous forms of sexual activity to a genito-reproductive focus; third, the replacement of overwhelming fixation on one parent by a stable post-obsessional relation to that parent; fourth, the emergence of a near-obsessional relation to a loved outsider; and, fifth, the development from a repressed hostility to the same-sex parent to a non-sexual but affective and affectionate relation to that parent (who is not to be seen as a rival for the love of the newly acquired outsider). This is the normal development path. The subject it describes is social and historical, both inter- and intra-personal. The unconscious energies within the subject may be partly repressed, but are always potentially causally active (often rooted from nodes at which the development process has gone awry).

The sense of the subject found here is far off the path which ran from Plato to Kant. Nor is it to be found on the line between Christianity and classical sociology. It may better be regarded as somewhere on a new route, stretching toward the postmodern conception of the subject, described as follows by Nikolas Rose:

> In place of the self, new images of subjectivity proliferate: as socially constructed, as dialogic, as inscribed upon the surface of the body, as spatialised, decentred, multiple, nomadic, created in episodic recognition-seeking practices of self-display in particular times and places.[31]

We can now come to a precise question concerning Julie. Where is she? Which path is she on? It is very tempting to say that she is at the cross-over point. But that would be illicit. These paths are the byways of historical hermeneutics, not transports for individual subjects. Kieslowski does not make things easy. Not only does he haze over the end of the film with a powerful, lyrical and typically Polish romanticism, he also had a pretty firm view of his own subjectivity as located on the 'old' path:

> If you don't understand your own life, then I don't think you can understand the lives of the characters in your stories, you can't understand the lives of other people. Philosophers know this. Social workers know this [...] I believe that composers do [...] it's absolutely necessary to those who tell stories about life: an authentic understanding of one's own life. By authentic I mean that it's not a public understanding, which I'll share with anybody. It's not for sale, and, in fact, you'll never detect it in my films. Some things you can find out very easily but you'll never understand how much the films I make or the stories I tell mean to me and why. You'll never find that out. I know it, but that knowledge is only for me.[32]

It may be, then, that locating Julie as a divided soul, broken up by the loss of part of her being and gradually coming to terms with the contingency of her fractured subjectivity, goes somewhat against the grain of Kieslowski's inclinations. We do get some unwitting support from him, though. He says:

> For all its tragedy and drama, it's hard to imagine a more luxurious situation than the one Julie finds herself in. She's completely free at the beginning because her husband and daughter die, she loses her family and all her obligations. She is perfectly provided for, has masses of money and no responsibilities.[33]

The luxury of Julie's situation is that she has no history as a subject. Kieslowski thought to make her free by killing her significant others, disabling her mother, and allowing her to overcome her only childhood neurosis. He could only do this if he saw Julie as a cipher, an empty vessel to be filled by the flood of history and care welling around her. His achievement was to avoid having this symbol of empty subjectivity seem to decide, to make the choice to be re-connected, to opt to be filled with the *caritas* which the music celebrates; rather it was the flood that surrounded her that pulled her in. In truth, the film was about the flood rather than about Julie. So the question of where Julie might be as a subject is a question to be posed about Julie before the accident, and the answer to that question is clear: she would have been an inhabitant of late twentieth-century Europe, a complex, divided, fragmented self. It was the trauma which allowed Kieslowski to empty her out, and site her on the 'old' path.

Angela Pope is a film director whose husband died of leukaemia a short time before she saw *Three Colours Blue*. She described how her own life had been:

> He was gone. I didn't sell up, move out, move on. Nor did I try to blot out the past. I didn't need to because I couldn't remember it, though I tried hard enough. I wore his clothes, read the books he read, tried to speak as he spoke, think as he had thought. None of it worked; the memories stayed stubbornly erased. (Much later they would come back, without my summoning, and with startling ferocity.)[34]

She goes on to describe how her public life at this time was a shell, but that, as if from nowhere, the world flooded in at a certain point. She felt the film was honest, and saw Kieslowski's sentiment ('Though I speak with the tongues of angels, but have not love, I speak as a hollow brass') as profound.

Both the film and its sobering real-world duplication demonstrate that memory is outside of willed control. This is a feature of the subject that the traditional line from Plato to Kant did not much dwell on, and it is a facet of limit-subjectivity[35] that may now receive increasing attention, a philosopheme whose time may have come. Much recent attention has been paid to the need for memory, the will to remember. Cathy Caruth's recent edited collection, *Trauma: Explorations in Memory*, thus is concerned with the Holocaust, Hiroshima and AIDS, and Shoshana Felman's lead article[36] in that collection is concerned with what it is to witness, to be a witness, to bear witness. The history of interiority may be said to begin with a book of confessions, nothing other than the making public of memory; and it is no coincidence that Derrida's programmatic explication of the *Memoirs of the Blind* exhibition at the Louvre (1990/91) explores the relation between drawing and memory and concludes with reflections on Augustine's question to God about the nature of tears (why are they sweet to those in misery? and Marvell's question of what tears see.)[37]

Were we able to erase memories at will then we could become senile and dependent as if by a series of strokes (no matter that we made them happen, since after the fact they would by definition not be recalled), and so the appalling vision is of Julie wishing to abandon her memories and (did she but realize it) become her mother. Memories are required keeping, there may be none that should be wilfully abandoned even were that possible. This is a key theme of Kieslowski's work as a whole, and – to return to the reality of balkanization finally – is a principle of European belonging which is forgotten at our peril. The lesson for philosophies of European integration is both positive and cautionary: positive, since it suggests that new political forms will not erase the formative regional narratives of identity formation, and will not therefore empty out European subjectivities to create the feared spectre of homogeneity *in vacuo* at the heart of European identity; cautionary, because the pursuit of European integration becomes an extraordinarily complex affair requiring a pervasive sensitivity to the defining histories of European subjectivities as they are currently constituted.

NOTES

1. Stjepan Mestrovic, *The Balkanization of the West* (London: Routledge, 1994), p. ix.
2. Harold Bloom, *The Western Canon* (London: Macmillan, 1994), p. 517.
3. Bloom, p. 521.
4. Bloom, p. 527.
5. Bloom, p. 524.
6. Pierre Bourdieu, *The Rules of Art* (Cambridge: Polity Press, 1996), pp. 286–7.
7. Bloom, p. 519.
8. Geoffrey Hartman, 'Public Memory and Its Discontents', *The Uses of Literary History*, ed. Marshall Brown (Durham NC: Duke University Press, 1995): pp. 73–92, here p. 73.
9. Hartman, p. 77.
10. Hartman, p. 80.
11. Walter Benjamin, 'The Work of Art in the Age of Mechanical Reproduction', *Illuminations* (London: Jonathan Cape, 1970), pp. 219–54, here pp. 223–4.
12. Hartman, pp. 77–8.
13. Noel Burch, *Theory of Film Practice* (London: Secker and Warburg, 1973), pp. 142–3.
14. Daniela Stok, ed., *Kieslowski on Kieslowski* (London: Faber and Faber, 1993), p. 212.
15. Nigel Andrews, 'Struggles for Liberty', *Financial Times* 14 October 1993.
16. An obituary contains the following: 'one of the things we talked about

was how awkward it was to give the characters in a film names. He agreed, but he took it further and talked about the great danger film makers found themselves in, of playing God with their characters.' (Engel, Andi. 'Krzysztof Kieslowski: Human Touch of a Master'. *The Guardian*, 14 March, 1996.) It is hard to know how the writer of serious fiction can avoid that, but perhaps an answer is to ensure that their characters' desires are not directed at the eternal, meaning that their beings are shown to be demonstrably wound up with multitudinous mortality.
17. Stok, p. 222.
18. Louise Nesselson, 'Trois Couleurs: Bleu', *Variety*, 20 Sept. 1993.
19. Other interpretations are, of course, possible. Contrast this interpretation with the following account from Wittgenstein: 'after Schubert's death, his brother cut certain of Schubert's scores into small pieces and gave to his favourite pupils these pieces of a few bars each. As a sign of piety this action is *just* as comprehensible to us as the other one of keeping the scores undisturbed and accessible to no one. And if Schubert's brother had burnt the scores we could still understand this as a sign of piety.' Ludwig Wittgenstein, *Remarks on Frazer's Golden Bough* (Retford: The Brynmill Press, 1979), p. 5.
20. Stok, p. 224.
21. Jacques Derrida, 'Freud and the Scene of Writing', *Writing and Difference* (London: Routledge, 1978), pp. 196–231, here p. 226.
22. Jacques Derrida, *Of Grammatology* (Baltimore: Johns Hopkins University Press, 1976), pp. 70–1.
23. As might be expected for a Polish film-maker working in French, the language of the King James Bible is *not* followed, and the key word in the text is not *charity* but *love*. It is in other words the sense of love as *caritas*, as giving rather than withholding which ultimately animates the film and its music.
24. I explicitly exclude the unsustainable Burckhardtian notion that a specific sense of self-conscious personhood emerged in the Italian Renaissance (see Peter Burke, 'Representations of the Self from Petrarch to Descartes', *Rewriting the Self*, ed. Roy Porter (London: Routledge, 1997).
25. 'We have to wait until Augustine before a theory [...] where the goods of the soul are stressed over those of worldly action, is formulated in terms of inner and outer.' (Charles Taylor, *Sources of the Self* (Cambridge: Cambridge University Press, 1989), p. 121.
26. In the *Timaeus*, Plato distinguished two kinds of cause: '[...] the necessary and the divine', and some scholars (see Godfrey Vesey, 'Responsibility and Free Will', *Key Themes in Philosophy*, ed. A. Phillips Griffiths (Cambridge: Cambridge University Press, 1989), pp. 85–100) have regarded mind as the essence of the divine, and therefore implied that Plato did have a well-formed view of humans as prime movers. The following passage from the *Timaeus*, however, describes Plato's view of mortals (and suggests that this is indeed a pre-echo of human causal powers, rather than an early version): '[God] ordered his own children to make the generation of mortals. They took over from him an immortal principle of soul, and, imitating him, encased it in a mortal

physical globe, with the body as a whole for vehicle and they built onto it another mortal part, containing terrible and necessary feelings: pleasure – the chief incitement to wrong; pain, which frightens us from good; confidence and fear; two foolish counsellors: obstinate passion and credulous hope. To this mixture they added irrational sensation and desire which shrinks from nothing, and so gave the mortal element its indispensable equipment' (Plato, *Timaeus* (Harmondsworth: Penguin, 1955), p. 95.)

27. See the discussion of voluntariness, purposive choice and practical reasoning in Anthony Kenny, *Aristotle's Theory of the Will* (London: Duckworth, 1979).
28. Friedrich Nietzsche, *Beyond Good and Evil* (Harmondsworth: Penguin, 1973), p. 48.
29. Suzanne Duvall Jacobitti, 'Thinking About the Self', *Hannah Arendt: Twenty Years Later*, eds Larry May and Jerome Kohn (Cambridge, Mass.: MIT Press, 1996), pp. 199–219, here p. 205.
30. Freud uses the condition of obsessional neurosis to explore the functioning of repression. He finds that 'obsessional neurosis has as its basis a regression owing to which a sadistic trend has been substituted for an affectionate one. It is this hostile impulse against someone who is loved which is subjected to repression [...] As a substitutive formation there arises an alteration of the ego in the shape of an increased conscientiousness [...] But the repression, which was at first successful, does not hold firm; in the further course of things its failure becomes increasingly marked. The vanished affect comes back in its transformed shape as social anxiety, moral anxiety and unlimited self-reproaches; the rejected idea is replaced by a *substitute by displacement*, often a displacement onto something very small or indifferent. A tendency to a complete re-establishment of the repressed idea is as a rule unmistakably present [...] Thus in obsessional neurosis the work of repression is prolonged in a sterile and interminable struggle.' (Sigmund Freud, 'On Repression', *On Metapsychology* (Harmondsworth: Penguin), pp. 139–58, here pp. 157–8.) It is not hard to see how an interpretation of Julie's behaviour might be made to fit quite easily into this syndrome (the inevitably neurotic nature of her relationship with Olivier being obscured by Kieslowski's romanticism).
31. Nikolas Rose, *Inventing Our Selves* (Cambridge: Cambridge University Press, 1996), p. 169.
32. Stok, p. 36.
33. Stok, p. 212.
34. Angela Pope, 'In Memory', *Sight and Sound* 6.8 (August 1996).
35. See Roy Boyne, 'Postmodernism, the Sublime and Ethics', *The Politics of Modernity*, eds Irving Velody and Arthur Still (Cambridge: Cambridge University Press, 1998).
36. Shoshana Felman, 'Education and Crisis, or the Vicissitudes of Teaching', *Trauma: Explorations in Memory*, ed. Cathy Caruth (Baltimore: Johns Hopkins University Press, 1995), pp. 13–60.
37. Jacques Derrida, *Memoirs of the Blind* (Chicago: Chicago University Press, 1993), pp. 126 and 129.

13 Europeans: Foreigners in Their Own Land[1]
Sylvie Gambaudo

Julia Kristeva addresses the issue of foreignness and national identity from two angles: historical and psychoanalytic.[2] She offers a summary of the subjective position of foreigners in Europe, extracting the history[3] of foreigners from History with a capital H. Beyond our traditional apprehension of that History, she also questions the definition of 'foreigner' and writes a more subjective history: that of the foreigner, as the one who is doubly bound between the memory of a lost past and the beckoning of an elusive future. In the gap that separates past and future lies the difficult reality of a European identity. Discussions[4] on 'Europe' often analyse and define the limits which draw the contours of Europe's emerging identity. In this effort, Europeans are gathered under a common geographical, political and economic banner. Allowances are made to preserve a certain sense of national control; some borders are open, some are not... Europeans are foreigners in their own land, caught between an identity they are losing and the identity of an other[5] that invites at the same time as it frightens them. Their foreignness is above all a collective reminiscence of a strangeness that they individually encountered. It is precisely this strangeness that the foreigner remembers, whatever his/her nationality, and whose history Kristeva writes.[6]

In *Etrangers à nous-mêmes*, Kristeva considers the concept of foreignness from two different focal points: that of the non-foreigner (the citizen, the native), the one who belongs to a given social group either through time (blood ties) or space (land ties), and that of the foreigner. In the first instance, the foreigner is the passive recipient of the insider's socio-political history, the ideological fluctuations of which define and write the foreigner's history and identities accordingly.[7]

In the second instance, the foreigner is the actor of his/her own history but also of the insider's psychical history. Kristeva takes up Freud's concept of 'heimlich/unheimlich' and uses it to analyse foreignness.[8] Freud suggested that the subject's entry into the symbolic sphere is marked by the repression of what threatens the integrity of his/her ego, that is to say, symbolization stems from a process of estrangement from the pre-linguistic sphere. The subject must become an other, a stranger, in order to become a subject; the symbolic subject is a foreigner in exile from his/her pre-linguistic territory. What was part of the baby's experience of its pre-linguistic time (the here-and-now experience of being without language, without separation, without estrangement) has now become strange, a foreign space, the strangeness the subject must repress in order to be represented. However, repression is never perfect and the human subject experiences over and over again this process of repression (Freud's 'return of the repressed'). With repetition, repression itself becomes familiar or the process of estrangement is familiar territory. It follows that the foreigner is the living testimony of a story of estrangement, upon whom natives can project their own anxieties in acts ranging from the legal granting of rights and prohibitions to unlawful acts of racism. The foreigner stands as an outsider, outside 'our' society ('we', the natives, the citizens), outside 'ourselves', a victim of 'our' fear of the other-than-'us', a passive marker of the ideology of a given time to which 'we', by contrast, belong.

Freud's idea can be applied to the process of Europeanization in two ways: first, the effort to create a united Europe requires the European subject to give up his/her attachment to the nation-state and to create a new symbolic identification with a European nation. On a metaphorical level, this process of repression of what was considered 'natural' (the native believes s/he was born into a national identity) and the identification with the symbol 'European' induces a reminiscence of that other estrangement and its affective charge. Second, the suggestion that identity can be undone on a national level and re-created or displaced onto a European level exposes identity as a construct; the subject's identity is thus exposed as an illusion masked by a tacit, collective agreement that identity is stable and inherent. Consequently, there is a collective hesitation, even mistrust, for the symbolic function (represented by the State, political leaders) which is failing to reassure the subject of his/her identity.

Moreover, Kristeva argues that, in the first process of estrangement, what is repressed is 'the processes and the representative contents no longer necessary for pleasure, self-preservation and for the adaptative growth of the individual as a speaking subject and a living organism'.[9] These processes and representative contents deal with the questions of death, of origin (the feminine, birth) and possibly the drives acting as a frontier between the organic and the psyche.

In the context of Europeanization, it can be argued that the subject who previously acknowledged and identified with the authority of the symbolic function is now facing a time anterior to the existence of that symbolic function; if the symbolic fails, the subject is called to address again questions of origin and death. The process of Europeanization could then be considered as a threat to the integrity of the subject's ego, rather than as a unifying process. In other words, the creation of a European identity signifies, at the same time, the destruction of identity.

It is therefore unsurprising that Europe should see a resurgence of xenophobic fervour and an accrued interest in nationalistic groups. Both are a reaction against the fragmentation of the nation, reaction precisely because they are a re-enactment of affects now transposed onto contemporary European issues. If the advent of the European subject is also the 'come back' of the foreigner, if it is to renew its symbolic contract with its 'citizens', the making of Europe must address issues of origin and death.

The media have long been exploiting the gold mine that foreignness is, even more so today when the issue of national identity has been re-actualized by the question of Europe. Foreignness and its associated emotional charge is being recuperated and marketed in various productions[10] precisely because the foreigner's strangeness induces a dualistic re-action: s/he can be both attractive and repulsive. His/her differences confer to him/her powers and knowledge that the native, in his/her sameness, does not possess and is both attracted to and threatened by. Present representations of the foreigner, in a time of globalization and loss of a clearly defined enemy, are moving away from the 'Kung Fu' image – that is, the other as an enigmatic traveller, with exotic customs, a 'sexy' accent or look, whose image we can define, control and buy/sell. We now look for 'our' foreigners beyond the realm of human consciousness in the proliferation of cyborgs and aliens who are invading our lives, X-entities we cannot even name, but which fascinate us and which we must ultimately destroy. In the light of the issues of origin and death mentioned above, it is interesting to note the success of a series such as *The X-files*, which clearly transcends the boundaries of origin and death; viewers are attracted to and repulsed by the prospect of an origin which transcends the limits of human reproduction and the questioning of a death which might offer something other than the utter destruction of the subject.

To sum up, Europeans, inasmuch as they share a common identity, exist doubly: first as constructs of the natives, that is to say Europeans are the product of their own construct; secondly they exist as the lived experience of foreignness. Both events, although diametrically opposed in their dynamic, are linked because they happen on the body of the European subject. This double-bind which retains Europeans caught in a precarious position is also a chance to recognize, in Kristeva's words, that we are all 'strangers to ourselves': either they, as national natives, can recognize their own strangeness and address it in a renewal of identity, or they will not afford themselves the risk to put their national identity under threat and will repress again their own strangeness. But, if they choose Europe over the nation, will they then be capable of building a democratic society in which Europeans, in their foreignness, will be able to live together without ostracizing the strangeness of the other and without levelling identities to a European sameness?

Le Vieil Homme et les Loups offers an attempt at staging the question of otherness and its problematic relation to the social sphere. *Le Vieil Homme et les Loups* is an effort to articulate several issues centred around the theme of cultural crisis. Julia Kristeva's novel displays a certain pessimism with regard to the way she portrays 'society', a term which, considered in its global dynamic, encompasses all human socialization and readily applies itself to the questioning of a European society.

Le Vieil Homme et les Loups could be described as a murder mystery. Its opening section, 'the invasion', is set in 'Santa Barbara', a town paralysed by the tyranny of an unknown entity, 'the wolves', who have invaded the town and commit murders at random, keeping the inhabitants in a state of permanent terror. Three characters are prominent in this first part: Sceptisius Clarus, the old man, a paternal and philosophical figure who refuses to bow to the wolves' might; Alba Ram, the old man's pupil and a hazy character whose persona, thoughts and actions appear unclear (to the reader and to herself), and Vespasian, Alba's condescending husband, whose relationship with the old man seems to be one of contained courteousness. Vespasian is having an affair with 'la collègue du lifting' (the lifting colleague), a seemingly happy-go-lucky character whose purpose in life is to lift other people's spirits and bodies. The first section of the story is told in the third person and conveys a feeling of confusion, of being in a twilight zone closer to the atmosphere of dreams than reality. The second section, 'série noire', sees the arrival of Stéphanie Delacour, ex-inhabitant of Santa Barbara and a journalist enquiring about one murder. Her enquiry, conducted in the first person, leads her to remember childhood traumas, to consider the identity of the other protagonists, to re-define her own identity as an exile, and after the death of the old man in the third section, 'Capricio', to re-live and mourn the death of her own father and seek the true face of the wolves. In other words, the novel deals with issues of death, exile, strangeness and renewal of identity.

Le Vieil Homme et les Loups is based on much of Kristeva's personal experience as a Bulgarian native. Santa Barbara, a name reminiscent of 'Sainte Barbarie', Saint Barbarity, could be any town, anywhere on the planet. It presents aspects of many cities, with markers which identify Santa Barbara as both western and eastern: readers from the East recognize the invasion of the wolves as emblematic of the Red Armies invading eastern Europe, while readers in the West will remember Santa Barbara as an American television series (I will come back to the series later). The message then implies that it does not matter where the reader is: at any point on the planet, people are facing the same situation of crisis. The crisis identified by Kristeva can be described as follows:

She is concerned about the disillusionment of the people of the East,[11] who, after encountering the failure of socialist ideals, are left in a state of distress and turn to the West, and in particularly western Europe, to provide them with the democratic answers that will help them rebuild their social space. Kristeva expresses her concern that the 'new nomenklatura' might be a masquerade of the old, a new 'loup'[12] to disguise the fact that the old regime is not entirely dead, but operating under a more pervasive disguise. Indeed, Kristeva sympathizes with the predicament of former dissidents from the East who, in a context where wheeling and dealing, political passivity and incompetence are *de rigueur*, are at a loss to define what they now might be dissenting against.

Kristeva is critical of the two models currently available for the shaping of Europe. These two models, eastern and western, rest on the role played by authority figures in the process of identity formation. If authority is exercised too rigidly, as was the case in eastern Europe, the symbolic function does not permit any deviation from the norm set by that authority; the existence of a foreignness (as defined earlier) within the individual's identity is negated and its expression forbidden and punishable, be it political or artistic. In reverse, if authority is not exercised, and Kristeva suggests that this is the case in western Europe, the symbolic function cannot take place, that is to say the individual is unable to position his/ her self in relation to that authority; here again, the sense of identity is negated since there is no symbolic entity to identify with or against.

Kristeva is indeed pessimistic about the state of democratic societies in western Europe. She is very critical[13] of the political arena in democracies which she defines as a 'technocratic setup' within which the political leaders are

> responsible but not guilty – and this means that all subjective and moral dimensions have been reabsorbed, eliminated, by the inexorable march of a bureaucracy that is more and more anonymous and responsible to itself alone. There are no more culprits [...]: since good and evil don't exist, total bureaucracy, another version of totalitarianism, has trivialized and animalized the human.[14]

In the absence of a clearly defined positioning of authority, the place of power is being left vacant. Instead, we are being offered a moralizing euphoric discourse, a consensual ideology which erases problems rather than addresses them and around which we rally. As no one seems to be in charge, an increasing and alarming number of individuals are losing interest in political issues.

Santa Barbara is representative of both eastern and western realities. It stands at the junction between two opposite processes, a place where inhabitants seem to have lost their identity and the desire to reconstruct themselves. They operate collectively, the one identical to the other, a town of nobodies in a world of illusions. In Santa Barbara, people sense that crimes[15] are being committed, but there are no bodies to be identified as victims and nobody can be identified as the criminal(s). The inhabitants know of crimes because of rumours heard behind closed doors but never addressed openly. Even the character of Stéphanie, from whom the reader expects some kind of logic and organization of the plot, ends up identifying the dead body of Alba, only to meet Alba alive again later, and as a self-proclaimed criminal. No one is willing to take a position of knowledge, as victims or as criminals, and those who do either mistake appearances for the truth (Stéphanie) or die (the old man). Yet, even the death of the old man, which would have proved that Santa Barbara is hiding its crimes, is inconclusive as the reader does not find out whether he dies murdered (victim of someone else's crime) or as a reaction to the shock of seeing the truth in a deadly vision of crime (victim of his own crime). Everyone is, at some point in the story, a victim and a criminal, with a blurring of the frontier that separates the two identities. In the absence of a clear definition of 'crime', be it in the evilness of the criminal or the innocence of the victim, the very notion of 'crime' disappears, and the official knowledge is that there is no crime in Santa Barbara. It is also, for Kristeva, an absence of the sense of what is good and bad, that is to say a vacancy of the voice of authority (the State, the author-narrator, the reader, the inhabitants of Santa Barbara) which disables us from taking a position for or against that authority.

The impression left by Santa Barbara is that of a town built on illusions, with everybody being excited about the spectacle of crime they heard of, but that no one seems to care about as a real life event, as if the inhabitants had become bored with or blasé in the face of the banality of reality. As in the American series of the same name, Santa Barbara is a place where life occurs on the surface and the surface has been modified, disguised, lifted to a state of ever-lasting excitement: not only excitement for the body-beautiful, as for the fans of the series *Santa Barbara*, but also excitement for the illusory spectacle of life and death as presented by the media. Behind that fabricated surface, there is nothing to be found of the human subject; it is this vulgarization of subjectivity, of human life, mainly but not solely by the media, that Kristeva sees as criminal, because illusion has become the norm and because we revere those mirages like sacred images of true life.[16]

For Kristeva, this situation is barbarous and it is precisely this combination of East/West issues, totalitarianism, collapse of idealistic values, malaise, banality, which converge in Santa Barbara under the guise of wolves. Moreover, as a psychoanalyst, Kristeva sees a parallel between the socio-economic situation and the disquieting loss of interest in psychical life. Three solutions to the impoverishment of psychical activity are presented to us:[17] pharmaceutical answers, in the character of Alba who resolves her depression through the personal use of drugs, and later through administering a concoction of drugs and poison to Vespasian, as an answer to the anxiety caused by their relationship problems; media answers, with soporific ready-made images of trivia as discussed above; religious answers, with the resurgence of fundamentalism, be it religious or, as mentioned earlier, nationalistic.

This impoverishment also has repercussions on a linguistic level with the 'withering away of language just as there is a withering away of culture'.[18] Languages, like cultures, display a general laziness which can be perceived in the tendency to copy and recreate the structures of the American English language, with a particular predilection for the phrases recurring in media productions (video games, film industry, television series), often but not necessarily American. Kristeva envisions two possibilities to protect the diversity of languages and cultures from being homogenized on the American model, a protection vital in a Europe rich with its linguistic diversity: either a reactive turning back to tradition, to an idealized past we are nostalgic for precisely because it is lost (this is the domain of the purists and the conservatives), or the open grafting of aspects of other cultures and mentalities onto the language under threat, in order to insert within that language the seeds of awareness and awakening.

In *Le Vieil Homme et les Loups*, Kristeva grafts onto French the Latin language, which carries a sense of loss, sorrow and mourning as Latin is a dead language to us. Hence, Kristeva privileges subversing (sub-verse, like an undercurrent breaking the course of the linguistic and cultural flow) over the implementation of drastic linguistic measures in which no one takes responsibility since responsibility is projected onto the linguistic imperialism of the invasive 'other' (as far as the French are concerned, the culprit is American cultural imperialism; this was very prominent at the time of Jacques Lang's Ministry of Culture and still carries on with events such as the Toubon bill in which threatening the French language becomes a legally punishable offence).

These three cultural phenomena, combined with the levelling of languages and identities on the American model, are symptomatic of the impoverishment of western culture and the vacancy of the psyche which seeks elsewhere for its answers: a culture of illusion, running on empty images of false hopes which draw the contours of our 'psychic laziness, fleeting narcissistic mirages'[19] which rest on 'a careful shunting aside of the reality of suffering and the necessity to confront such suffering with a full knowledge of the facts'.[20]

Faced with the knowledge of these facts, Kristeva then addresses the question of whether there might be different solutions than those mentioned above. As far as Kristeva is concerned, her work revolves round three issues which all deal with aspects of language: psychoanalysis and literature which are epitomized in the process of writing, in the French sense of 'écriture'. 'Ecriture' is of importance in the context of Europe and literature, as it is one space where Kristeva believes a renewal of identity is possible; literature is then vital in the process of Europeanization of the self. 'Ecriture' can be defined as a type of literary practice which defies discursive pretensions, on the writer's part, to omniscience and neutrality;[21] to the contrary, 'écriture' carries within its own discourse the heterogeneity particular to human experience.[22] Hence, Kristeva defines writing as a process enabling the writer, be it as analysand or as artist, 'to put the neutral surface of abstract words into contact with a whole dynamic of recollection that leads us at once to recall traumas, the pains or the pleasures, and the most archaic sensations'.[23] Style, 'one possibility of being in contact with our unconscious [...] our sensations',[24] occurs when the memory of these pains and sensations are translated into language. Writing is a journey of reconciliation between the subject's body and his/her memory, which appears to the reader as changing style. Hence, the novel form would appear to offer the most potential, as it pretends to tell a story and therefore a movement in time and space which theoretical texts, for instance, cannot convey so easily. I mentioned earlier the importance of addressing issues of origin and death in the transition from national to European identity; 'écriture' in literature offers the space where the writer recalls his/her origin (the archaic memory of pre-linguistic bond to the maternal space) and is able to express his/her foreignness and its relation to death.

Kristeva's style in *Le Vieil Homme et les Loups* displays this process/trial[25] as the narrator displaces any fixed position the subject appears to be in. On the one hand, the murder mystery genre enables the narrator, especially in section two, to break the linearity of the story, as the fragments of evidence that she finds on the way trigger several stories that the narrator imagines related to the murder. On the other hand, the atmosphere of the novel is, overall, disturbing, as the scrambling of voices and genres prevents the reader from taking position: clipped dialogues, the abundance of allegory and metaphors, the narrator's voice being displaced from first to third person, block the reader's effort to settle comfortably into one fixed reading identity. These shifts confer a multiplicity of identities on both the narrator and the reader. The narrator's journey is a reminiscence of his/her foreignness re-lived with its affects through 'écriture' and enabling a renewal of identity. This journey is also shared by the reader through a process of transference. 'Écriture' is not a totalizing mode of writing pretending to arrest its progression at perfect meaning; rather, it is an endless process in which homogeneity and heterogeneity interact in the production of a renewed identity, that is to say, an identity of multiplicity rather than sameness. In this dynamic, Europe holds a privileged position as it already treasures, within its symbolic frontiers, the diversity of languages, cultures, histories...

In *Le Vieil Homme et les Loups*, this dynamic is exemplified in Stéphanie, a character who stands out at the end of the novel, as a positive identificatory figure. Stéphanie embodies the foreigner, in the Kristevan understanding of the term and which I referred to at the start of this essay. She is both from Santa Barbara and an outsider, an exile from the place. From the moment of her arrival, she positions herself as an exile from her past in the town and lists what she recognizes as familiar in the same town ('heimlich'/ 'unheimlich'). Her journey as a character proceeds from this reminiscence which leads her, not only to investigate crimes, but also to reflect on the other protagonists' relationship with the wolves, finally to question her own psychical space. Stéphanie's arrival breaks the fragmented course of the first section; she steps into a situation of crisis and chaos and brings, to begin with, a sense of hope for order through the detached and non-committal attitude she displays. In this sense, Stéphanie endows the story with a psychoanalytic tone, as she exemplifies the same positioning as an analyst at work, in both her postures and her thinking processes. However, she soon turns the analysis on herself as the event of death calls for a deeper reminiscence of her past. Especially in the third part, Stéphanie faces the unconscious upheaval that her encounter with her own foreignness and death has opened; she then begins to address her relationship with mortality and origin.

Her path is contrasted by Alba and Vespasian's closing of psychical activity; Alba, in her depressed state, remains untouched and untouchable, a truly repressed character whose capacity to question her psychical space is being made impossible by the fact that she chooses hatred and crime without guilt and without responsibility; similarly, Vespasian portrays the caricature of male violence, destructive, murderous, a monstrous character who does not appear to have any kind of inner depth to his personality. Both Alba and Vespasian embody the death of psychical life; they are more like automatons than human beings and therefore their subjectivity has become meaningless, a series of unquestioned and unquestionable automated tasks.

In relation to racial crimes, Kristeva stated:

> Should we condemn, be indignant, punish? Absolutely. Necessarily. I am afraid, however, that [...] in simply pointing out evil, we run the risk of authentifying and fixing it.[26]

In Santa Barbara, crime is not fixed, which enables the novel to move beyond a mere detective story. At the end of a detective story, order is restored when the culprit is brought to justice and given a cross to carry; that cross is both a punishment for disrupting our social peace and in some way a projection of our own guilt for secretly experiencing the erotic pleasure (in abjection or attraction) that the spectacle of crime triggers.[27] The eroticism of crime brings out, in the human subject, a form of bestiality of which the wolves of the novel are reminiscent. Stéphanie realizes that 'Society is founded on a crime committed together.'[28] Santa Barbara's social order is a reversed sense of order; as representative of a society, Santa Barbara's existence rests on a fantasy of crime and the assurance that crime as a fantasy goes on, as the pulling force that gathers members of its society; chaos is the norm; order (finding culprits, denouncing good and evil) would bring this social edifice down.

Two questions support the novel's intrigue: what crime is being committed? and who commits those crimes? Stéphanie moves from investigating the crime of others (the inhabitants) to questioning the possibility of another, more invisible crime, the crime of the other within the self and which concerns and threatens an entire social organism. It is a movement away from scapegoating (the social rests on a good vs bad dynamic in which the innocent 'I' is able to take a good position in contrast to 'you', the stranger, the criminal)[29] and towards identifying scapegoating as the crime. Scapegoating the other, the different, the foreigner means that the 'I' does not take any responsibility or guilt for the crime committed and, as an innocent party, this 'I' can denounce and clearly fix crime in the other's subjectivity and therefore reinforce the dynamic of 'xenophobia' which cements the social. In *Le Vieil Homme et les Loups*, 'crime' is identified not as an event but as a generic term bearing the function of control of the inhabitants who then reproduce the same dynamic of control onto the next social layer (the wolves-Vespasian-Alba, for instance). The wolves, the ones who commit the crimes, symbolize this invisible dynamic; it is the entire society which is responsible for closing up the psychical potential of its members and rejecting the responsibility onto an invisible other, the wolves themselves.

The only characters who do not fall prey to the wolves are Stephanie and the old man who both turn the dynamic onto themselves, thus breaking the contagion. The old man, in all his wisdom, dies of too much awareness, murdered by the wolves. If the wolves represent the crime of others, the old man dies because they could not bear to be exposed. If the wolves represent the old man's own crime, then he died for having had the unbearable vision of his own and others' otherness and of a social space reduced to the acting of a spectacle of murder. The question of whether the wolves belong to others or are his own remains open at the end of the novel. Stephanie, on the other hand, 'dies', in the psychical experience of her encounter with death, and emerges from the ashes of her inner journey renewed and prepared for another investigatory challenge.[30]

At the end of *Le Vieil Homme et les Loups*, the reader is left with a diffused feeling of discomfort. On the one hand, the novel addresses contemporary problems which the reader, as a social subject, feels concern him/her. It could even be argued that the reader cannot avoid the issues raised in the novel because of the use of metaphors: '*métaphore* operates, giving form to infantile psychic inscriptions that are located on the border of the unnameable'.[31] Hence, the narrator addresses, beyond the realm of consciousness (and resistance), the reader's own psychical imprints. On the other hand, the narrator's strategy has been to disturb the reader's sense of identity, as a reader. By de-centring several times the narrative positioning, the narrator questions the reader's own position as a reader and displaces his/her identity into a multiplicity of positions. Hence, the narrative path followed by Stéphanie, from order to disorder and finally to subjective truths, is also that of the reader: what began as a comfortable reading activity turns into a disrupting journey, at the end of which the reader is left alone to gather the scattered pieces of his/her reading experience and renew his/her definition of his/her own image.

Le Vieil Homme et les Loups is not specifically a novel about Europe. It is a novel about human subjectivity and the emotional difficulties the search for an identity entails. It is precisely for that reason that the novel cannot be grounded in a particular place. On the one hand, this would have given the protagonists a stable and unquestioned identity by virtue of having been created/born there, thus undermining the problem faced by individuals in their search of their identities; the heroes of Santa Barbara are from nowhere specific; they are created/born foreigners, with no nation, no state to position their origins *a priori*; yet they are from somewhere since they exist and belong in the continuum of human history. On the other hand, Santa Barbara is a town built out of real life details, gathered together as the product of the narrator's imagination and calling on the readers' memories and fantasies about their own place of origin. These two aspects converge in a novel which has much to tell about the difficult reality faced by Europeans; it lends itself for reflection in a Europe seeking a common origin on which to build a shared sense of identity. In a culture like the European culture where instant images prevail, it is both refreshing and puzzling to be met by a writer who so strongly believes in the therapeutic role a certain type of literature can play.

NOTES

1. I would like to acknowledge the help I received from Tracy Davis and Professor Roy Boyne.
2. See Julia Kristeva, *Etrangers à nous-mêmes* (Paris: Arthème Fayard, 1988); translated as *Strangers to Ourselves* (NY: Columbia University Press, 1991); in this chapter, all translations from *Etrangers à nous-mêmes* are my own unless stated otherwise. See also Anna Smith, *Readings of Exile and Estrangement* (London: Macmillan, 1996) in particular Chapter 1: 'Strangers to Ourselves', pp. 11–50.
3. 'History', the common tale of foreigners, the untold story of the History books. The interest of Kristeva's work lies in the way she exposes Historical silences and gathers them to write about an other's history.
4. I am referring to the popular view that Europe stems from a bureaucratic organization, whose decisions on and definition of Europe are then redistributed nationally in political speeches and through the media. The role of bureaucracy will be discussed later.
5. 'An other' refers first to the idea that identity is a process not a thing and that we can consider identity as ever changing into another with the individual always in the process of becoming an other than what s/he is; second, in the process of symbolization, the individual cannot be reduced to his/her symbol and is always other than what s/he is. See for instance the work of Jacques Lacan.
6. Julia Kristeva, *Le Vieil Homme et les Loups* (Paris: Fayard, 1991); translated as *The Old Man and the Wolves* (New York: Columbia University

Press, 1994); in this chapter, all translations from *Le Vieil Homme et les Loups* are my own unless stated otherwise. See also M. Ross Guberman, *Julia Kristeva: Interviews* (NY: Columbia University Press, 1996), in particular Chapter 15: 'Interview: The Old Man and the Wolves', pp. 162–75. I shall return to *Le Vieil Homme et les Loups* in more detail in the second part.
7. It is interesting to note that as far as the European Union is concerned, there seems to be a 'hierarchy of belonging' based upon the economic strength of a given state: the stronger and the more stable the economy, the more weight the state has in the shaping of Europe. The definition and shaping of a European identity would then stem from a financial dynamic, acting as both its symbol and locus.
8. See *Etrangers à nous-mêmes*, especially Chapters 1, pp. 9–60 and 8, pp. 249–85.
9. *Etrangers à nous-mêmes*, pp. 272–3.
10. Foreignness is to be understood in its wider sense of the one who is strange, different, alien, other than the common mortals; it seems that foreign heroes, or heroes dealing with that which is foreign, have proliferated and multiplied over the past decade and to give an exhaustive list of these productions is beyond the scope of this chapter. However, some television series have become so prominent (shown several times a week on different channels in the UK, regularly repeated, ongoing for more than a year, generating their own cultural sub-groups and market) that they can be mentioned here as representative of this cultural phenomenon: *Star Trek*, *Highlander*, *The X-files*, *Millennium*, *Forever Knight*, *Poltergeist*.
11. Julia Kristeva interviewed by Edith Kurzweil, first published in *Partisan Review*, 1985; translated in Guberman (1996): 'Psychoanalysis and Politics', Chapter 14, pp. 146–61.
12. In French, 'un loup' is also a black velvet mask, worn at masked balls to disguise one's identity.
13. Julia Kristeva interviewed by Bernard Sichère (1992), first published in *L'infini*; translated in *Partisan Review* and in Guberman (1996): 'The Old Man and the Wolves', pp. 162–75. Quotations are from Guberman's book.
14. *Julia Kristeva: Interviews*, 174.
15. 'Crimes' is to be understood in both a literal (reminiscent of the Red Army) and figurative sense (the withering away of human identity).
16. In a dramatic turn of events, the press, accused of symbolic crimes against the human subject, is now being tried and judged for its responsibility in the death of the Princess of Wales. Before her death, the privacy of individuals, the marketing of human life as spectacle, the building and selling of human identity were issues addressed only sporadically. It can be argued, as the newspaper *Libération* did, that the social events and the media coverage of the time preceding Diana's funeral is building yet another myth about her identity; see *Libération*: 'Le mythe parfait' by Serge July, 2 September 1997.
17. See 'The Old Man and the Wolves' in *Julia Kristeva: Interviews*, pp. 162–75.

18. *Julia Kristeva: Interviews*, p. 169.
19. Ibid., p. 173.
20. Ibid.
21. Theoretical discourse comes to mind, but we can also consider most discourses pretending to hold the truth, by removing the fallible narrator from the text, hence endowing him (and I do mean him, as 'her' would imply a questioning of the 'gendered truth') with special powers of insight, beyond the text itself: historical, political, as well as fictional discourses exemplify this type of writing.
22. See, for instance, Roland Barthes, *Le Degré zéro de l'écriture* (Paris: Seuil, 1953); republished 1972; Julia Kristeva, *Sens et non-sens de la révolte* (Paris: Arthème Fayard, 1996).
23. *Julia Kristeva: Interviews*, p. 55.
24. Ibid.
25. 'Le sujet en procès', see Julia Kristeva,: *La Révolution du langage poétique: l'avant-garde à la fin du XIXe siècle: Lautréamont et Mallarmé* (Paris: Seuil, 1974); translated as *Revolution in Poetic Language* (New York: Columbia University Press, 1984).
26. Julia Kristeva, *Lettre ouverte à Harlem Désir: 'Pourquoi?'* (Paris: Rivages, 1990), p. 10; translated as *Nations Without Nationalism* (New York: Columbia University Press, 1993). Translations from the French text are my own.
27. Apart from the obvious success of the 'mediazation' of crime (for example, O.J. Simpson, the proliferation of serial killers' representations in films), the spectacle of criminals being hanged, in Great Britain, provoked in the crowd of spectators erotic feelings ranging from orgasms (death as sexual excitement) to vomiting (abjection of the death drive). Kristeva recounts in 'Pourquoi?' (*Lettre ouverte à Harlem Désir*, p. 9) that 'Hitler cynically asserted that antisemitism was the only authorized form of pornography' at the time of the Third Reich.
28. *Lettre ouverte à Harlem Désir*, p. 18.
29. For this matter, during their last electoral campaign, the British Labour Party was displaying a poster which read 'Young offenders will be prosecuted'. With such a message, we have a circular dynamic of responsibility and guilt which fits Kristeva's criticisms: a young person commits an offence; society is exposed as producing little 'monsters' and passes the blame on to the authorities; the authorities are in turn exposed as incompetent and 'soft' in the face of rising criminality and the lowering of the age of criminals and they display a message in which the young are targeted, with an emphasis on the 'young' as a social group other than simply 'offenders' or 'the old'. Moreover, the careful removing of any perpetrator of the punishment through the use of the passive means that no one is taking responsibility for administering the law ('young offenders will be prosecuted', by whom?). Hence, the place of authority is vacant or passive and the young become the scapegoats of social unrest.
30. See Julia Kristeva, *Possessions* (Paris: Arthème Fayard, 1996).
31. *Julia Kristeva: Interviews*, pp. 163–4.

Index

Adventurers, The, 56–60
Algerian War, 108–9
L'Allée des Soupirs, 111–13
Alliance Révolutionnaire Caraïbe, 107
Americans, 35–6, 41–2, 98, 119, 130–1, 136
Antillanité, 102
ARC, see Alliance Révolutionnaire Caraïbe
Aristotle, 217
Arnold, Matthew, 18, 132
Augustinian, see St Augustine
Auschwitz, 65, 66, 69, 71–2, 73, 74, 75, 76
Austen, Jane, 31, 48
Austria, 44–61

Bakhtin, Mikhail, 179
balkanization of literary studies, 207–10
Belgium, 9–11, 25, 140, 148
Benjamin, Walter 209
Beyond Good and Evil, 3, 218
Bhabha, Homi K., 34, 196, 201
Bildungsroman, 35, 36, 40
Black Album, The, 89
Blair, Tony, xx
Bloom, Harold, 207–10
Bodin, Jean, 33
Booker Prize, 94
Bourdieu, Pierre, 208
Bradbury, Malcolm, 119, 129, 138–53
Brancusi, Constantin, 159, 166–7
Britain and the continent/Europe 8, 9, 16, 20, 26, 54–5, 140, 147–9, 194–5
British, 44
 see also English
British–German relations/attitudes 45–6, 50, 59, 61

Britishness, xiii, 60
 see also Englishness
Brontë, Charlotte, 3–26
Buddha of Suburbia, The, 85, 88, 89–94, 95, 96, 98–9
Burke, Edmund, 32, 33
Byron, Lord, x, 5, 6

camp, 66, 69, 70, 71, 72–3, 74, 75, 76, 81
 see also Lager
canon of English literature, 86, 88–9, 99, 122
canon of European and Western literatures, 85, 88–9
Caribbean French, 101–14
Cartesian, see Descartes
Cartland, Barbara, xi, 46, 47, 50–5
Chamoiseau, Patrick, 102, 103–5, 106
Changing Places, 41, 152
Charlemagne, 174, 175
Chasse au Racoon, La, 108–11
Chronique des sept misères, 103–4, 106
chronotope, 179, 186, 188
Collected Works of Billy the Kid, The, 94
Commonwealth literature, 86
Condé, Maryse, 106–8, 113
Confiant, Raphaël, 102, 105–6, 111–13
Créolité, 102

Days of His Grace, The, 174, 185
Decalogue, The, 211
Delors, Jacques, 204
Départements d'Outre Mer, 101–14
Derrida, Jacques, 214–15, 221
Descartes, 217, 218
Destin, 160, 164, 165
Discourses, 175

Index

displacement, 66, 197, 200, 202
DOM, see Départements d'Outre Mer
East of Wimbledon, 120, 121–8, 129
Eating People is Wrong, 145
écriture, 233–4
Eliade, Mircea, 164–5
Eliot, George, x, 6
Eminescu, Mihai, 166, 168, 169, 170
English, 39, 55, 97, 98, 132–3, 136, 192
  butler, 120, 128, 129, 132–3, 135
  countryside/landscape, 119, 196, 201
  gentleman/gentleman ideal, 120, 125, 128, 129, 130, 132, 196, 203
  language, 86, 143
  see also British
Englishness, xiii, 32, 34, 50, 53–4, 122, 125, 126, 128, 129, 132–3, 134–5, 136, 192, 194–203
English Patient, The, 85, 88–9, 94–9
Enigma of Arrival, The, xx, 192, 197–203
Enlightenment, 24, 32, 33, 109
Erasmo, 160
Erasmus, 162
ethnocentrism, 33
Etrangers à nous-mêmes, 225
eurocentric, eurocentrism, 85, 89, 99, 203
Europa, ausente, 161
Europa, nuestra utopia, 163
Europe, 81, 87, 119, 121, 136, 159, 160, 161–3
  definition of, ix, x, xiii, 65, 71, 75, 170, 176
  eastern, xxi, 37, 38, 69, 78, 80–1, 138–9, 141, 142, 145–7, 149–52, 161, 229–30 see also Romania and Uscatescu
  history of, 87, 173–91
  in Uscatescu's work, 159–71
  languages in, 76–7
  western, 78, 80–1, 142, 229–30
Europeans, 130–1, 176, 225, 228, 237
Europeanness, 171
European Community/Union, xix, 9, 80–1, 108, 138–53, 163, 194
European identity, ix, xiv, 65–6, 68–9, 77, 78, 101, 102, 108, 113, 170, 171, 173, 176, 187, 192, 203, 204, 222, 225
European integration, xiv, xix, 192, 194, 203, 222
Europeanization, 226, 227, 233
European novel, xi
European subjectivity, xiv, 207–22
European subject, 226
Eurosceptics, 21
Eyre, Jane, 6–8, 9, 12, 25–6

Falklands War, 195
Favel Alone, 182, 183
Favel Ensam, 182, 183
federalists, 149
Few Steps towards Silence, A, 186–7
film, European, 207–10
First Night, 60
foreigner, 97–8, 143, 225–6
foreignness, 225–8
Forster, E.M., 18
free trade, 18–19, 23
French, 44, 60, 98, 131
  identity, 108
  identity in the Caribbean, 108, 113–14
  literary history, 102
  in the West Indies, the, 101–2, 103
Frenchness, 112
French West Indies, 101–14
Freud, Sigmund, 217, 218–19, 225–6

Germans, 35, 36–7, 40–1, 44–61, 131
Germanness, 39, 45–6, 73
GONG, see Groupe d'Organisation Nationale Guadeloupéenne

242 *Index*

Grand Prix Littéraire de la Femme, Le, 106
Gravy Train, The, 138, 140, 141–6, 147
Gravy Train Goes East, The, 138, 140, 141, 143, 146–53
große Atempause, Die, see *La Tregua*
Groupe d'Organisation Nationale Guadeloupéenne, 107
Hans nådes tid, 174, 185
Heidegger, Martin, 160, 167
history, 51, 152, 174, 175, 177, 178, 182, 183, 184, 186, 225
see also past and Europe, history of
Hodge, Jane Aiken, 56, 60
Holocaust, 70, 72
Holt, Victoria, 47, 48
Howard's End, 18
Hume, David, 32–3

Ibbotson, Eva, 47
identity, 88, 90, 93, 95–6, 159, 173, 175, 176, 182, 183, 187, 197–204, 222, 226
see also European identity, national identity, Romanian identity
Innocent, The, 35, 37–42
integrationists, 149
intergovernmentalists, xix, 149
In the Skin of a Lion, 94
Ishiguro, Kazno, 120–1, 128–36
Italians, 67, 68, 79
Italianness, 67

James, Henry, 8
Jameson, Fredric, 87
Jeanne, Max, 108–11, 113
Johnson, Eyvind, 173–88
Judas Kiss, The, 49

Kant, Immanuel, 217–19, 221
Kieslowski, Krzysztof, xiv, 207–22
Kim, 91
Kipling, Rudyard, 91

Konzentrationslager, 69; see also camp and *Lager*
Kristeva, Julia, 225–37
Kureishi, Hanif, 85, 88, 89

Lager, 66, 69, 70–6
see also camp
Lägg undan solen, 184
Last Act, 60
Leading Lady, 60
Lessing, Gotthold Ephraim, 184
Levi, Primo, 64–81
Lewis, Matthew, 31
Life's Long Day, 182
literary studies, balkanization of, 207–10
literature
role and function of, xi, xiv, xxi, 187, 208
problems of definition, 86
Livsdagen lång, 182
Lodge, David, 35–6, 39, 41, 152
Luceafarul, 169

Machiavelli, 162, 175
Manchester School, 19
McEwan, Ian, 35, 39
memory, 215, 221–2
Middlemarch, x
Midnight's Children, 88, 98
Millenarium, 168
Monk, The, 31
Monnet, Jean, xxi, 142
Montesquieu, 33
Morning Gift, The, 47
Mort de l'Europe, La, 160, 161

Några steg mot tystnaden, 186–7
Naipaul, V.S., xx, 192, 196, 197–203
narrative perspective, 39
nation, 33, 34, 68, 97, 119, 136, 166, 177, 192–4, 203
and novel, 34, 177, 196
and narration, 34, 196–7
national character, 33, 67, 68
national identity, xi, 33, 67, 119, 122, 159, 167, 171, 174, 193–4, 197, 203, 225

Index

nationalism, 97, 142, 166, 193–4
nationality, xi, 94, 97, 98, 177
nation-state, xix–xx, 93, 192–4, 204
Nègre et l'Amiral, Le, 105–6
Négritude movement, 102
New Labour, 196
Nietzsche, Friedrich, 3, 4, 218
Nineteen Eighty-Four, xii
Nobel Prize, 173
No End, 211
Noica, Constantin, 161
non-foreigner, 225
Northanger Abbey, 31, 32, 34, 48
novel
  autobiographical, 197
  European, xi
  gothic, 5, 6, 31, 48
  historical, 36, 37–8, 40, 106
  international, 35–6, 38, 40, 173–4
  spy, 37–8, 40
  television, 138, 139

'Of National Characters', 32–3
Ondaatje, Michael, 85, 87, 88, 94
On the Night of the Seventh Moon 47–9
Orwell, George, xi
otherness, 33, 40, 79, 136
  see also foreigner and foreignness
Out of the Shelter, 35–7, 39, 40–2

Paradise Lost, 122
past, 45, 179–85, 187
  see also history
Pays Mêlé, 106–7
Philosophical Essays Concerning Human Understanding, 32
Plato, 217, 218, 219
poetry, 167–70
Politik als Beruf, 159
popular literature, 44–61
post-colonial counter-discourse, 197
post-colonial literature, 86–7, 192, 196, 197
post-independence literature, 87
Prix Anaïs Nin, Le, 106

Prix Carbet, 113
Prix Goncourt, 103, 106
Prize of European Unity, 160
Prize of Latin Union, 160
Problema de Europa, El, 161
Proceso al humanismo, 160
Professor, The, 9, 10–12, 19–20, 21, 22–3
Profetas de Europa, 160
Put Away the Sun, 184
Puterbaugh Prize, 106

racism, 103, 111
Radcliffe, Ann, 5, 21, 31
Rates of Exchange, 138–9, 143, 146–7, 152
Reawakening, The, see *La Tregua*
Reflections on the Revolution in France, 32, 33–4
Reluctant Bride, The, 47, 52–5
Remains of the Day, The, 120–1, 128–36
Renan, Ernest, xx
romance
  gothic, 44
  historical, 44–6, 50, 56, 59, 60–1
Romance of the Forest, The, 31
Romania
  culture, 159, 163–71
  identity, 163–71
Rules of Art, The, 208
Running in the Family, 94
Rushdie, Salman, 88, 98

Salisbury, Carola, 47
Schindler's List, 209, 210
Scottish National Party, xi–xii
Secret for a Nightingale, 47, 48
Sentimental Journey through France and Italy, 31–2
Se questo e un uomo, 65, 69, 73
Shadowed Spring, The, 47–8
Shirley, 9, 13–15, 16–18, 21, 23–5
Small World, 41
Spanish National Prize for Literature, 160
Spielberg, Stephen, 209, 210
St Augustine, 218, 221

stereotypes (national), xx, 32, 36–7, 39, 40–1, 44-6, 93, 120, 128, 132, 136, 140
see also under individual nationalities, e.g. French
Sterne, Laurence, 31–2
supranationalists, xix

Taylor, Charles, 218
Texaco, 103, 104–5, 106
Thanatos, 167–8
Thatcher, Margaret, 195, 196
Three Colours Blue, 211–22
transcultural literature, 85–9
translation, 65–6, 70–1, 73, 75, 78
travel accounts, 119
travelogue, 31–2, 70
Traversée de la Mangrove, 107–8, 113
Treaties of Rome, xix

Tregua, La, 64–81
Trois Couleurs Bleu, 211–22

Uscatescu, George, 159–71

Very Naughty Angel, A, 46, 50–2, 53
Vieil Homme et les Loups, Le, 228–37
Villette, 3–4, 6, 9, 15–16, 20

Weber, Max, 159
Why Come to Slaka, 138
Williams, Nigel, 120, 121–8, 129
Wordsworth, William, 4–5
world fiction, 85–9, 93, 98–9
World War II, 35, 40–1, 45, 55, 59, 65, 68, 81, 86, 95, 103, 104, 105, 106, 111, 148, 164, 171, 173
Wuthering Heights, 11